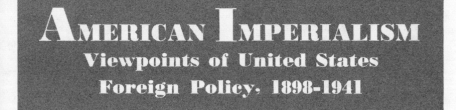

AMERICAN IMPERIALISM
Viewpoints of United States
Foreign Policy, 1898-1941

DOLLAR DIPLOMACY

A Study in American Imperialism

Scott Nearing
and
Joseph Freeman

ARNO PRESS & THE NEW YORK TIMES
New York ★ 1970

Collection Created and Selected
by
CHARLES GREGG OF GREGG PRESS

Library of Congress Catalog Card Number: 74-111703
ISBN 0-405-02040-6

ISBN for complete set: 0-405-02000-7

Reprint Edition 1970 by Arno Press Inc.
Manufactured in the United States of America

DOLLAR DIPLOMACY

DOLLAR DIPLOMACY

A Study in American Imperialism

by

SCOTT NEARING

and

JOSEPH FREEMAN

MODERN READER PAPERBACKS
NEW YORK AND LONDON

PREFACE

"Dollar Diplomacy" was adopted as a title for this volume because it seemed to include, more completely than any other short phrase, the growth of United States economic interests abroad, and the diplomatic and military support accorded them by the Federal Government. No thorough study has been made of United States extra-territorial economic interests. United States state papers, with minor exceptions, have not been published since about 1915. Consequently, "Dollar Diplomacy" is not a History of American Imperialism, but a description of certain type cases in which United States economic and diplomatic interests have come into collision with the economic and political interests of certain "undeveloped" countries. These cases were picked, first, because they represented distinct phases in imperial development, and second, because sufficient first-hand material was available to make possible a reasonably competent study. The History of American Imperialism is still to be written.

The book has two chief purposes: first, to indicate how far the United States is following an imperial policy, and second, to suggest some of the outstanding characteristics of United States foreign policy.

The authors do not claim originality either for the ideas or for the material collected in this volume, but so far as they are aware, these data have not been assembled elsewhere in this form, and with this general purpose in mind. Where first-hand sources were available, they have been used. Acknowledgment is made for data taken from secondary sources. Complete references covering practically all footnotes appear in a bibliography at the end of the volume.

Scattered through the text are a number of maps and charts,

intended to summarize certain aspects of the problem which lend themselves to that form of treatment. A few of the less easily accessible documents are printed in the appendix.

Acknowledgments are due to a number of men and women who have assisted generously in the preparation of this volume. Melchior Guzman and Adrian Richt secured and translated many of the Latin-American documents, and Adrian Richt prepared much of the material on Cuba. Robert W. Dunn permitted the authors to use statistical information which will shortly appear over his name in book form. The manuscript was read, in whole or in part, by Professors Edwin M. Borchard, Charles A. Beard, Harry Elmer Barnes, Raymond L. Buell, Edward Mead Earle, and Thomas S. Adams, and by Lewis Gannett and James Weldon Johnson. Without committing themselves to the interpretation, emphasis and conclusions presented in the manuscript, all of them made helpful suggestions.

The authors wish to thank Miss Ann Coles, who prepared the maps and charts, Miss Ruth Stout, who typed the manuscript in its final form, verified the references and read the proof, and Miss Natalie Brown, who prepared the manuscript for the publisher. Miss Marion M. Shields and her staff did an immense amount of typing on the manuscript in its preliminary stages.

A special word of appreciation is due the Economics Division of the New York Public Library. All of the members of the Economics Staff have been courteous, patient and extremely efficient in locating material and in verifying the wide range of data which appear in the following pages.

THE AUTHORS.

New York City, June 10, 1925.

CONTENTS

CONTENTS

MAPS AND CHARTS

INTRODUCTION: RECENT IMPERIAL EXPERIENCE

One by one the principal nations of Europe emerged from Feudalism, passed through the commercial and the industrial revolutions, and entered the stage of financial imperialism. In the course of this transformation the centre of economic power shifted first from landlords to traders and manufacturers, and later to bankers.[1] During this process, Western Europe evolved an economic system under which the road to income and power lay through the control of various forms of industrial wealth: resources, tools, machinery, banks, stores—the "jobs" upon which the masses of men depended for a living.

The owners of the new wealth, or "capital" as it was called to distinguish it from the "land" that made up the bulk of property in an agricultural society, became, through their ownership of industrial capital, the masters of the very large economic surpluses arising out of machine production. Upon their shoulders rested the responsibility for investing these surpluses within the home market or of exporting them into some undeveloped, foreign territory.

The masters of investment were not wholly free to make this decision. Economic necessity dictates that every modern industrial society must develop foreign markets for its surplus products; must control sources of food, fuel, minerals, timber, and other raw materials; must secure business opportunities for the investment of surplus capital. European capitalists were therefore compelled to seek markets, raw materials, and investment opportunities, many of which lay in the Americas, Africa, Asia, and Australia, where the business opening, or the return on invested capital, yielded the greatest net advantage.

[1] Hilferding, "Finanzkapital." Hobson, "Evolution of Modern Capitalism." Veblen, "The Engineers and the Price System."

At these points of maximum return, goods were sold and capital was placed.

By 1914 economic interest had compelled the chief business groups of Europe to establish large foreign holdings in one or more of the undeveloped continents—Africa, Asia, Australia, the Americas.[1] Proceeding upon the dictum that "the flag follows the investor," each one of these industrial nations organized a military and a naval machine large enough to protect the foreign interests of its traders and investors. Between 1870 and the beginning of the World War, the building of this military machine constituted the largest single charge on the budget of each of the principal European nations. After its establishment, the military machine was used, first, to play a more or less active rôle in the internal life of those countries in which the owners of the military machine held important economic interests; and second, to defend the property of the investors against a possible attack from any rivals who might be inclined to interfere with their holdings.

The rôle which the investing country played in the life of the undeveloped territory varied all the way from minor political intrigue to the establishment of sovereignty. The most successful of the industrial countries (Britain) secured an empire "on which the sun never sets," including some of the choicest garden spots of the earth. Lillian C. Knowles[2] has recently made a study in which this imperial process is carefully described.

Economic expansion and the development of financial imperialism were not confined to Europe. Following the opening of Japan to western influence, the same processes were repeated there. A feudal and agricultural society was converted through the industrial revolution into a commercial and manufacturing community with a growing economic surplus, an increasing population, a capitalist or investing class, and a corresponding broadening of imperial interests.[3]

---

[1] Hobson, "Export of Capital." Hobson, "Imperialism."
[2] Knowles, "Economic Development of the British Overseas Empire."
[3] Viallate, "Economic Imperialism," p. 72 ff.

This process of discovering foreign markets, of establishing permanent foreign economic interests and of exercising political pressure upon the regions in which the economic interests exist, has found its chief expression in Europe, yet it is not peculiar to any nation, but corresponds to a certain stage in the development of economic surplus. J. A. Hobson[1] notes that imperialism "implies the use of the machinery of government by private interests, mainly capitalist, to secure for them economic gains outside their country." W. S. Culbertson[2] describes imperialism as "an over-seas economic expression of western civilization." The first of these definitions interprets imperialism as a business venture; the second presents it as an inevitable phase of capitalism. Historically it would be correct to say that imperialism signifies the rise of the trading class to power. Looked at from this angle,[3] imperialism becomes a phase through which society passes at a certain stage in its economic development.[4]

The United States, like Japan and the countries of Europe, has been passing through those economic stages which followed the commercial and industrial revolutions; like the nations of Europe, it has established a system which places surplus wealth in the hands of a small, private investing class; like them, it has been engaged in multiplying capital at home. To what extent has it followed their example in seeking foreign markets, in exporting capital, and in opening new fields for American enterprise on foreign shores? The answer is to be found in the recent economic and diplomatic history of the United States.

[1] Hobson, "Imperialism," p. 100.
[2] "Annals," v. 112, p. 124.
[3] Wissler, "Man and Culture," p. 347.
[4] Lenin, "Imperialism, the Final Stage of Capitalism."

DOLLAR DIPLOMACY

I

AMERICAN ECONOMIC EXPANSION

1. *Five Generations of Expansion*

American economic interests have been steadily expanding since the middle of the eighteenth century, when the thin line of settlers, scattered along the Atlantic seaboard, penetrated the hinterland and pushed across the Allegheny mountains. First, there was the settling of the Northwest territory, then the movement into the Southwest. The third period, ending with the nineties of the last century, saw the tide of men and capital flow across the plains and beyond the Rockies and the Sierras to the Pacific. Then, with the opening years of the new century, there began the fourth period of expansion—the movement of American business enterprise into regions over which the flag·of the United States did not fly. This last period is ordinarily referred to as the period of economic imperialism.

Before 1900 there were American traders in foreign countries, and American prospectors and industrialists had penetrated Mexico, Cuba, Hawaii, Canada, and other neighbouring territory. No considerable amount of capital had been exported, however, as the domestic demand for capital more than covered the available amount of the investment surplus.

Throughout the half century that has elapsed since the organization of the Standard Oil Co. (1870), the economic life of the United States has been expanding with extreme rapidity. The movement of the country from an undeveloped, agricultural, debtor nation, exporting raw materials and borrow-

I

ing capital for improvements, to a developed, manufacturing, creditor nation, exporting manufactured goods and capital and importing raw materials, was hastened by the war. The movement was in full swing, however, before the war began, and war or no war, it must have continued because of the strategic economic position held by the United States.

2. *The Economic Position of the United States*

The strong economic position of the United States is due to its abundant resources and raw materials; its extensive machinery and capital equipment; its well organized labour force, and the resulting productive efficiency. These three elements have provided an immense volume of wealth, of income and of investible surplus that have made possible its rapid advance to a position of world economic power.

The natural economic position of the United States is very strong: a vast land area of three millions of square miles, compactly grouped around a central river valley of great fertility; wide variations of climate; numerous and excellent harbours; a network of rivers; timber in abundance; large supplies of the important fuels and metals.

The second important item in the economic position of the United States is the mechanical equipment with which production is carried on. During the years that preceded the Spanish-American War, while the United States was still short of capital, it was able to borrow largely from Europe. Then, in the later years, when so much of the surplus of European countries was going into military and naval preparations, the relative isolation of the United States made it possible for that country to devote practically the entire surplus to the building of machinery and equipment.

It is very difficult to put the resulting economic advantage into terms of farm animals, agricultural machinery, blast furnaces, cotton spindles and the like. While the United States contains but seven per cent of the world's land and six per cent of the world's population, it reports a third of the railroad mileage, a fourth of the telegraph mileage, a sixth of the world's postoffices, and four-fifths of the world's automobiles. The figures for volume of manufacturing capital and equipment do not exist in any complete form. The value of manufacturing capital, however, was 1.7 billions in 1870; 9.8 billions in 1900; 18.4 billions in 1910 and 44.5 billions in 1920.[1]

Human drive is the force that makes the social machinery move, and skilled human drive is the determining element in economic efficiency. There are about forty-five millions of gainfully employed persons in the United States, beside about twenty-one millions of housewives and housekeepers who do not work for gain. Among the forty-five millions, two-sevenths are engaged in agriculture, three-sevenths in manufacturing industry, and the remainder are scattered between trade, transport, mining, domestic service, and the professions. Here is a great body of trained men and women, augmented, during a century, by a constant influx of adults from Europe.

Europe contributed large amounts of capital to the United States. Interest was paid on the loans, and ultimately the principal was returned. Europe, between 1830 and 1920, has furnished about thirty millions of immigrants to the United States for which the United States paid nothing. These human contributions have been particularly plentiful in recent years. Between 1870 and 1900, 10.7 millions of immigrants came to the United States from Europe. Between 1900 and 1920, 12.5 millions arrived. These immigrants, mostly adults, were raised and trained at European expense, and then, in the prime of life, they came to the United States and spent their energies in building American industry.

The combination of abundant resources, large capital equipment and a highly organized labour force has resulted in a phenomenal growth of American productivity. By the time of the Spanish American War (1898) the American industries had been put on an effective basis. During the next fifteen years, while the population of the country increased 30 per cent:[2]

[1] U. S. "Statistical Abstract," 1923.
[2] Idem.

```
Wheat production increased....................  70 per cent
Corn production increased.....................  27
Cotton production increased...................  58
Coal production increased.....................  90
Petroleum production increased................ 317
Pig iron production increased.................  69
Steel production increased....................  131
Copper production increased...................  89
Cement production increased................... 406
```

These gains, supplemented by those made during the period of the war, have put the United States in a position where it produces a quarter of the world's supply of wheat, half of the world's supply of iron and coal, three-fifths of the world's supply of aluminum, copper and cotton, two-thirds of the world's supply of oil, three-quarters of the world's supply of corn, and nine-tenths of the world's supply of automobiles.

3. *Wealth, Income and Surplus*

Census estimates [1] place the wealth of the United States for 1922 at 322 billions of dollars. Of this amount, $176 billion are in the form of real property and improvements; $19.9 billion in railroads and their equipment; $15.8 billion in manufacturing machinery, tools and implements; $15.4 billion in street railways and other public utilities, and $36 billion in products and merchandise. Clothing, personal adornments, furniture, private automobiles, and the like totalled only $40 billion, or less than an eighth of the whole.

Comparisons with other countries are difficult owing to the chaotic state of Europe. Harvey E. Fisk has attempted to meet this difficulty by reducing the post-war wealth estimates to a common denominator of 1913 dollar values. On this basis his post-war wealth figures are: [2]

Great Britain	$70,000 million
France	57,900
Germany	55,000
Russia	45,000
Italy	21,250

[1] U. S. Census Bur., "Estimated National Wealth," 1924.
[2] Ingalls, "Wealth and Income," 2nd ed., p. 350. Fisk, "Inter-Ally Debts," p. 263.

Japan	$15,000 million
Austria-Hungary	14,000
Belgium	5,000
United States	230,000

O. P. Austin, statistician for the National City Bank of New York, has made an estimate as follows:

Estimated National Wealth
(in billions of dollars)

	1922	1912
United States	320.8	186.3
United Kingdom	88.8	79.3
France	67.7	57.1
Germany	35.7	77.8
Italy	25.9	23.0
Russia	—	56.1
Canada	22.1	10.9
India	21.9	—
China	19.1	—
Argentina	13.2	11.7
Brazil	13.0	—
Australia	9.7	6.1

The total wealth of the United States has been increasing with great rapidity. In 1850 it was placed at $7 billion; in 1870 at $30 billion; at $88 billion in 1900, and at $322 billion in 1922.[1] There has been a corresponding increase in the income of the United States, from $31.4 billion in 1910; $36 billion in 1915; to $72 billion in 1920 and $59 billion in 1922.[2] Just what amount of this income appears in the form of a surplus that is available for use in enterprises outside of the United States it is impossible to say. Ingalls attempts an answer by estimating the "savings that are made each year out of the national income."[3]

	Total Income	Savings
1912	$33 billion	$ 5 billion
1914	33	5
1916	45	14
1918	61	22
1920	72	11
1922	59	5

[1] National City Bank, "Economic Conditions," Dec. 1924, p. 203.
[2] U. S. "Statistical Abstract."
[3] Ingalls, supra, p. 203.

These wealth and income figures are little more than estimates, but they give some idea of the surplus wealth possibilities of the United States, particularly in comparison with the wealth and income of the principal countries of Europe.

The stage of surplus wealth production which has now been reached by the United States places that country automatically in the category of the great financial empires. This point is well stated by W. S. Culbertson, in his analysis of the three chief stages in the recent economic development of the western world: the first is the period of territorial conquest; the second is the period of developing productive efficiency; the third is "the growth of a modern type of economic imperialism. The roots of this development are found in the nature of capitalism itself. The capitalist organization of machine production tends to produce more goods than can be sold at a profit. Capital also tends to accumulate rapidly. In other words, consumption both of goods and of capital tends to lag behind production. The capitalist class, therefore, which is in control of modern business, is constantly seeking new markets in which to dispose of goods and new opportunities for the investment of surplus capital." [1]

Since the United States has reached the stage of financial imperialism, there are three directions in which its foreign economic policy will normally develop:

1. The search for resources and supplies of raw materials upon which home industry depends for its survival.

2. The search for markets which will absorb surplus products.

3. The search for outside (extra-territorial) business opportunities. This last is sometimes described as the search for investment. It is more than that. It is a search for new fields in which business enterprise—trade, manufacturing, mining, lumbering, etc., may be carried on.

These three lines of expansion are now being followed by American business enterprise. Behind this enterprise are the immense funds of wealth and surplus that give it driving power.

[1] "Annals," v. 112, p. 5.

4. *Importing Raw Material and Food*

All industrial nations are compelled to import some of the raw materials out of which industrial products are made, and some of the food upon which the industrial population depends for its maintenance. The United States is no exception to this general rule.

There are two groups of raw materials which are bought outside the United States. First, those which the United States does not produce at all, such as rubber; sisal jute and raw silk; cocoanut oil (largely produced in the Philippines). Second, those raw materials which are found in the United States but in such small quantity or in such crude form that it is cheaper to buy the commodity abroad. In this second class are paper-pulp, petroleum, iron ore, tin, nickel, platinum, antimony, asbestos, lead bullion, nitrate. Wool, skins and hides are also largely imported because of the shortage of the domestic supply.

Although the United States produces a volume of food sufficient to maintain the population, there are certain food products that are imported in very large quantities. Among them are meat, fish, cheese, coffee, olive-oil, cocoa, sugar, bananas, lemons, dates and figs.

Since the middle of the last century the United States imports have passed through a significant development. In 1850 "crude materials for use in manufacturing" made up only 6.8 per cent of the total imports, while "food stuffs partly and wholly manufactured" made up 12.4 per cent; "manufactures for further use in manufacturing" comprised 15.1 per cent and "manufactures ready for consumption" made up 54.9 per cent of the whole. Against about seven per cent of raw products, the United States was importing over 82 per cent of manufactures or semi-manufactures.

By 1910, this situation was materially altered. Imports of "crude materials for use in manufacturing" were 36.4 per cent; "manufactures ready for consumption" had fallen to 23.6 per cent, while the other items held about the same proportions. During this period, therefore, the United States purchases from abroad were shifting from manufactured products to raw materials.[1]

The value of crude materials imported increased between 1850 and 1920 by nearly 150-fold. The value of manufactured products increased during the same time only nine-fold.

This change in the character of American imports, from manufactured products to raw products, has of necessity made a corresponding change in the source of United States purchases abroad. The manufactured products came from the manufacturing countries of Europe. The crude materials came, in the main, from Canada, Mexico, Central America, the West Indies and the Philippines.

5. *Foreign Markets*

Pressure toward the marketing of goods abroad comes from two directions. On the one hand the surplus products of highly specialized industry frequently cannot be disposed of within the country in which they are produced. In the second place the raw materials and other products of foreign origin can be paid for, in the long run, only by the export of commodities. Hence the business interests in every great economic nation are compelled to market outside of the national boundary lines. During the period of the World War, the United States became, second to Great Britain, the leading foreign trading nation of the world.

Like other industrial countries, the United States has been for a century an exporting nation, but the character of its exports, particularly since the middle of the nineteenth century, has undergone a very considerable modification.

Seventy years ago or thereabouts nearly two-thirds of all United States exports were crude materials for use in manufacturing, and more than four-fifths of the exports were crude materials and food stuffs. Manufactures ready for consumption comprise only a little more than one-tenth of the total exports of this period.

By the end of the century, manufactures ready for consump-

[1] U. S. "Statistical Abstract," 1922, p. 666 ff.

tion had increased to nearly one-sixth of the total, while crude materials for use in manufacturing had diminished to about one-third of the whole. From 1910 onward the change was comparatively rapid. Crude materials dropped to one-fourth of the total. Crude materials and crude food stuffs combined constitute less than two-fifths of the exports, while food stuffs partly or wholly manufactured, manufactures for use in further manufacturing, and manufactures ready for consumption, now comprise more than three-fifths of all United States exports.[1]

So long as the United States was exporting raw materials and food stuffs, the logical destination of these commodities was Europe. The transformation in American economic life which has made the United States in its turn a leader among manufacturing nations has shifted the export bulk from the raw material field to the manufactured field, and has, of necessity, shifted the export market at the same time.

The dramatic way in which this change in the destination of exports has occurred is well illustrated by figures showing the exports to the various continents.[2] Since 1850 exports to South America have been relatively constant. At that date, 5.9 per cent of all United States exports went to South America. In 1922 the percentage was again 5.9 per cent. Meanwhile, there have been variations. Exports to Africa comprised 1.5 per cent of the total in 1922. Since 1895 they have been relatively constant. Exports to Oceania were 2.7 per cent in 1922. They have increased slightly. The real change in United States exports may be found by comparing exports to Europe with exports to North America and Asia. During the early years of American imperialism, three-quarters of all American exports went to Europe. At the present time this proportion has been reduced to nearly one-half. During the same period the exports to Asia have increased five-fold and those to North America have risen from one-sixth to one-quarter of the total. Europe, a manufacturing centre, absorbs primarily raw materials and food. Asia and the Americas—

[1] U. S. "Statistical Abstract."
[2] U. S. "Foreign Commerce and Navigation."

markets for manufactured goods—have attracted the increasing attention of American business interests.

Europe is still the best market for American products. Her people buy approximately half of the commodities exported by the United States. Of this more than two-fifths goes to the United Kingdom while over one-seventh is absorbed by Germany. The United Kingdom, Germany and France together purchase seven-tenths of all the exports sent by the United States to Europe. There were, in 1922, seven European countries each of which bought more than $50 million worth of goods from the United States. The United Kingdom heads the list with $855 million; Spain comes at the end with $71 million.

United States exports to North America go chiefly to Canada, which takes more than half of the total exports to North American countries. Add Cuba and Mexico, and more than ninety per cent of the exports to North America are accounted for.

Total exports to South America are only about half of the exports to Canada alone. Argentina, Chili, Brazil and Colombia are the chief markets. Exports to Asia are practically confined to China and Japan, the latter country taking half of the entire Asiatic exports. Almost all of the exports to Oceania went to Australia and New Zealand, in the ratio of four to one. There is practically no market for United States goods in Africa.

The change in the type of goods exported and in the destination of the exports is obvious enough. The United States is ceasing to export raw materials for the use of manufacturing countries; is making up her own raw materials; is importing those that she lacks, and is marketing the manufactured product.

6. *The Export of Capital*

The export and import of goods need involve nothing more than a transitory economic relation. The trader, at best, is none too permanent. The export of capital, on the other hand, means that American investors have taken title to mines, railways, plantations, factories, and other property of a perma-

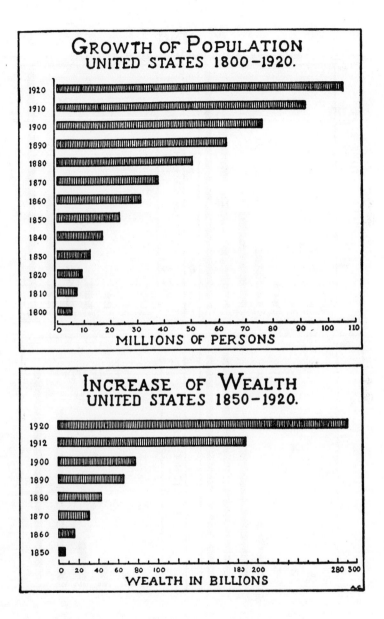

GROWTH OF POPULATION
UNITED STATES 1800–1920.

MILLIONS OF PERSONS

INCREASE OF WEALTH
UNITED STATES 1850–1920.

WEALTH IN BILLIONS

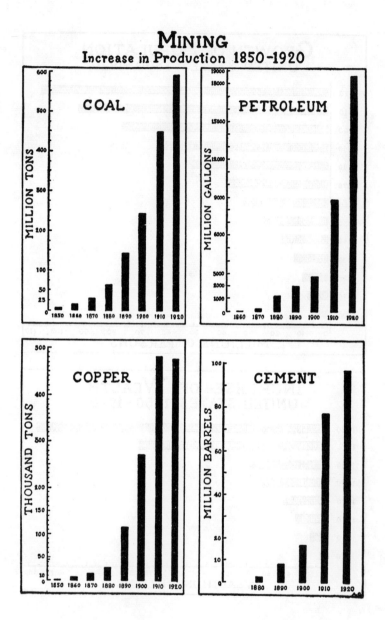

INDUSTRY
1850-1920

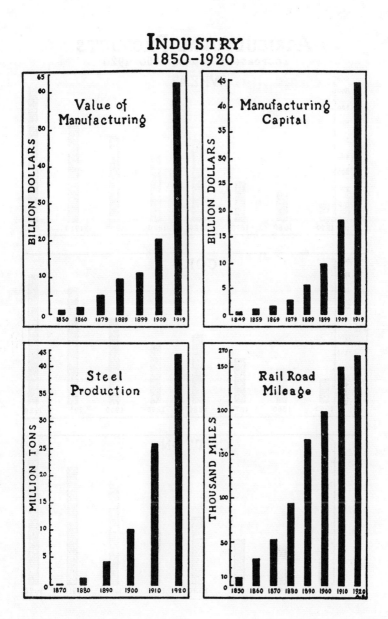

AGRICULTURAL PRODUCTS
Increase in Volume 1850-1920

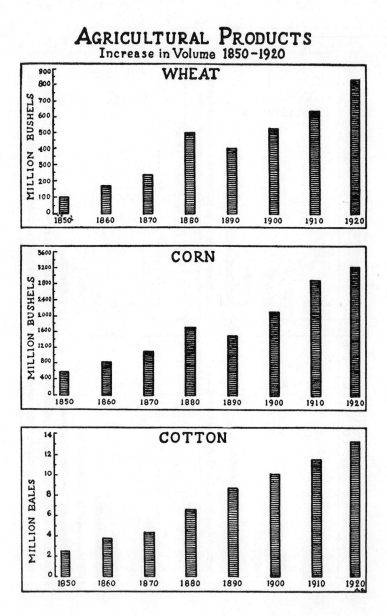

nent character lying outside of the territory over which the United States Government exercises jurisdiction. American business enterprise has passed beyond the political boundaries of the United States and is seeking business opportunities in Mexican oil fields, Cuban sugar plantations and Central American railroad systems.

This stage in economic development has frequently been described.[1] The leading industrial countries of Europe have all experienced it at the point where the economic surplus could find a more profitable investment market abroad than it could find at home. At the beginning of the present century the United States had reached this point in its economic development, and the experiences of the war compressed into a decade a process that would have extended, ordinarily, over a much longer period. Today the United States, as a leading investing nation, finds itself, not only with some twenty billions of dollars of economic interests abroad, but with a steadily growing demand for further investments. The United States has become, and must remain, an exporter of capital so long as there are surpluses of capital seeking investment and markets in which such investments can be made.

During the years 1904 and 1905 large Japanese loans were floated in American and European financial markets, and in March, 1907, when $115 million of these loans were refunded, half of the load was carried by American banking firms. These transactions may be described as the first real adventure of the United States financiers into the fields of international financing.[2]

United States investors, in 1900, held about $500 million worth of foreign securities, distributed as follows: Canada, $150 million; Mexico, $185 million; Cuba, $50 million; other Latin-American countries, $55 million; Europe, $10 million, and China and Japan, $5 million.[3] As an offset to these security holdings, there were about $3,000 million of foreign money in-

[1] Hobson, "Export of Capital," chs. I and II. U. S. National Monetary Commission, "Publications," v. 20, p. 155 ff.
[2] "Annalist," v. 16, p. 452.
[3] Fisk, "Inter-Ally Debts," p. 306.

vested in American securities, chiefly railways.[1] Sir George Paish puts the total of foreign investments in the United States at $6,000 million.[2] The Bankers Trust Company suggests the possibility of $7,000 million.[3] This situation left the United States a heavy net debtor to the outside world.

Within the next decade the volume of United States foreign investments climbed rapidly. In 1909 it was $2,000 million, and by 1913 it had reached $2,500 million.[4] Half of this amount was in Latin America and more than a quarter in Canada. The war with Spain, 1898, had given the United States the Philippines, Porto Rico, and a temporary protectorate over Cuba; Hawaii had been annexed during the war, hence the political basis for economic expansion had been laid at the same time that the economic developments of the United States provided a large fund of investible surplus.

The United States was still a net debtor to the outside world in 1913, but the total of United States investments in foreign countries was increasing far more rapidly than the total of foreign investments in the United States.

The war of 1914 greatly expedited the transformation of the United States from a debtor into a creditor nation. During the war years, the United States not only bought back some three billions of American securities owned abroad, but, in addition, advanced to the outside world, in the form of materials, credits, etc., some nine billions of dollars. During the four and a half war years the exports of the United States were $22,974 million, while imports were $11,166 million, leaving a balance of eleven billions in favour of the United States.[5]

This tendency toward foreign investment, stimulated by the war, continued to operate even after the depression of 1920–21 cut short post-war prosperity. D. R. Crissinger,[6] Comp-

[1] Hobson, "Export of Capital," ch. VI. "Yale Review," v. 9, pp. 265–285.
[2] U. S. National Monetary Commission, supra, p. 175.
[3] Fisk, supra, p. 310.
[4] Ibid., p. 306.
[5] American Economic Association, "Proceedings," 1920, p. 22.
[6] "Economic World," n. s. v. 24, p. 413. "Review of Economic Statistics," v. 1, p. 246 ff.

troller of the United States Treasury, summarized "Our contributions to financing the outside world" between August, 1914, and August, 1922, in this way:

	Millions
American securities repurchased from abroad..........	$ 3,000
American Government loans........................	10,000
Interest accrued on the above......................	2,000
Commercial credits extended abroad.................	3,000
Dollar securities bought from foreign countries......	2,731
Foreign money securities sold here..................	620
Foreign currencies bought by America...............	500
	$21,851

Post-war exports of United States capital have been large. Foreign securities floated in the United States totalled: [1]

$ 622 million in 1920
675 " " 1921
897 " " 1922
398 " " 1923
1,208 " " 1924

The flotations for 1924 included $567 million to Europe; $244 million to Canada and Newfoundland; $207 million for Latin America and $189 million for Asia.[2]

These foreign securities, sold on the American market, "do not present the entire outward movement of capital." "In addition, a large number of short-term bank credits were opened during the year and a considerable amount of direct industrial investment was made. It is extremely difficult, however, to obtain accurate data for these items."[3]

Besides these security purchases and credit transactions, United States interests have continued the expansion of their holdings in Canada and in Latin America. "An American Corporation took over the telephone lines in Spain." American interests bought the Anglo-Chilean Nitrate and Railway Co. from British holders.[4]

[1] U. S. "Federal Reserve Bulletin," v. 10, p. 96. U. S. "Commerce Reports," Jan. 26, 1925, pp. 184–186.
[2] Ibid., p. 186.
[3] Ibid., p. 184.
[4] Idem.

Capital exports for 1925 promise to exceed those for 1924. On March 13, 1925, the New York Times carried a list of pending foreign loans running over a billion dollars and predicted that the total of foreign securities sold in the United States in 1925 would exceed a billion and a half.

The decade following 1914 has witnessed the repayment of practically the entire debt owed by American business to foreign investors, and the piling up of obligations totalling more than twenty billions, held by American business men and by the United States Government against the business men and governments of foreign nations.

7. *United States Government Credits*

United States foreign economic assets are about equally divided between the obligations of European governments to the government of the United States and the commercial credits, investments, and enterprises of the business world. This economic classification leads to a geographic classification. United States government credits have been granted almost exclusively in Europe; United States foreign business assets are chiefly in the Americas.

The sums now owing by European governments to the government of the United States total about $12 billion. Nine and a half billions of this amount represent original war loans; about a billion represents credits due for surplus war supplies sold by the government of the United States to European governments, and the balance covers accrued and unpaid interest.

The principal debtors are Britain, with a total indebtedness of $4,577 million; France, with a total indebtedness of $4,137 million; Italy, with an indebtedness of $2,097 million, and Belgium, with an indebtedness of $471 million. Armenia, Austria, Czechoslovakia, Esthonia, Finland, Greece, Hungary, Latvia, Lithuania, Poland, Roumania, Russia and Jugoslavia owe much smaller amounts.[1]

[1] U. S. Treasury Dept., "Annual Report," 1923/24, p. 230.

8. *The Distribution of Business Investments*

United States business investments abroad represent so novel an experience that they have not as yet been made the object of such exhaustive studies as J. A. Hobson's "Imperialism," or C. K. Hobson's "Export of Capital." Still, the Department of Commerce has made several estimates, the Guaranty Trust Company and the Federal Reserve Board list and publish state, municipal and corporate bond-issues floated by foreign interests in the United States, and a number of private studies have dealt at considerable length with investments in particular regions.

W. R. Ingalls [1] estimates the total of the United States commercial investments in foreign countries at $2,977 million in 1916, and $3,993 million in 1920. The investments for 1920 are distributed as follows: South America, $535 million; Central America, $93 million; Canada, $1,450 million; Mexico, $800 million; Cuba, $525 million; Europe, $470 million, with scattering investments in other countries.

The Bankers Trust Company [2] distributes the "investments of the American people in foreign countries in 1923" as follows: North America, $3,556 million; Central America, $4 million; South America, $823 million; West Indies, $354 million, making a total for the Americas of $4,737 million. In the same table, the investment in Africa was placed at one million; in Asia, $476 million; in Europe, $2,194 million, and in Oceania $22 million.

Department of Commerce estimates on United States investments run very much higher than those of the Bankers Trust Company, and seemingly with good reason. It is difficult to understand, for example, how Central American investments can be written down at four millions, and investments in the West Indies at $354 million, in the Bankers Trust Company table, when United Fruit Company properties in Central America and United States sugar properties in Cuba alone would far exceed these amounts.

[1] Ingalls, "Wealth and Income," ch. III.
[2] Fisk, "Inter-Ally Debts," p. 310.

The Department of Commerce estimates of United States foreign investments at the end of 1924 are as follows:[1]

	Millions
Europe	$1,900
Asia and Oceania	690
Latin America	4,040
Canada and Newfoundland	2,460

9. New Fields for American Enterprise

Foreign trade and the export of capital have opened up new and vast fields to American enterprise. The great stores of natural resources, the large capital equipment, and the technical efficiency of United States industry create surpluses which are finding better paying investment opportunities outside of the United States than inside the country. The pressing demand for certain raw materials, such as rubber, oil and silk, which are not produced in sufficient quantity within the United States, forces American enterprises to seek out and hold the sources of such products. The war loans, the largest single item among United States foreign assets, have placed sixteen European countries in a position of debtor to the United States Treasury.

The United States, like other industrial countries which are passing from the supplying of raw materials to the marketing of manufactured commodities, faces the necessity of making this adjustment in its economic relations. United States exports in 1922 were more than a sixth of the total exports of the world. In 1922, they were $3,765 million, as compared with $3,190 million for the United Kingdom; $1,673 million for France; $783 million for Japan and $443 million for Italy. Although these exports comprised only a small percentage of the total volume of American economic products, the United States has taken a position as one of the competitors in the world struggle to establish and maintain foreign markets.

The post-war income of the United States is estimated to be as great as the combined incomes of Great Britain, France, Italy, Russia, and Germany. There is no satisfactory way of estimat-

[1] U. S. "Trade Information Bulletin," no. 340, p. 12.

ing investible surplus for these countries, but the relative position of the United States is evident enough.[1]

10. *Political Implications of Economic Imperialism*

The United States Government and United States investors hold claims against foreign governments and foreign properties aggregating more than twenty billions of dollars. The bulk of the government loans are in Europe, and most of the business investments are in Canada and Latin America. These facts are not controverted. They are merely a statistical record of American business abroad. Regarded from a social standpoint, however, they are the economic structure of American imperialism.

Economic activities are reflected sooner or later in the realm of politics. It is therefore only a question of time when foreign investments will modify foreign policy. This is a commonplace in Europe, where empires like Britain and France are accustomed to deal with the political issues arising out of foreign investments. The problem is new, however, in the United States. Less than a generation has elapsed since the United States first became an investing nation; it is only in the last decade that the political problems of foreign investment have presented a real issue in the public life of the United States.

While it is not possible to assert that there is an inexorable sequence in the relation between economic investment and diplomatic policy, the experience of the United States during the last dozen years, confirmed by previous experiences of European financial empires, would indicate a development which might be briefly described as follows: (1) Migration of capital takes place, but without any political implications, as in the economic relations between the United States and Canada. (See Chapter II.) (2) Capital, migrating to foreign countries, soon makes demands upon the foreign governments within whose jurisdiction investments are located. These demands are made under the authority of concessions, bankers' contracts, and the like. While the distinction between non-political migrations of capital and capital migrations in response to concessions

---

[1] Fisk, supra, p. 265.

is not very sharp, it ordinarily appears in modified political behaviour. Bolivia is now in the twilight zone between peaceful migration of capital and political control by American bankers. (See Chapter II.) (3) American interests have been working for three decades to secure concessions in China. The efforts to control oil in the Near East have covered more than a dozen years. (See Chapter III.) (4) The influx of American capital and the participation of its representatives in local political activity leads to active interference with the internal affairs of foreign countries, such as Hawaii and Mexico. This interference has taken the form of the encouragement and subsidizing of revolution. (See Chapter IV.) (5) Where United States investors do not receive satisfactory treatment from local authorities they apply to the United States Government for support. In a number of such cases, the armed forces of the United States have intervened in the internal affairs of countries like Haiti, Santo Domingo, and Nicaragua. (See Chapter V.) (6) After a territory has accepted United States control, military occupation ceases. (See Chapter VI.) (7) The sequence is completed by the armed conquest of territory (the Philippines, Chapter VII) and by the purchase of territory (the Virgin Islands, Chapter VII) without consulting the wishes of the populations that are transferred to American sovereignty.

This cycle is best illustrated in the relations between the United States and the Caribbean countries, since it has its freest expression where a strong country is dealing with a weak one. The war established important economic relations between the United States and her European peers, resulting in a heavy mortgage debt held by the United States against Europe. (See Chapter VIII.)

Throughout this whole process economic interests work hand in hand with the officials of the United States Government. In the course of this co-operation a technique of imperialism has been developed which is now well advanced and which is accepted and practised alike by Democratic and Republican administrations. (See Chapter IX.)

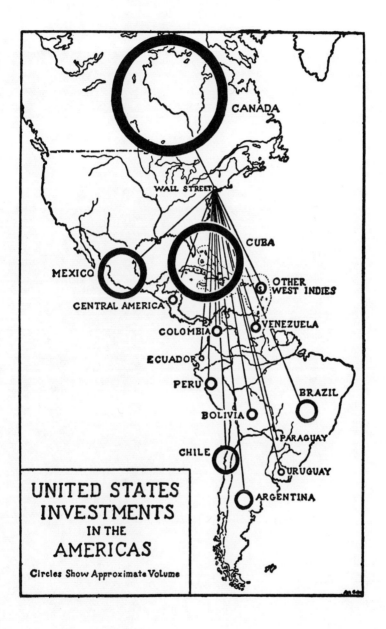

CANADA

WALL STREET

CUBA

MEXICO

OTHER
WEST INDIES

CENTRAL AMERICA

COLOMBIA

VENEZUELA

ECUADOR

PERU

BRAZIL

BOLIVIA

PARAGUAY

CHILE

URUGUAY

UNITED STATES
INVESTMENTS
IN THE
AMERICAS

ARGENTINA

Circles Show Approximate Volume

II

ECONOMIC PENETRATION

1. *The Opening Wedge of Imperialism*

Peaceful economic penetration, the opening wedge of imperialism, results from the migration of capital.

Capital is probably more fluid and mobile at the present time than is labour. During the past century, capital from industrial countries has penetrated the most remote parts of the world—first in shipping and trading ventures; later in mining, agricultural, manufacturing, public utility and similar enterprises. C. K. Hobson [1] gives a detailed account of British overseas investment; the opening chapter of this book tells the same story for the United States, and the principle of capital migration with minor variations applies to the other leading industrial countries. Just as fluid capital (credit) is transferred from New York and Boston to Kansas City and Denver, fluid capital is transferred from Paris and London to Buenos Ayres, Cape Town and Toronto. National boundary lines make the movement of capital more difficult; wars temporarily restrict it, but in the long run it is easier to get a visa for a financial transaction than it is for a passport permitting emigration. "In modern times," writes C. K. Hobson [2] "emigration of capital has been more and more separated from emigration of persons. It has become possible for persons to move from one land to another and to retain full rights and adequate control over the capital which they have left behind them. In the same way, persons who remain in their own country can send their property abroad while retaining their rights to it, and obtaining periodic payments for the service performed by it."

[1] Hobson, "Export of Capital."
[2] Ibid., pp. 77-78.

The migration of capital is most easily studied in the case of two neighbouring countries like Canada and the United States having the same language and business customs. In such a situation, given a reasonable degree of security and stability, the movement of capital will be almost as free as it is between the various states of the United States. This is particularly true when there is a surplus of capital on one side of the boundary and a shortage of it on the other.

2. *Financing a New Civilization*

Like the United States, Canada was settled and is occupied by Europeans and their descendants, while more than nine-tenths of the Mexican population is Indian. Canadian industrialism grew very slowly prior to 1900 and during the last twenty years it has made great progress, particularly under the pressure of war demand. Twenty-five years ago, the United States farmers and United States bankers both had ample room for expansion inside their own borders. With the exhaustion of free land, however, the abundant and undeveloped Canadian resources assumed a position of vital importance to the farmers, miners, lumbermen and other business interests in the United States.

Canada is larger than the United States by half a million square miles. Its total productive land is rated at 537.8 millions of acres (as compared with 293.8 millions in the United States). The forest acreage of Canada is rated at 800 millions compared with an acreage of 500 millions in the United States. Canada has one-sixth of the total coal reserves of the world, while in Newfoundland alone there are 3,635 million tons of iron ore (as compared with about 4,200 million tons in the United States). E. C. Eckel [1] notes that there are deposits across Canada from New Brunswick to British Columbia which have never yet been adequately surveyed.

These extensive tracts of agricultural land, timber land, coal deposits and iron reserves, make Canada the logical field for expansion from the United States. Within a few years the

[1] Eckel, "Iron Ores," pp. 378-385.

United States will cease to produce a sufficient supply of wheat and meat to feed its own population. The Canadian wheat fields will then become indispensable. Already the timber supply of the United States is seriously depleted and the forest reserves of Canada are being drawn upon for paper stock and for lumber. The coal of Nova Scotia particularly and the iron of Newfoundland constitute economic advantages of huge importance to United States heavy industry.

3. The Growing Canadian Demand for Capital

Canada herself has been slow to develop her resources. Although the Canadian territory was colonized at the same time as that of the United States, various factors have operated to prevent the growth of Canadian population and of Canadian industry. At the present time, while the area of Canada is greater than that of the United States, the population is only about seven per cent of the population of the United States, and the disparity between the wealth of the two countries is equally striking. The completion of transcontinental railway lines toward the end of the nineteenth century laid the basis for a new Canadian expansion in the course of which both British and United States capital have penetrated the Dominion to a very considerable degree.

4. British Bankers Supply the First Canadian Capital

Until about 1900, the amount of British capital invested in Canada was small. With the opening of the Canadian West, however, and the development of mining, manufacturing, lumbering and farming, a new field was created which British investors were glad to seize. So rapid was the development of Canadian demand for capital that by 1910 Canada had more British capital invested than any of the other dominions.[1]

In 1913 Canadian flotations in London amounted to 47 million pounds sterling out of a total of 245 million pounds of capital subscriptions made in the United Kingdom, or nearly one-fifth of the whole. This movement continued to the very

[1] "Annals," v. 68, p. 29 ff.

eve of the war: in the first six months of 1914 over 37 million pounds sterling of British capital found the same outlet.[1]

C. K. Hobson estimates [2] that in 1913 British investors placed 44 million pounds sterling in Canada as compared with 18 million pounds in Australia, 18 million pounds in the United States, 15 million pounds in Brazil, 11 million pounds in Argentina, and lesser amounts in other countries. The total foreign holdings of British investors for 1913 he placed at 515 million pounds sterling in Canada, 378 million pounds in India and Ceylon, 370 million pounds in South Africa, 319 million pounds in Argentina, and 754 million pounds in the United States.

At the outbreak of the war, Canada was thus the principal recipient of the new investment funds from Great Britain (the chief investing nation of the world at that time) and, with the exception of the United States, Canada had more British investments than any other country of the world.

5. *United States Investors Enter the Field*

The Monetary Times Annual for 1914 estimates the United States investments in Canada as follows:

$$1909 \ldots \ldots \ldots \ldots \$279 \text{ million}$$
$$1911 \ldots \ldots \ldots \ldots \quad 417$$
$$1913 \ldots \ldots \ldots \ldots \quad 636$$

British investments in Canada for 1910 were estimated at 365 million pounds sterling.[3] Five years before the war American investments in Canada were less than one-sixth of those of Great Britain, while at the outbreak of the war they were about one-fourth of the British investments.

Even in 1914, however, the economic dependence of Canada upon the United States was considerable. While the bulk of her exports went to the British Isles, the bulk of her imports came from the United States. Thus in 1913 Canadian exports of Canadian produce totalled $356 million of which nearly

---

[1] "Annals," v. 68, p. 217.
[2] Ibid., p. 29.
[3] Ibid., p. 218.

half ($170 million) went to the United Kingdom and $140 million to the United States. In the same year Canada imported goods to the value of $671 million, of which nearly two-thirds ($437 million) came from the United States, while only $139 million came from the United Kingdom.[1] Thus Canada was borrowing extensively in Great Britain and using a part of the money to pay for the goods that she was buying in the United States.

Meanwhile two other movements of importance were taking place. Farmers from the Middle West were migrating into the Canadian wheat belt, while business houses from the United States were establishing branch plants and branch offices in the principal Canadian business centres.

6. The Effects of the War

The war increased the demand for Canadian goods. Canadian exports were $377 million in 1913 and $1,179 million in 1917.[2] These exports consisted in part of food and raw materials but they also represented a very great increase in the manufacturing industry. Thus the steel production of Canada was 743 thousand gross tons in 1914 and 1,695 thousand gross tons in 1918;[3] exports of cotton fabrics were 356 thousand yards in 1914 and 846 thousand yards in 1917; exports of drugs and chemicals, $1,695 thousand in 1914 and $9,164 thousand in 1917; exports of woollens in 1914, $81,555, in 1917, $725,148.[4]

The amount of capital invested in Canadian manufacturing industries increased from $1,959 million in 1915 to $3,230 million in 1919.[5] Similar expansion took place in mining, power development and other enterprises requiring large capital investments. During these same years Canada was floating war loans and making other unusual capital demands upon her population.

[1] "Canada Year Book," 1922–23, pp. 474–5.
[2] Ibid., p. 470.
[3] "Mineral Industry," 1923, p. 355.
[4] "Canada Year Book," 1918, pp. 308–316.
[5] Ibid., 1922–23, pp. 415–416.

Capital, in sufficient volume to meet this demand, was not available in Canada. It could no longer be imported from Great Britain because of the pressure of war demand there. There was only one source from which it could be readily derived and that was the United States. By 1919 the net flow of the United States capital into Canada was estimated at $220 million, and for 1920 it rose to $325 million.[1] Ingalls estimates that in 1920 the total of American capital in Canada was about $1,800 million as compared with $279 million in 1909 and $636 million in 1913. Here was an increase of more than six-fold between 1909 and 1920 and of nearly three-fold between 1913 and 1920.

Following the war, in the spring of 1920, a period of industrial depression set in, which gave the United States investors new opportunities to penetrate the Canadian field. The disorganization of European economic life rendered continental investments uninviting. The evident stability of industrialism in Canada provided an unusually strong incentive for United States economic expansion in that direction. The Canadians themselves were forced to call for this assistance because, like the business men in every other country, they had expanded at an exceptionally rapid rate during the war and with the depression of 1920 many of them were caught in a position where they could not meet their obligations. Consequently they were forced to rely upon financial assistance from the strongest financial centre in their neighbourhood, namely New York. Then too, with the cessation of the war demand, many of the newly established manufacturing industries found themselves without a market for their product and were forced either to close down completely or else to make terms with American banking interests that would carry them over the period of depression.[2] The American Economist states that between 1920 and 1923 the per cent of Canadian manufacturing controlled in the United States increased from about 50 per cent to about 60 per cent. According to the editor of the Economist this was

[1] Ingalls, "Wealth and Income," pp. 61-2.
[2] "American Economist," v. 71, pp. 77-8.

due in part to the failure of Canadian investors to hold their economic position in the face of hard times and in part to the rapid movement of the United States manufacturers to establish plants in Canadian territory.

7. *Nationality of Canadian Capital*

Before the war, the bulk of imported Canadian capital was British. At the end of the war—certainly by 1920—the total volume of United States capital in Canada was probably equal to the total volume of British capital in Canada. An article by W. L. Mackenzie King [1] states that: "It was estimated in 1920 that the investments of the United States in Canada stood at one billion 272 million 850 thousand, the chief items being $714 million in bonds, $150 million in branch industries, $94 million 276 thousand in insurance company investments, and $197 million in the timber mills and mines of British Columbia." In the same article, Mr. King writes: "Before the war and during the early years of the war British investments in Canada were far in excess of those of the United States. Today, however, the banking authorities in New York affirm that there is as much American as British money invested in Federal, provincial, municipal and industrial securities."

Manufacturing capital is still controlled by Canadians, but the United States has outstripped British investors in this field. As far back as 1918, 34 per cent of Canadian industrial stocks were owned in the United States.[2]

Estimates of British and United States investments in Canada for 1923 are:[3]

	United States Capital	British Capital
	(in millions of dollars)	
Railways	$425	$850
Government and Municipal bonds	701	456
Industries		
Forestry	325	60
Mining	235	100

[1] "Manchester Guardian Commercial," v. 7, p. 370.
[2] Canada, Com. Int. Ser., "Canada as a Field for British Branch Industries."
[3] "Financial Post Survey," 1925, p. 195.

	United States Capital	British Capital
	(in millions of dollars)	
Fisheries	$ 5	$ 3
Public Services......................	137	116
Other industries.....................	540	145
Mortgages and Land..................	75	185
Banking and Insurance...............	35	80
	2,478	1,995

The same figures are summarized and contrasted with 1918:

Outside Investments in Canada
(in millions of dollars)

	1918	%	1923	%
Great Britain...........	$1,860	77	$1,995	42
United States...........	417	17	2,478	52
Other	140	6	323	6
	$2,417	100	$4,796	100

8. *Canadian Bond Sales*

The rapid movement of United States capital into Canada is well illustrated by the Canadian bond sales during the past fifteen years. In 1910 one-sixth of the Canadian bonds were marketed in Canada, a negligible number in the United States and the balance in Great Britain. During the years which followed the outbreak of the war, the volume of bonds marketed in Canada and in the United States steadily increased while the British market for Canadian bonds has been practically eliminated.

Summary Bond Sales in All Markets [1]
1910–1924 (figures in millions of dollars)

Year	Sold in Canada	Sold in United Kingdon	Sold in United States	Total
1910	39.3	188.1	3.6	231.0
1911	44.9	204.3	17.6	266.8
1912	37.7	204.2	30.9	272.9
1913	45.6	277.5	50.7	373.8
1914	32.9	185.9	53.9	272.9
1915	114.3	41.2	178.6	335.1
1916	102.9	5.0	206.9	356.9
1917	546.3	5.0	174.7	726.0

[1] "Monetary Times," v. 74, no. 2, p. 80.

Summary Bond Sales in All Markets (continued)
1910–1924 (figures in millions of dollars)

Year	Sold in Canada	Sold in United Kingdon	Sold in United States	Total
1918	727.4	14.6	33.3	775.4
1919	705.4	5.1	199.4	909.9
1920	101.8	—	223.0	324.9
1921	213.3	12.2	178.1	403.6
1922	250.2	—	242.2	492.4
1923	427.9	2.4	84.5	514.8
1924	336.8	3.6	239.5	579.9

Another significant aspect of the sale of bonds is provided by Canadian state and municipal financing. The Federal Reserve Board [1] lists the Canadian state and municipal loans then outstanding in the United States. The total number of loans is 189. The total amount is $233,964,244. The largest (Province of Quebec) is for $7,000,000. The smallest (Prince Rupert, B. C.) is for $2,500. They include water, school, road, light and power, sewer, and other bonds. Six of the loans were floated in 1913 and 1914; 58 in 1915 and 1916; 16 in 1917 and 1918, and 49 in 1919 and 1920.

9. Branch Plants in Canada

No complete study has been published showing the number of United States branch plants in Canada. G. W. Austen [2] states that "There are six or seven hundred openly known branches of American industries in Canada, such as the International Harvester, the Canadian General Electric, the General Motors, but there are hundreds of companies with Canadian names, Canadian directorates, and supposedly Canadian management that, in reality, are financially controlled in New York, Chicago, Boston, Pittsburgh, or other centres."

The Canadian Commercial Intelligence Service [3] notes the rapidity with which United States capital has penetrated the Canadian field. "During the calendar years 1919 and 1920 the influx of industries became more pronounced than ever before.

[1] U. S. "Federal Reserve Bulletin," v. 7, pp. 945–7.
[2] "American Economist," v. 71, p. 77.
[3] Canada, Com. Int. Ser., supra, p. 117.

For example, during these years in Toronto alone there were established 46 additional U. S. industries, as compared with 18 Canadian and 4 British." A. G. Sclater of the Union Bank of Canada puts the number of United States branch plants in Canada at "over seven hundred" and "the number is increasing yearly." [1]

The economic position occupied by the United States business interests in Canada is thus summarized by F. S. Chalmers.

"The United States owns one-third of all the industries in Canada and one-third of all the producing mines; it owns a large part of the timber resources not vested in the Crown, and has extensive interests besides in Canadian water powers, real estate and other assets. Investors in the United States hold, besides, a third of all the bonds issued by Canadian provinces, a third of all the debentures issued by Canadian municipalities, and are developing an increasing interest in the bonds of the Dominion Government. . . .

"British investments in Canada are, roughly, two billion dollars, which is less than the pre-war figure by a small fraction. United States investments in Canada may be accepted as having now definitely passed that mark and are close to two and a half billions. . . .

"Strong imperialists in Britain may 'view with alarm' the displacement of British ownership of Canadian enterprise by United States ownership. But protests or discussions would be futile. Capital knows no allegiance to nationality. . . . The investment possibilities of Canada, regardless of boundary lines or political affiliations, have been the underlying factors in the movement.' [2]

10. *The Technique of Peaceful Economic Penetration*

Abundant resources, parallel economic and social development and the proximity of the Canadian field, all combine to make Canada the logical depository for large volumes of United States capital. This capital migration which has been active for less than twenty-five years has, nevertheless, reached such proportions that many of the important Canadian economic activities are already under the financial domination of American banking and other business interests. Temporarily

[1] "Manchester Guardian Commercial Supplement," Sept. 18, 1924, p. 38.
[2] "Annalist," v. 22, p. 208.

the influx of American capital into Canada has been checked by the rapid decrease in capital demand due to the general world depression following the war. British investors have been quite generally eliminated from the Canadian field and ultimately important Canadian resources must almost inevitably be developed by importations of United States capital.

These capital migrations have taken place without the exercise of any force or threat of force. They have occurred just as logically as the migration of eastern capital into the frontier communities of the newly developing West. In this case the frontier lies to the north and the presence of a political boundary furnishes no serious obstacle. Despite changes in the political complexion of the governments at Ottawa and at Washington, the economic forces represented by these capital migrations continue to draw United States business interests into the Canadian field.

11. *Economic Penetration under Government Control*

Economic penetration acquires a political aspect when capital is brought into a country under a special permit from the government. These permits range all the way from licenses to concessions, but in every case they establish a relation between the holder of the permit and the government which grants it. This is particularly true where the permit is for an unlimited or for an indefinite term. In that case, the holder of the permit is almost compelled to take such steps as are necessary to preserve friendly relations with the permit-issuing authority.

A good case in point is an executive decree granting to Swift and Co. the right to construct a pier in the port of La Plata. The decree is dated Buenos Ayres, June 22, 1918, and reads as follows:

"The Chief Executive of the Nation Decrees:
"Art. 1. The concession will have a precarious character, the Government having the right to declare it ended at any moment when it considers it convenient, without any right of complaint on the part of the concessionary company.

"Art. 2. The work will be executed according to the details of the plans attached, and under the supervision of the General Direction of Hydraulic Works, which may introduce in the course of the same modifications which it deems necessary."

The other three sections of the decree provide that the concessionary company must pay the legal taxes and abide by the regulations in force, and must also pay the expense of the government inspection of the work.[1]

Similarly, the United Fruit Co., with docks at Sama, Cuba, applied to the Government for an authorization, legalizing these docks. A decree (No. 283) was therefore issued in much the same way that any license bureau in the United States would issue a license.[2]

12. *The Bolivian Loan of 1922*

Peculiarly exacting are the conditions which are ordinarily imposed when the bankers of a powerful country lend money to the government of a weaker country. Numbers of such loans have been made in the past by European bankers;[3] and during recent years United States bankers have entered the field. Most of the United States bank loans have been made to the governments of Latin-American countries. Many such loans carry guarantees which place the borrowing government at the mercy of the banking syndicate.

The Bolivian Loan of 1922 is an excellent illustration of the type of bankers' contract frequently met with in the case of Latin-American loans.

Authorization for a loan not to exceed $33 million was provided in the Bolivian law of May 24, 1922. The contract of May 31, 1922, entered into between the Government of Bolivia on the one hand and the Stifel and Nicolaus Investment Co., Spencer Trask and Co., and the Equitable Trust Co., on

---

[1] Argentina, "Boletin Oficial," June 27, 1918, pp. 608-9.
[2] Cuba, "Gaceta Oficial," July 17, 1906, pp. 421-2.
[3] Hobson, "Imperialism," p. 63 ff. Viallate, "Economic Imperialism," ch. III.

the other, provided for the issuance of a $26 million bond issue. The terms of the contract require the borrower to pay annually ten per cent of the original principal amount of issue, in monthly instalments. After paying the interest of eight per cent, the balance is turned into a sinking fund, which will be used for the repurchase of bonds after May 1, 1938. The issue matures May 14, 1947. The bonds are exempt from present and future Bolivian taxation.[1]

As a guarantee that the loan of 1922 will be paid, both as to principal and interest, the Republic of Bolivia "affects and encumbers with a first lien or pledge and charge in favour of the Trustees, the following shares of stock, funds, revenues and taxes as security for the full payment of the principal, premium and interest of the Bonds and all other expenses and amounts required for or incident to this Contract or to the service of the loan:

a. "All of the shares not less than 114,000 of the Banco de la Nacion Boliviana belonging to the Republic and which the Republic represents are sufficient at present to control said Bank." The Republic agrees to deliver to the Trustee under the contract either bearer certificates or certificates of stock "representing said shares." Should the capital stock of the Banco de la Nacion be increased at any time during the life of the loan, "the Republic shall acquire such proportion of additional shares as shall be necessary for said control; the shares so acquired shall immediately thereafter be pledged as security for the loan." Thus the control of the Bolivian National Bank is assured to those who are administering the loan.

In addition to these shares of the bank stock, the Republic pledges, as security for the loan:

b. All revenues representing dividends on these shares of stock.

c. The tax upon mining claims or concessions.

d. Revenues from the alcohol monopoly.

[1] U. S. "Trade Information Bulletin," no. 194, pp. 13-15. Bolivia; Hacienda, "Memoria," 1922, pp. 41-140.

e. Ninety per cent of the revenue received by the Republic from the tobacco monopoly.

f. The tax on corporations other than mining and banking.

g. The tax upon the net income of bank.

h. The mortgage tax.

i. The tax on the net profits of mining companies.

j. All import duties.

k. All export duties.

l. All funds, revenues, and taxes now or hereafter allocated by special laws to the construction of the Potosi-Sucre Railroad.

m. First mortgages and liens upon all the properties and earnings of the Railroads constructed from Villazon to Atocha and from Potosi to Sucre, including their franchises and other property and their net earnings.

Should the railroads above mentioned be sold as a result of the foreclosure of the mortgage, "the purchaser shall have the right to operate the said railroads for a period of 99 years from the date of such purchase" and the company that is organized to operate the railroads "as also the entire business and property thereof, shall, in respect to said railroads be free from taxes and imposts of all kinds."

As a further guarantee, the Republic agrees not to contract any external loan prior to Dec. 5, 1924, without the consent of the Bankers, and after that time, "and so long as any Bonds of the present loan shall remain outstanding," the Republic will not contract any further loans unless, for two years immediately preceding such a proposed loan, the revenues pledged to the service of the present loan shall have produced annually "at least one and one-half times the amount required for the service of the present loan," and unless, during those years the Republic shall have raised enough revenue to meet all of its ordinary general expenses, without borrowing or without selling capital assets.

These provisions place in the hands of the loaning Bankers the virtual control of the Bolivian National Bank, the property and revenues of certain Bolivian railroads, and the revenues of the Republic, at the same time practically precluding additional loans during the life of the present loan.

13. *The Fiscal Commission*

For the practical administration of the provisions contained in the Bolivian Loan Contract, a Permanent Fiscal Commission is provided, consisting of three members. "The President of the Republic shall appoint the three Commissioners; of these, two to be appointed upon recommendation of the Bankers." These two members of the Commission, recommended by the Bankers, may be removed "at any time, at the request of the Bankers."

The Commission "shall act by majority vote; and shall elect as its chairman and Chief Executive one of the two Commissioners who shall have been recommended by the Bankers."

This Bankers' representative, so long as any bonds of the loan remain outstanding, "shall be elected a member of the Board of Directors of the Banco de la Nacion Boliviana, and the Republic shall take such action as may be necessary to secure his election and continuance in office as such."

Section 3 of this article provides that "the total cost of the Commission shall constitute a part of the service of the Loan and shall be included in the amounts to be deposited monthly in the Banco de la Nacion Boliviana."

As for the duties of the Commission, they are simple and inclusive. So long as any bonds of the loan remain outstanding, and beginning not later than August 1, 1922, "the collection of all taxes, revenues and income of the Nation shall be supervised and fiscalized by the Permanent Fiscal Commission, the creation of which has been authorized by Law of March 27, 1922."

These provisions for the organization and functioning of the Permanent Fiscal Commission place the entire revenue of the Republic under the control of three men, two of whom are selected by the loaning Bankers, and one of whom, as Chief Executive, sits on the Board of the Bolivian National Bank and helps to determine its policy. The costs of this Commission are paid out of the revenues which it controls.

The Permanent Fiscal Commission holds the economic key to the life of the Republic and the Bankers control the Commission. As yet there has been no default, and no political issues have been raised, but this loan contract ties the representatives of the loaning Bankers into the heart of Bolivian political life by placing in their hands the control of Bolivian public revenues. Should a default take place, the members of the Commission automatically become the central figures in the Bolivian political world, and the Loan of 1922 takes precedence over all other public considerations. There is, in this relation, an international issue of the first magnitude between the Government of the United States and the Government of Bolivia. While the issue may never arise, the fact remains that representatives of an American banking syndicate are administering the finances of a sister Republic.

14. *Economic Penetration and Political Interference*

There is no boundary line between economic penetration and political interference. Modern imperial practice calls upon governments to "protect life and property." When, therefore, a nation like the United States reaches the stage at which its property owners acquire extensive economic interests outside the nation's boundaries, the political protection of these interests follows as a matter of course.

Investments in Canada, although they are more extensive than United States investments in any other foreign territory, have never as yet involved serious political issues. Latin-American investments, on the other hand, have given rise to various diplomatic tangles, resulting in the use of the army and the navy in a number of instances.

Although it is impossible to name the point at which economic penetration will lead to political interference, the history of modern imperialism suggests that such a point is quite generally reached. And certainly recent United States relations with Latin America indicate that the United States is as likely to reach the interference point as is any other imperial power.

III

SPHERES OF INFLUENCE

1. "Spheres" in China

The years which witnessed the opening up of the vast resources of China to international capital also witnessed the entrance of two new powers into the arena of imperialism: Japan, which was thrust into the foreground by her victory in the Chino-Japanese War of 1895; and the United States, which emerged as a first class power with her victory over Spain in 1898. In that same year the first great "battle of concessions" was waged in China.

China with her abundant resources and her population of four hundred millions was an ideal place for the investment of the surplus capital in the hands of European and American business men and bankers. A new technique of imperialism was evolving. "The days of territorial expansion by discovery and colonization or conquest by force of arms" gave way to the "more crafty kid-gloved methods of dominating weak and improvident nations through the insidious operations of political finance." [1] A new terminology including such phrases as "sphere of interest" and "sphere of influence" was evolved to describe the new "conquest by railway and bank."

A sphere of interest is "a portion of territory wherein a nation has expressly or impliedly declared that it will permit no other nation to exert political influence, and that itself will lead in the exploitation of natural resources." [2] The control of a sphere of interest was exerted in the following way:

First, the foreign investors secured a strategic base on the seacoast; this was followed by building a railway for the

---

[1] "Far Eastern Review," v. 11, p. 277.
[2] Reinsch, "World Politics," p. 114.

successful exploitation of the natural resources and the domination of the economic life of the "sphere." The next step was to establish a bank or to obtain a first option on loans or concessions, especially those covering railways and mines. To safeguard their particular interests, the governments behind the investors then forced China to agree not to alienate the territory under their economic control, and entered into mutual agreements to respect each other's spheres of interest.

2. The American Sphere of Interest: Manchuria

This new imperialist technique was applied to the economic subjugation of China after the Chino-Japanese War of 1894–5 had demonstrated the helplessness of the Celestial Empire. Russia acquired as her sphere of interest North Manchuria and Outer Mongolia, with Port Arthur as a strategic base;[1] Japan acquired South Manchuria and Inner Mongolia with Formosa and the Pescadores as a strategic base;[2] Germany leased Kiaochow, and thus obtained the Shantung peninsula as her sphere of exploitation;[3] Great Britain by the acquisition of Waihaiwai laid claim to the Yangtse Valley, Thibet and the Szechwan province;[4] while France controlled Southwestern China, including Kwangtung, Kwangsi and Yunnan, and Kwangchowang.[5]

In this "battle of concessions," lasting up to 1900, the United States obtained no strategic base, but her victory in the Spanish-American War had given her the Philippines. These islands, combined with its large Pacific seaboard, made the United States a Far Eastern power. Furthermore, her merchants had been carrying on an extensive trade, chiefly with Manchuria, for over half a century. Hence, when the financiers of the various powers made bids for the construction of the great central trunk line from Peking to Canton by way of Hankow, the American Chinese Development Company entered the race.

[1] MacMurray, "Treaties and Agreements," v. 1, p. 119.
[2] Ibid., pp. 19–20.
[3] Ibid., p. 112.
[4] Ibid., pp. 1, 94, 104, 152.
[5] Ibid., pp. 28, 124, 128.

This company had among its participants the Standard Oil Co. and the American Sugar Refining Co.[1] The American interests obtained the concession for the southern portion of this line in 1898.[2]

The contract for the northern section of the railroad was given to a Belgian concern. The American China Development Company went to the expense of making two surveys and building about thirty miles of railroad from Canton north; but the death of its directing spirit, Ex-Senator Brice, forced it to suspend work. In 1905 J. P. Morgan purchased the Belgian interest[3] but did not go on with the project, not being interested at that time in Chinese investment. Eventually the Hankow-Canton railway contract was cancelled, and the Chinese Government bought out all the property of the American China Development Company.[4] This first venture of American finance in China ended badly, but it was used later as a precedent for claims to the exploitation of Manchuria, and proved to be the beginning of a tenacious fight carried on by bankers and by the State Department for economic control of that area.

3. The Open Door Policy

One year after the American China Development Company obtained the concession for the Hankow-Canton railway, Secretary of State John Hay announced to the great powers the policy which the United States Government would follow in regard to the international battle for the exploitation of China. With a view to preventing the partition of China, and especially the absorption of Manchuria, which American business men considered their particular sphere of interest, Secretary Hay in 1899 made the formal declaration of the Open Door Policy.[5]

[1] Reinsch, supra, pp. 128-9.
[2] MacMurray, "Treaties and Agreements," v. I, pp. 519-22.
[3] Croly, "Willard Straight," p. 287.
[4] U. S. "Foreign Relations," 1905, pp. 124-5. MacMurray, supra, pp. 519-22.
[5] Overlach, "Foreign Financial Control in China," p. 199.

The Open Door Policy recognized special interests and spheres of influence, but insisted on equal opportunity in trade. In its formal aspects, the proposition submitted by Secretary Hay requested a declaration from "the various powers claiming 'spheres of influence' in China to the effect that each in its respective spheres of interest or influence—

"First. Will in no way interfere with any treaty port or any vested interests within any so-called 'sphere of interest' or leased territory in China.

"Second. That the Chinese treaty tariff of the time being shall apply to all merchandise landed or shipped to all such ports as are within said 'sphere of interest' (unless they be 'free ports') no matter to what nationality it may belong, and that the duties so leviable shall be collected by the Chinese government.

"Third. That it will levy no higher harbor dues on vessels of another nationality frequenting any port in such 'sphere' than shall be levied on vessels of its own nationality, and no higher railroad charges over lines built, controlled, or operated within its 'sphere' on merchandise belonging to citizens or subjects of other nationalities transported through such 'sphere' than shall be levied on similar merchandise belonging to its own nationals transported over equal distances." [1]

The purpose of the Hay doctrine was clear enough. American business men had no other means of gaining entrance into the markets of China. "There were created, through a variety of circumstances," according to Thomas W. Lamont, "a series of 'spheres of influence,' all tending to impair the independence and sovereignty of China. This policy served to divide up China commercially into almost water-tight compartments, and the nations like the United States which had no compartment could not do much trading." [2]

4. The Boxer Rebellion

This doctrine was communicated at a time when the Chinese were beginning to grow restless under foreign exploitation.

---

[1] U. S. "Foreign Relations," 1899, pp. 131–133, 142.
[2] Lamont, "New Consortium for China," p. 2.

The restlessness culminated in the Boxer uprising of 1900. The revolt was crushed by the Powers, but its aftermath had important consequences on American policy in China. Secretary Hay took advantage of the occasion to reaffirm the Open Door doctrine in a circular communication sent to Great Britain, France, Russia, Germany, and Japan on July 3, 1900, in which he urged the Powers to co-operate to "bring about permanent safety and peace to China, preserve Chinese territorial and administrative entity, protect all rights guaranteed to friendly powers by treaty and international law, and safeguard for the world the principle of equal and impartial trade with all parts of the Chinese Empire".[1] This doctrine was accepted on paper by the Great Powers, chiefly because the "balance of world power was delicately adjusted" and "they feared the consequences of independent action."[2]

Despite the formal acceptance of the Open Door doctrine, American interests in Manchuria continued to be threatened by Russian capitalists. In 1901, Russia, taking advantage of the Boxer Rebellion, established a measure of military control in the province. More important, she opened in the same year the Chinese Eastern Railway and established the Russo-Chinese Bank. She secured the privilege of importing oil free of tax into China. As a result the sales of the Standard Oil Company in Manchuria fell off.[3]

The policy of the United States toward China was clearly formulated by President Roosevelt in a speech delivered at San Francisco in 1903, in which he proclaimed that the United States was a great Asiatic Power:

"The extension of the area of our domain has been immense; the extension in the area of our influence even greater. America's geographical position in the Pacific is such as to ensure peaceful

[1] U. S. "Foreign Relations," 1901; "Appendix. Affairs in China," p. 12.
[2] Straight, "Politics of Chinese Finance," p. 3.
[3] Plebs League, "Outline of Modern Imperialism," p. 48. Pan, "Trade of the U. S. with China," pp. 227–232.

domination of its waters in the future, if we only grasp with sufficient resolution the advantages of that position." [1]

5. *The Manchurian Bank Project*

The fight of American capital for control of Manchuria did not begin in earnest, however, until the Russo-Japanese War of 1905, and seemed temporarily to sidetrack one of the chief contestants in that sphere. In this war, which was the result of Russian and Japanese rivalry in Manchuria, the Japanese were in part financed by Edward H. Harriman and his bankers, Kuhn, Loeb & Co.[2] The American government took an active part in the negotiations. The completion of the Panama Canal at this time gave the United States a strategic point for the struggle for commercial and political supremacy in the Pacific. The treaty of peace was signed on American soil at Portsmouth, New Hampshire. These facts were not without significance. American interests were conciliated by a reaffirmation of the Open Door doctrine in Articles III and IV of the treaty, applying specifically to Manchuria, America's sphere.[3]

Immediately after the signing of the Portsmouth Treaty, Harriman concluded a memorandum for an agreement with Marquis Ito and Marquis Katsura of Japan for joint American and Japanese ownership of the South Manchurian Railway, together with the various coal, timber and mining concessions which went with the railroad. At the time this agreement was made, the railroad was still Russian property, but was due to be transferred to Japan by Article VI of the then unratified Portsmouth Treaty. Harriman wanted the South Manchurian Railway as part of his scheme to build a railway line around the world; Japan was willing to agree to share the road with Americans while the treaty was still unratified. But one month after the ratification of the treaty, Japan and China signed

---

[1] Roosevelt, "Works," v. 1, p. 393.
[2] Croly, "Willard Straight," p. 239.
[3] Bland, "Recent Events in China," p. 306.

the King agreement of December 22, 1905, by which American capital was to be excluded from the South Manchurian railroad. The scheme was opposed by powerful Japanese statesmen and never went through.[1]

American financiers did not give up their fight for the control of Manchuria. When the South Manchurian Railway scheme fell through, Harriman laid the plans for another line which would meet his purpose. His plans received powerful assistance from the State Department, particularly from the American consul-general at Mukden, the principal city in Manchuria. After conference with Harriman in the United States, the American consul-general reached an agreement with Governor Tang Shao-Yi of Manchuria for the creation of a Manchurian Bank with a capital of 20 million gold dollars to act as financial agent for the Manchurian government. This bank was to be established by American financiers and was to stabilize the Manchurian currency and promote railway and industrial enterprises, particularly the line from Hsin Mintung to Aigun, to be part of Harriman's round-the-world scheme. A memorandum to that effect was forwarded to Harriman in the United States on August 7, 1907. On that day the consul-general at Mukden wrote these significant and prophetic words in his diary: "Tang approves draft. Letter mailed! Fraught with tremendous possibilities. If adopted it means we play principal part in the development of Manchuria. Our influence in China tremendously enhanced."[2]

Consul-General Straight returned to New York in 1908 with the draft of the agreement for the Manchurian Bank. A series of conferences followed involving E. H. Harriman, Jacob H. Schiff, and Otto Kahn for the bankers; the United States State Department and the Chinese representative, Governor Tang of Manchuria, who had come to the United States expressly for the purpose of putting through the Manchurian bank deal. At

---

[1] Bland, supra, pp. 309–10. Straight, supra, p. 4. Croly, supra, p. 239. MacMurray, supra, v. I, p. 554.
[2] Croly, supra, p. 241,

no time did the Chinese representative negotiate directly with the American financiers; all these negotiations were carried on through the State Department.[1]

The negotiations for the Manchurian Bank fell through, however, owing to the death of the Emperor of China and Empress Dowager in November, 1908, and the fall of the party in power which was negotiating the loan for China.[2]

In the same month—on November 30, 1908—Secretary of State Root and the Japanese ambassador at Washington entered into an agreement pledging their governments to respect each other's spheres of interest in China. The Root-Takahira agreement reaffirmed the Open Door principle in the Pacific, and pledged Japan and the United States to maintain the status quo in that region.[3]

6. *The Battle for Manchurian Railways*

The death of the Empress Dowager of China and the fall of Yuan-Shi-Kai from power in 1908 brought the manœuvres for a Manchurian bank controlled by American financiers to a standstill. But Edward H. Harriman and his bankers, Kuhn, Loeb & Co., were not ready to give up their plans for the exploitation of Manchuria. Harriman was still intent on his plan of a railroad which should girdle the globe. For such a railroad he needed a line running from some point on the trans-Siberian line to a port on the Pacific free from ice most of the year. He had been carrying on since 1906 a series of negotiations with the Russian Government for the purchase of the Chinese Eastern Railway. Russia was willing to sell this line, provided Japan, her rival in Manchuria, would give up her strategic advantage by selling to the American Bankers the South Manchurian Railway. Japan refused to do this. Harriman's next move was to plan for a parallel line running from Chinchow at the head of the Gulf of Pechili to Aigun on the Amur River.[4]

[1] Croly, supra, p. 277.
[2] Bland, supra, p. 314. Straight, supra, p. 5.
[3] U. S. "Foreign Relations," 1908, p. 510; see also Appendix III.
[4] Croly, supra, p. 297.

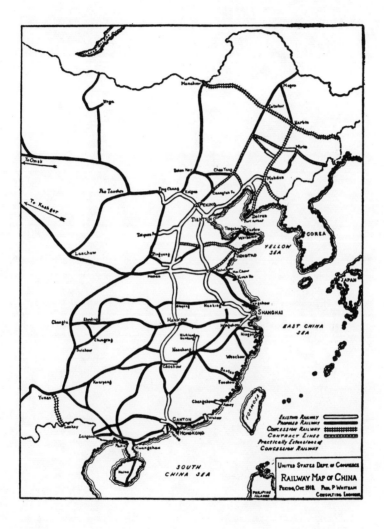

To Omsk

To Kashgar

Urga

Manchow

Mopan

Tsitsihar

Harbin

Mirin

Pao Taochow

Paton Hoi

Chao Yang

Mukden

Ping Chang

Kalgan

Changtun Fu

Dalren

Port Arthur

PEKING

TIENTSIN

Tingchow Chefoo

Weihaiwei

COREA

Taiyuan Fu

YELLOW SEA

Pingyang

TSINGTAO

Laochow

Honan

Kalsal

Han Chow

Kiran Ho

JAPAN

Hsinyang

Hankiang

Kingchow

SHANGHAI

Changlu

Ehchang

HANKOW

Hangchow

Ningpo

EAST CHINA SEA

Chungsing

Shihkiachr Nanchang

Suichow

Nanchang

Wenchow

Kweiyang

Chaochow

Santao

FORMOSA

Foochow

Yunan

Changchow

Amoy

Loohoy

Wuhew

CANTON

Langson

Pakoi

HONGKONG

Kwangchow

Hoinn

SOUTH
CHINA SEA

EXISTING RAILWAY
PROPOSED RAILWAY
CONCESSION RAILWAY
CONTRACT LINES
Practically Extensions of
CONCESSION RAILWAY

UNITED STATES DEPT. OF COMMERCE
RAILWAY MAP OF CHINA
PEKING, OCT. 1918.   PROF. P WHITHAM
CONSULTING ENGINEER

PHILIPPINE
ISLANDS

For the successful carrying out of this plan and of other and more important moves in Manchuria, the American bankers interested would need the fullest possible co-operation from the State Department. Assistance was promised them by the new administration. In advising against a reduction in armaments, President Taft, in his inaugural address of March 4, 1909, declared:

"In the international controversies that are likely to arise in the Orient growing out of the question of the open door and other issues the United States can maintain her interests intact and can secure respect for her just demands. She will not be able to do so, however, if it is understood that she never intends to back up her assertion of right and her defense of her interest by anything but mere verbal protest and diplomatic note." [1]

This declaration of intentions was the first avowal of the policy which, under the Taft administration, won the title of "Dollar Diplomacy." An opportunity soon presented itself. In May, 1909, the Chinese Government made an agreement with German, British, and French bankers for a loan to construct the Hukuang railways, involving the lines from Hankow to Szech and from Hankow to Canton.[2] Immediately a group of American bankers was organized to finance any concessions for railroads which American capitalists might obtain from the Chinese Government. This group was headed by J. P. Morgan & Co., to whom the management of the business was entrusted, and included Kuhn, Loeb & Co., the First National Bank, the National City Bank, and Edward H. Harriman.[3] The American bankers at once began to struggle for admission into the international group of bankers which was to float the Hukuang loan. Secretary Knox, four days after the announcement that China had signed an agreement with the German, British and French bankers, applied to China for the admission of the American group.[4]

[1] U. S. "Congressional Record," v. 44, p. 3.
[2] Blakeslee, "Recent Developments in China," p. 127.
[3] Croly, supra, p. 281.
[4] U. S. "Foreign Relations," 1909, p. 144.

However, as the loan had been under negotiation for several years, the Tripartite bankers and the Chinese Government objected to the delay which would be involved in reopening negotiations for admitting the American bankers. But the State Department was insistent.[1] While the financial representative of the Morgan group was negotiating with the Tripartite bankers in London, Secretary Knox brought diplomatic pressure to bear upon China. The American Chargé d'Affaires at Peking was ordered by the State Department to "solemnly warn the Government of China that there appears no reason to doubt that, as a result of early meetings in Paris and Berlin, the American group will reach with the European bankers an agreement for participation in the present loan by American capital." The American envoy was also to inform China that "Americans would welcome an opportunity to arrange for the whole loan, if necessary, by reason of further persistency of the individuals who refuse to meet the situation broadly." [2]

Other emissaries of the United States Government were equally busy fighting for participation by American bankers in the Hukuang loan. Ambassador David Jayne Hill informed the German foreign minister that he did not think his government "would find it possible to neglect the interests of American capital and enterprise in the East." [3]

All these diplomatic efforts seemed futile. The Chinese Government drifted, hoping the Powers would quarrel among themselves. At this point President Taft stepped in. Breaking all diplomatic precedent, he sent a personal message to Prince Chun, regent of the Chinese Empire, in which he stated:

"I am disturbed at the reports that there is certain prejudiced opposition to your Government's arranging for equal participation by American capital in the present railway loan . . . I send this message not doubting that your reflection upon the broad phases of this subject will at once have results satisfactory to both countries. . . . I have resorted to this somewhat unusually direct communication with your Imperial Highness, because of the high

[1] U. S. "Foreign Relations," 1909, pp. 144–178.
[2] Ibid., p. 179.
[3] Ibid., p. 151.

importance that I attach to the successful result of our present negotiations." [1]

As a result of this pressure, China and the four powers made a virtue of necessity. The American group was admitted. A preliminary agreement for the Hukuang loan was drawn up by the German, British, French and American bankers at Paris on May 23, 1910.[2]

The final agreement for the Hukuang loan, however, was not signed until May 20, 1911.[3] It was signed by the Imperial Government of China, the Deutsch-Asiatische Bank, the Hongkong and Shanghai Banking Corporation, the Banque de l'Indo Chine, and the American group, J. P. Morgan & Co., Kuhn, Loeb & Co., First National Bank, and the National City Bank. In this agreement the Imperial Government of China authorizes the bankers of the four Powers to issue a five per cent Gold Loan for six million pounds sterling. The term of the loan was forty years. The security was to be the likin, salt, and rice taxes. British, German, and American engineers were to work on the sections in which their groups were interested. The loan was made that year.[4]

7. Chinchow-Aigun Railway Concession (1909)

Willard Straight, former consul-general at Mukden, was now agent for the Morgan group in China. He had been active in obtaining participation in the Hukuang loan. He was also negotiating with the Manchurian authorities for the proposed Chinchow-Aigun Railway, which was to give American capital a strategic point against its Russian and Japanese rivals. On October 2, 1909, an agreement was signed by which the Morgan group was to furnish the sum necessary to build a railway between Chinchow and Aigun, to be constructed by a British firm, Pauling & Co.[5]

[1] U. S. "Foreign Relations," 1909, p. 178.
[2] Ibid., 1910, p. 280.
[3] MacMurray, "Treaties and Agreements," v. 1, p. 866.
[4] Lamont, "New Consortium for China," p. 3.
[5] MacMurray, "Treaties and Agreements," v. 1, p. 800.

The Chinchow-Aigun agreement was signed on October 2, 1909, between the Viceroy of Manchuria and the Governor of Fengtien and the representative of the American group. The group consisted of J. P. Morgan & Co., Kuhn, Loeb & Co., the First National Bank, and the National City Bank. The contract was also signed by the British engineers, Pauling & Co. By this agreement, the provinces of Manchuria and Fengtien were to borrow from the American bankers the sum necessary to construct the railway from Chinchow to Aigun at a rate not to exceed five per cent. The interest and amortization were guaranteed by the Imperial Government. The security was to be the railway line. At the same time an agreement was drawn up between the American bankers and Pauling & Co. that at least one-half the material and equipment purchased in Europe and America for the construction of the railway should be American and that certain American engineers to be recommended by the American bankers should be employed to work on the construction of the road.[1]

When the Morgan representative returned with the agreement for the Chinchow-Aigun line in his pocket, the State Department thought it saw its way to realize Harriman's old scheme of neutralizing the Manchurian railways by placing them in the hands of an international group. On November 6, 1909, therefore, Secretary Knox sent a note to Britain, calling attention to the new agreement between the Chinese Government, the American financiers, and the British construction company, and making the following proposals: That China should be given a large international loan from the interested Powers (1) to bring the Manchurian Railways under an economic, scientific, and impartial administration by some plan vesting in China the ownership of the railroads through funds furnished for that purpose by the interested powers willing to participate. (2) Such loan should be for a period ample to make it reasonably certain that it could be met within the time fixed and should be upon such terms as would make it attractive to bankers and investors. (3) Nationals of the participating powers

[1] MacMurray, "Treaties and Agreements," v. 1, p. 802.

should supervise the railroad system during the term of the loan, and the governments concerned should enjoy for such period the usual preferences for their nationals and materials upon an equitable basis *inter se.* (4) Japan and Russia should participate in the plan as well as Great Britain and Germany.[1]

In this way American bankers, with the help of the State Department, hoped to prevent the absorption of Manchuria by Russia and Japan. But once more Japan refused to give up her advantage in Manchuria, and Russia would not give up the Chinese Eastern so long as Japan held on to the South Manchurian.[2]

France, Russia's ally, and Britain, Japan's ally, backed up their allies, and thus Knox's neutralization scheme was turned down by the Powers involved. Instead of prying their rivals loose in Manchuria, the American financiers, as a result of the Knox diplomacy, had forced Russia and Japan, who five years before had fought a bloody war, into an entente. On July 4, 1910, Russia and Japan signed an agreement to respect each other's spheres of interest in Manchuria.

Balked once more in their attempt to acquire shares in the Chinese Eastern and South Manchurian railways, the American bankers returned to their contract of October 2—that is, they proceeded with the Chinchow-Aigun railway. But Japan and Russia were not only unwilling to let American bankers control their railroads; they would not allow a rival road to be built. Although the contract of October 2 had been ratified by a Chinese Imperial Edict, and China was nominally a sovereign nation, Russia and Japan both protested to the State Department that the proposed Chinchow-Aigun railway was inimical to their interests in Manchuria. Britain tacitly supported her ally; and since the United States was not in a position to oppose the three great Powers single-handed, the Chinchow-Aigun scheme was allowed to lapse temporarily.

But by this time America's rôle in the Far East and the intimate connections between the State Department and the

[1] U. S. "Foreign Relations," 1910, p. 234.
[2] Ibid., pp. 249, 251.

financial houses with investments in that part of the world had become firmly established. The policy was clearly expressed by W. W. Rockhill,[1] United States minister to China during the Hukuang loan and Chinchow-Aigun negotiations, when he said:

"It seems clear to me that so long as we shut our eyes to the undoubted fact that, in the East at least, from Stamboul to Tokyo, politics, finance, and trade go hand in hand, and that neither the profits of trade can be fully reaped nor our influence and prestige be adequately upheld without incurring the responsibilities incident to political and financial activity, we must be content to play a modest effaced rôle in the Far East, unworthy, in my opinion, of our great country and its vast interest in the Pacific."

8. The Six Power Loan

The international battle for financial concessions in the Hukuang loan had two immediate effects on China: first, the Celestial Government was impressed by the power of American bankers, backed by the government at Washington, to break their way into European combinations for the exploitation of China; second, the empire was confronted with the apparition of possible and probable bankruptcy and the possibility of the complete control of China's finances by foreign capitalists.[2] The Manchu dynasty was tottering under the strain of foreign exploitation; unless it could stabilize the currency of the country, ruin seemed likely. A plan for a loan of 50 million dollars for the purpose of stabilizing the currency and developing the resources of Manchuria was worked out. The financial concession was offered to the American group. This plan was a new version of the agreement drawn up by Governor Tang of Manchuria and the American consul-general at Mukden in 1907 for the creation of a Manchurian bank. In effect the American group was making another attempt to carry through its plan for obtaining an "economic stranglehold" on Manchuria.

When this plan became known in the chancelleries of Europe,

[1] Overlach, "Foreign Financial Control in China," p. 214.
[2] Bau, "Foreign Relations of China," p. 63.

the British, French and German bankers suggested that the Manchurian currency and development scheme be undertaken jointly by the financiers of the four Powers. At first, the American group refused, although it had just invoked the Open Door Policy in order to obtain a share in the Hukuang loan. Later it was forced to accede to the demand for several reasons: (1) the desire of American finance to strengthen its position in Manchuria against Russia; (2) the necessity for limiting financial competition; (3) the inability of American banks to float any large volume of Chinese securities on the American market, as America was not yet a large investor in foreign securities and big industries were still absorbing American capital. The era of international financial trusts had begun.[1]

On April 15, 1911, an agreement was drawn up by the bankers of the United States, Great Britain, Germany and France for floating the Manchurian currency and development loan.[2] The agreement was signed by the Imperial Chinese Government, J. P. Morgan & Co., Kuhn, Loeb & Co., the First National Bank, and the National City Bank; the British Hongkong and Shanghai Banking Corporation; the German Deutsch-Asiatische Bank; and the French Banque de l'Indo Chine. The agreement provided for the loaning of 10 million pounds sterling (approximately 50 million dollars) for rendering uniform the Imperial Chinese currency and providing funds for the promotion and extension of industrial enterprises in the three Manchurian provinces. The rate of interest was to be five per cent and the time of the loan was forty years. As security the bankers of the four Powers were to have a mortgage on the taxes on tobacco, production, consumption, and salt. These taxes were declared in the agreement to be free from all other loans, liens, charges or mortgages. The bankers were to have first claim on them in case of default. China could not abolish nor decrease these taxes without the permission of the bankers.

[1] Croly, "Willard Straight," p. 370. Bland, "Recent Events in China," p. 324.
[2] MacMurray, supra, v. 1, p. 841.

This drastic agreement was known as the Chinese Currency Loan. It marked a new stage in the financial control of China. Willard Straight, the American consul-general who had engineered the Manchurian Bank agreement, was the financial representative of J. P. Morgan & Co. and had engineered the Currency Loan. Two days after the signing of the loan, he wrote to Morgan: "The significance of the Loan Agreement signed on Saturday will be better realized five years hence than it is today. It is the first tangible result of the new policy inaugurated by Secretary Knox." In his diary, on the day the agreement was signed, he wrote: "The Currency Loan is finished. Dollar diplomacy is justified at last."[1] The agreement, in fact, laid the foundation for the first Chinese Consortium, which later developed into the present Consortium. It attempted to create a monopoly for the bankers of the four Powers involved. Article XVI provided that "should the Chinese Government decide to invite foreign capitalists to participate with Chinese interests in the Manchurian business contemplated under this loan, or to be undertaken in connection therewith, the contracting Banks shall first be invited so to participate." In this way, the American bankers were ready to disregard the Open Door Policy which had proved so useful to them when other Powers attempted to set up a monopoly for the exploitation of Manchuria. Against the monopoly engineered by American finance, Russia and Japan protested, demanding to be admitted on equal terms.

In the midst of these discussions the Chinese revolution of 1911 broke out. The Boxer uprising eleven years before had been a protest against the first scramble by European and American business men for concessions. The revolution of 1911 was a protest against the Manchu dynasty under whose weak and corrupt rule the intrigues of the second scramble for concessions had rendered China a vassal of foreign finance. When the Chinese Republic was established and the various Chinese factions had finally adjusted their differences, the coalition government under Yuan Shi-Kai informed the Four

[1] Croly, supra, p. 402.

Power Consortium that China proposed to borrow $125,000,000 for general administrative reorganization. The respective governments of the groups were informed also that it was desirable that Russian and Japanese bankers be included in the consortium.[1] After long and complicated negotiations the Chinese were prepared to sign a contract embodying all the important demands of the bankers of the six Powers. The terms of the draft agreement were approved by the governments, who insisted in addition that foreigners be employed in important administrative posts, and as tax collectors and customs supervisors.[2]

This was in 1913. In that year Woodrow Wilson began his first term as President of the United States. The American bankers asked the new president what his attitude toward the proposed Six Power Loan would be. The form of the inquiry was a request that the new administration ask the American group to participate in the loan. Two weeks after taking office, President Wilson issued a statement on the new policy of the American Government toward investments in China, in which he withdrew official support from the American group headed by J. P. Morgan & Co. The statement read in part:

"We are informed that at the request of the last administration a certain group of American bankers undertook to participate in the loan now desired by the Government of China. . . . The present administration has been asked by this group of bankers whether it would also request them to participate in the loan. . . . The administration has declined to make such request because it did not approve the conditions of the loan or the implications of responsibility on its own part which it was plainly told would be involved in the request.

"The conditions of the loan seem to us to touch very nearly the administrative independence of China itself; and this administration does not feel that it ought, even by implication, to be a party to those conditions. The responsibility on its part which would be implied in requesting the bankers to undertake the loan might conceivably go to the length in some unhappy contingency

[1] Straight, "Politics of Chinese Finance," p. 11.
[2] Blakeslee, "Recent Developments in China," pp. 119–161. U. S. "Foreign Relations," 1913, pp. 170–171.

of forcible interference in the financial, and even the political, affairs of that great oriental state, just now awakening to a consciousness of its power and of its obligations to its people. The conditions include not only the pledging of particular taxes, some of them antiquated and burdensome, to secure the loan, but also the administration of those taxes by foreign agents. The responsibility on the part of our government implied in the encouragement of a loan thus secured and administered is plain enough and is obnoxious to the principles upon which the government of our people rests." [1]

This official indictment of the tactics and aims of financial imperialism contained an important passage which showed that the chief motive behind it was the fact that the first Wilson administration represented the industrial, rather than the financial, interests of the country. "The government of the United States," the passage declared, "is earnestly desirous of promoting the most extended and intimate trade relations between this country and the Chinese Republic. The present administration will urge and support the legislative measures necessary to give American merchants, manufacturers, contractors, and engineers the banking and other financial facilities which they now lack, and without which they are at a serious disadvantage as compared with their industrial and commercial rivals." [2]

As a result of the withdrawal of government support the American banking group dropped out of the Six Power Consortium, indicating the necessity of the diplomatic support for financial imperialism. The withdrawal of the American group left a Five Power Consortium, "under whose auspices the so-called Reorganization Loan of 25 million pounds was made in 1913." [3] Again, though the ambition of American finance to exploit China did not materialize at the time, it served to bring out clearly the dominant rôle which American capital was beginning to play in the Far East. This rôle was bringing it into sharper and sharper conflict with Japan, which was also striving to dominate the Pacific. An editorial on the Six Power

[1] "American Journal of International Law," v. 7, pp. 335–341.
[2] Ibid., pp. 338–9.
[3] Lamont, "New Consortium for China," p. 4.

loan in the Asahi Shimbun (a Japanese paper) of Osaka of
May, 1912, declared:

"The United States, having no territorial concessions and no
geographical facilities, has assumed the political and financial
guidance of China. . . . By bold and skillful diplomacy she has
outmanœuvred Japan, Russia, and England, whose rights and
interests are predominant, and forced them to take a back seat." [1]

The outbreak of the World War in 1914—a climax in the
clash of imperialist interests in various parts of the world, and
not least in China—put a stop to active concession hunting.
The United States, for a time the only investing country not
involved, did a slight business during the carnage. In May
1916 the American International Corporation, a Morgan subsidiary organized for foreign business, obtained a contract
for a loan from the Chinese Government for the improvement
of the South Grand Canal in Shantung province. The agreement provided for a loan of $3,000,000 at seven per cent for
thirty years secured by the land and the taxes on the land
affected by the improvement on the canal and by the tolls and
taxes on the canal. [2] In the same month the Siems and Carey
Co. of Chicago obtained a concession for building 1500 miles
of railroad in China. [3]

The year 1917 found the United States an active participant
in the World War. It also found Russia in the midst of a
social revolution, and thus definitely out of the imperialistic
race in China. The two remaining rivals in Manchuria could
now come to an understanding. It has already been pointed
out that at the height of competition for spheres of interest
the competing groups agree to respect each other's spheres.
For the purpose of reaching an understanding on China a
Japanese mission headed by Viscount Ishii arrived in the
United States and on November 2 signed a secret agreement
with Secretary Lansing that was to have far-reaching effects.
The Lansing-Ishii agreement frankly committed the United

[1] Bland, "Recent Events in China," p. 331.
[2] MacMurray, "Treaties and Agreements," v. 2, p. 1287.
[3] Ibid., pp. 1313-1324.

States to an acceptance of imperialism in the Far East. Under its terms the United States recognized "that Japan has special interests in China, particularly in the parts to which her possessions are contiguous." While disclaiming any intention of infringing on the "independence or territorial integrity of China," both governments pledged themselves to adhere to the Open Door Policy or "equal opportunity for commerce and industry." The two governments also agreed to oppose the acquisition by any other power of privileges which would infringe on such independence as China had or impair the Open Door principle.[1] Such an agreement was obviously an interference in the political affairs of "that great oriental state" against which Wilson had set his face four years before. In fact China protested against the Lansing-Ishii agreement, declaring that she "would not be bound by any agreement entered into by other countries, and that she would respect special interests of another nation due to territorial propinquity only in so far as they are provided in the existing treaties." [2]

Attempts to solve the contradictions raised by the conflict of imperialistic interests in China were made at the 1919 Peace Conference in Paris. One of the most acute problems involved the province of Shantung. This had been the German sphere of influence since 1898. In 1914 Japan took advantage of the outbreak of the war to seize the leased port of Kiauchow in Shantung and to extend her control to other parts of the province, stationing troops at strategic points. On January 18, 1915, Japan presented twenty-one demands to China, calling for a transfer of Germany's privileges in Shantung to Japan and demanding additional privileges, giving Japan complete control of the province. Japan demanded, among other things, control of South Manchuria and Eastern Inner Mongolia, including a practical monopoly of railway, mining and financial concessions, as well as police and military control.[3] These

---

[1] U. S. Congress, 66:1; "Sen. Doc." 106, p. 225.
[2] Bau, "Foreign Relations of China," p. 81.
[3] MacMurray, "Treaties and Agreements," v. 2, p. 1231.

demands were followed by an ultimatum threatening action. China was forced to sign treaties on May 25, 1915, granting the demands.[1]

During the negotiations, the government at Washington notified Japan and China that the United States "cannot recognize any agreement or undertaking which has been entered into or which may be entered into between the Governments of China and Japan impairing the treaty rights of the United States and its citizens in China, the political or territorial integrity of the Republic of China, or the international policy relative to China commonly known as the Open Door Policy." [2]

Japan, determined to keep Shantung if the Allies won the war, fortified herself by a secret agreement with Great Britain supporting her designs.[3] When the Paris peace conference considered the Shantung question, the Japanese delegation threatened to withdraw from the conference and boycott the proposed League of Nations unless Japan's claims to Shantung were ratified. President Wilson agreed to sustain Japan, chiefly for fear that if Japan withdrew from the peace conference she "would begin building up alliances of her own in the East." [4]

9. *The New Consortium*

Japan's victory at the peace conference was a blow to America's Open Door Policy, and the attempts of American business and finance to break down spheres of influence in China. The victory was offset, however, by the formation of the Chinese Consortium of 1920. Under American pressure China had entered the war on the side of the Allies in 1917. In order to finance China, the Department of State on June 30, 1918, called together representatives of the American bankers who had been interested in Chinese investment. The group consisted of thirty-six banks, headed by a managing committee of seven institutions consisting of: J. P. Morgan & Co.,

---

[1] MacMurray, "Treaties and Agreements," v. 2, p. 1216.
[2] Ibid., p. 1236.
[3] Baker, "Woodrow Wilson and World Settlement," v. 2, p. 250.
[4] Ibid., p. 258.

Kuhn, Loeb & Co., the National City Bank, the First National Bank, the Chase National Bank, the Continental and Commercial Trust and Savings Bank of Chicago, Lee, Higginson & Co., and the Guaranty Trust Co. of New York.[1] The bankers were willing to organize a combination for the purpose of floating Chinese loans, under conditions stated in a letter which they wrote to the State Department on July 8, 1918.[2] These conditions were:

(1) That Chinese loans be floated by a Four Power Group consisting of "financial members to be recognized by the respective Governments of Great Britain, France, Japan and the United States."

(2) That all members of the American Group should relinquish any concessions to make loans which they now hold, and all loans to China should be considered as Four Power Group business.

(3) That the United States Government "should be prepared in principle to recognize the change in our international relations, both diplomatic and commercial, brought about by the war."

(4) That the United States Government should "at the time of issue . . . make it clear to the public that the loan is made at the suggestion of the Government."[3]

To this frank request that the Government support the bankers in their Chinese business Secretary of State Lansing agreed. In a letter sent the following day, July 9, he declared:

(1) That "the Government has suggested that this loan be made and would have no hesitancy in formally stating that fact at the time of issue."

(2) That the Government "is willing to aid in every proper way and to make prompt and vigorous representations and to take every possible step to ensure the execution of equitable contracts made in good faith by citizens in foreign lands."[4]

[1] Lamont, supra, p. 4.
[2] Carnegie Endowment for International Peace, "The Consortium."
[3] Ibid., p. 2.
[4] Ibid., pp. 3-5.

The governments involved in the plan were formally notified by the State Department, and in the correspondence which followed we are able to see how completely the Government had changed its policy since Woodrow Wilson withdrew support from the old Six Power Loan of 1913. Not only was Washington willing to support the bankers, but the British Foreign Office was notified on October 8, 1918, that

"It can be definitely stated that the United States Government did not mean to imply that foreign control of the collecting of revenues or other specific security pledged by mutual consent would necessarily be objectionable, nor would the appointment under the terms of some specific loan of a foreign adviser—as, for instance, to supervise the introduction of Currency Reform." [1]

While the governments were exchanging notes on the Consortium, the bankers of the four Powers involved met in Paris to discuss terms. Thomas W. Lamont of J. P. Morgan & Co., who was in Paris at the time as financial adviser to the American delegation, took a leading part in the bankers' conference as representative of the American group. On May 12, 1919, the conference drew up a preliminary agreement.

Two serious obstacles had to be overcome before any real agreement could be reached. In meeting these obstacles the American bankers and the State Department combined forces. "In the succeeding months, among the four Governments involved, the United States taking the lead in the matter, there followed a long diplomatic correspondence." [2]

The first obstacle was the unwillingness of the French and British governments to guarantee exclusive diplomatic support to their respective groups. The draft of the bankers' agreement drawn up at Paris on May 12 stated that the groups involved were entitled to the exclusive diplomatic support of their respective governments. The United States was willing to give the Morgan group such support. It must be remembered in this connection that by this time the war had made American bank-

[1] Carnegie Endowment, supra, p. 15.
[2] Lamont, supra, p. 7.

ers the creditors of all the European Powers, and that they had already declared that Japan and the United States would have to finance the French and British groups of the Consortium. France and Britain, however, were not willing to grant their groups a monopoly of Chinese loans. They urged that other British and French groups willing to invest in China should be permitted to operate. The plan of the Morgan group finally prevailed. A compromise proposed by the State Department and accepted by the British and French governments provided that:

"The Governments of each of the four participating groups undertake to give their complete support to their respective national group members of the Consortium in all operations undertaken pursuant to the resolutions and agreements of the 11th and 12th of May, 1919, respectively, entered into by the Bankers at Paris. In the event of competition in the obtaining of any specific loan contract the collective support of the diplomatic representatives in Peking of the four Governments will be assured to the Consortium for the purpose of obtaining such contract." [1]

The second obstacle was, from the point of view of the American bankers and of international relations, even more serious. Japan, seeking to monopolize Manchuria and Mongolia, proposed that these two regions be excluded from the operations of the Consortium. Britain and the United States at once protested against the proposal. The American group of financiers also protested. Intricate negotiations were carried on jointly by the Morgan interests and the Department of State. Thomas W. Lamont notified the Japanese bankers that "Mongolia and Manchuria are important parts of China, and any attempt to exclude them from the scope of the Consortium must be inadmissible." [2] Secretary Lansing wrote to the Japanese Government that in view of the Lansing-Ishii agreement, Japan could "with entire assurance rely upon the good faith of the United States and of the other two Powers associated in the Consortium to refuse their countenance to any operation

[1] Great Britain, "Miscellaneous," no. 9 (1921), p. 32.
[2] Carnegie Endowment, supra, p. 21.

inimical to the vital interests of Japan." [1] Meantime Lamont "with the approval of the State Department at Washington" [2] went to Japan in person. After protracted negotiations a compromise was reached which was accepted by all the Powers involved. The rôle of the State Department in financial negotiations of an international character is tersely expressed in its memorandum of April 3, 1920, declaring that "the American Government is prepared to agree to the terms of the compromise proposed by Mr. Lamont in Tokyo." [3] By this compromise the South Manchurian railway and a number of other lines "upon which substantial progress had already been made by the Japanese" [4] were excluded from the scope of the Consortium; but the projected Taonanfu-Jehol railway and the projected railway connecting a point on the Taonanfu-Jehol railway with a seaport were to be included in the operations of the Consortium. [5]

Japan having waived the reservations regarding Mongolia and Manchuria, the American group was now in a position to close the deal. On October 15, 1920, the Chinese Consortium agreement was drawn up and signed in the Chamber of Commerce Building in New York City by representatives of the Hongkong and Shanghai Banking Corporation, the Banque de l'Indo Chine, the Yokohama Specie Bank Limited, and the American Group consisting of J. P. Morgan & Co., Kuhn, Loeb & Co., the National City Bank, the Chase National Bank, the Guaranty Trust Co. of New York, Lee, Higginson & Co., and the Continental and Commercial Trust and Savings Bank of Chicago.

After the agreement was signed, China received her first formal notification of the Consortium. [6] Up to that point that "great oriental state" whose sovereignty had been so often guaranteed by the State Department had not been consulted.

[1] Carnegie Endowment, supra, p. 39.
[2] Lamont, supra, p. 8.
[3] Carnegie Endowment, supra, p. 54.
[4] Lamont, supra, p. 9.
[5] Carnegie Endowment, supra, p. 61.
[6] Ibid., p. 73.

10. *China as an American Sphere of Influence*

The Consortium agreement, backed by America's dominant economic position, achieves the end toward which American investors and the State Department have been striving since 1900. China has become an American sphere of influence.[1]

The purpose of the Consortium, according to the agreement, is to negotiate and carry out Chinese loan business, more specifically loans to the "Chinese Government or to Chinese Government Departments or to provinces of China or to companies or corporations owned or controlled by or on behalf of the Chinese Government or any Chinese Provincial Government." Articles 3 and 4 provide for complete equality among the groups in all business undertaken by the Consortium, and reserve freedom for each group to decline to participate in any business which it does not desire to undertake. Article 5 provides that, so far as possible, the parties to any operation shall not be jointly liable, but that each group shall be obliged to liquidate its own engagements. Under Articles 6 and 7 any group which cannot issue Chinese bonds in its own market may request the other groups to include its share in their own issue. This last provision indicates the true situation in the Far East today. America, creditor of half the world, has leaped to the front as the dominant western Power in the Orient.

"Owing to the war the British and French markets may be unable for some few years to come to purchase any large amount of foreign securities either of China or of any other nation. The American group, therefore, has by force of circumstances, jumped from an inconspicuous position in the old Consortium to one of prime importance in the new.

"In this, America, as represented through the group, should be equipped to play a very active part. If so equipped she will be able . . . to lay out, with her experienced partners of Great Britain, France and Japan, a sound and comprehensive plan for the economic and financial development of China. . . . Through her

[1] Carnegie Endowment, supra, p. 67.

representatives at Peking she will be able sympathetically to wield influence upon the present confused elements." [1]

The new Consortium is thus the fruition of the two major policies attempted by the State Department in regard to China. First, it marks the triumph of the Open Door, since it gives American capital free access to the markets of China; second, it revives the Knox neutralization scheme, since all the railroads and other public utilities constructed by the Consortium will be internationally controlled, with America and Japan playing the leading rôle.[2] The old spheres of influence will be abolished and China will be turned into one sphere of influence to be exploited by an international financial trust. "We shall see no more 'spheres of influence' set up in China." [3] Since President Roosevelt turned the Boxer indemnity into a fund for the education of Chinese students in the United States, this country has been the traditional friend of China, a pose which has not been modified by incidents like the Chinese Exclusion Act of 1905. Nevertheless the new Consortium must not be looked upon as "an eleemosynary institution," according to Thomas W. Lamont, for "it cannot possibly function unless it has a fair margin of profit." [4] Under the new Consortium the American group becomes the leading factor in the construction of the Hukuang Railways, for a share in which it fought so hard in 1909. The formation of the Consortium was fostered by the Wilson administration; on March 31, 1921, Secretary of State Charles E. Hughes notified J. P. Morgan & Co. that he approved of the objects of the Consortium.[5] The success of the American financiers in making China an international sphere of economic influence, thereby giving American capital free access to it, received international diplomatic recognition at the Washington Arms Conference which met from November 12, 1921, to February 6, 1922. It

[1] Lamont, supra, pp. 17–18.
[2] Ibid., p. 14.
[3] Ibid., p. 17.
[4] Idem.
[5] Carnegie Endowment, supra, p. 74.

is significant that the Conference dealt with the question—
Armaments and the Far East.

The agreements reached by the Conference regarding the
Far East marked the triumph of American policies. The
Open Door was reaffirmed once more, and the old Knox scheme
of halting the battle for spheres of influence was realized.

The Four Power Treaty signed at the Conference by the
United States, France, Great Britain and Japan, bound the
Powers to maintain the status quo in the Pacific. The four
governments pledged themselves to "respect their rights in
relation to their insular possessions and insular dominions in
the region of the Pacific Ocean." A supplementary treaty
stipulated that the term "insular possessions and insular
dominions" shall, in the case of Japan, apply only to the
southern portion of Sakhalin, Formosa and the Pescadores.

For the United States the most important section of the
Four Power Treaty was Clause IV, providing that as soon as
the treaty was ratified by the four Powers, "the agreement
between Great Britain and Japan, which was concluded at
London on July 13, 1911, shall terminate."[1] With Japan the
most formidable rival of American financial and political interests in the Far East, Senator Lodge could frankly tell the
Senate on March 8, 1922, that "the chief and most important
point in the treaty is the termination of the Anglo-Japanese
Alliance. That was the main object of the treaty." Senator
Lodge added that "the Anglo-Japanese Alliance was the most
dangerous element in our relations with the Far East and with
the Pacific."[2]

The Nine Power Treaty signed at the Washington Conference dealt with China directly. The United States, Belgium,
Great Britain, France, Italy, Japan, the Netherlands, Portugal
and China signed the treaty. The Powers agreed to respect
the sovereignty, independence, and territorial and administrative
integrity of China; they once more pledged themselves to
observe the Open Door principle. None of the Powers was to

[1] U. S. Congress, 67:2, "Sen. Doc." 126, pp. 889–91.
[2] U. S. "Congressional Record," v. 62, March 8, 1922, p. 3547, 3552.

take advantage of the chaos in China to obtain special privileges inimical to the other Powers. Regarding spheres of influence and the race for concessions the treaty provided that no government would seek, or support its citizens in seeking, special commercial or economic advantages over the citizens of the other Powers. The governments involved were not "to support any agreements by their respective nationals with each other designed to create Spheres of Influence or to provide for the enjoyment of mutually exclusive opportunities in designated parts of Chinese territory." China pledged herself not to discrimate unfairly against any of the Powers in the use of her railroads. [1]

China requested the Powers represented at the Washington Conference to express their avowed respect for her territorial and administrative integrity by restoring her right to fix her own tariff, and abolishing foreign courts on Chinese soil. China's tariff in the treaty ports was fixed at a maximum of five per cent ad valorem by the Anglo-Chinese treaty of Nankin signed in 1842. This tariff agreement was embodied in the treaty of 1844 between China and the United States.[2] Foreign supervision of the collection of Chinese customs dates back to 1853, when Shanghai was captured by the Taiping rebels and the customs were closed. The foreign consuls began to collect the customs, and the following year the American, British and French consuls obtained treaties from China providing for the establishment of a foreign board of customs inspectors. In 1858 foreigners began to enter the Chinese customs administration, and by 1922 the Chinese foreign minister was able to declare that not one of the forty-four tariff commissioners in the treaty ports was a Chinese.[3] At the Washington Conference the Chinese delegation maintained that the present five per cent tariff was a continual financial loss to their government, and that China could not be as stable as the Powers said they wanted her to be unless she regained her tariff autonomy.

[1] U. S. Congress, 67:2; "Sen. Doc." 126, pp. 893-6.
[2] Ibid., p. 172.
[3] Ibid., p. 187.

The Conference did not restore China's right to fix her tariff, but provided for a revision of the tariff so as to really equal five per cent under present world financial conditions, and for a conference to consider the tariff question. [1]

Similarly, the Chinese delegation complained that the extraterritorial courts maintained by the foreign Powers in China were a violation of her sovereignty, and asked for their abolition. Extraterritorial rights were obtained by the United States from China by the treaty of 1844. Other Powers obtained the same privilege shortly afterward. In the commercial treaty of 1903 with China the United States promised to give up extraterritorial rights "when satisfied that the state of the Chinese laws, the arrangements for their administration, and other considerations warrant it in so doing." [2] The same words were embodied in the British-Chinese commercial treaty of 1902 [3] and the Japanese-Chinese commercial treaty of 1903. [4] The Washington Conference did not abolish extraterritorial rights, but adopted a resolution providing for a commission to consider the question, specifying that the foreign Powers are free to accept or reject the commission's recommendations. [5]

In many ways the Washington Conference achieved politically what the Morgan group of bankers had already achieved economically by the Chinese Consortium. Not only was the Open Door Policy strengthened, but the Powers agreed not to seek further spheres of influence in China. The last point was emphasized by President Harding in a letter urging the Senate to ratify the Washington Conference treaties. He also declared that the Nine Power Treaty superseded the Lansing-Ishii agreement of 1917 recognizing Japan's special interests in China. [6] On April 16, 1923, it was announced that the governments of Washington and Tokio had formally agreed

---

[1] U. S. Congress, 67:2; "Sen. Doc." 126, pp. 897–901.
[2] MacMurray, "Treaties and Agreements," v. I, p. 431.
[3] Ibid., p. 351.
[4] Ibid., p. 414.
[5] U. S. Congress, 67:2; "Sen. Doc." 126, pp. 903–4.
[6] U. S. "Congressional Record," v. 62, p. 3559.

to cancel the Lansing-Ishii agreement. However, the Root-Takahira agreement of 1908, pledging the United States and Japan to maintain the status quo in the Pacific, is still in effect. [1]

The influence of the Chinese Consortium made itself felt in the Shantung agreement which was a by-product of the Washington Conference. The negotiations between China and Japan regarding Shantung were attended first by Secretary of State Hughes and Sir Arthur Balfour, later by other American and British representatives. The result was an arrangement which deprived America's chief rival in the Far East of an important strategic base, and turned over some of the concessions which Japan had monopolized to the Consortium. The agreement between China and Japan provided for the restoration of Shantung to China and the withdrawal of Japanese troops from the province. China was also to buy from Japan the Shantung railway running from Tsingtao to Tsinanfu with money borrowed from Japan for a term of fifteen years.[2] However, it was agreed that "the concessions relating to the two extensions of the Tsingtao-Tsinanfu, namely the Tsinanfu-Shunteh and the Kaomi-Hsuchowfu lines, will be thrown open for the common activity of an international financial group." [3] As the Consortium has a monopoly on Chinese loans, American bankers may become heavily interested in these railway extensions.

America's openly declared aim of achieving ascendency in the Pacific, which has been rigorously pursued by the inseparable combination of finance and diplomacy, has brought her into collision again and again, first with Russia and Japan, and later with Japan alone. As far back as 1907 Baron Kaneko declared: "We must do our utmost in disputing this command of the Pacific with the United States, and also do our best in the control of the Far Eastern markets." [4] More recently (1919) Prof. John Dewey, returning from the Far East, wrote:

[1] "New York Times," April 16, 1923, p. 3:1.
[2] U. S. Congress, 67:2; "Sen. Doc." 126, pp. 125–31.
[3] Ibid., p. 128.
[4] "Pacific Era," v. I, p. 15.

"'In the interests of truth it must be recorded that every resident of China, Chinese or American, with whom I have talked in the last four weeks has volunteered the belief that all the seeds of a future great war are now deeply implanted in China." [1]

Japan looks upon the Far East as her exclusive economic empire. She has developed an Asiatic Monroe Doctrine proclaiming "Asia for the Asiatics." Her attempt to keep Mongolia and Manchuria out of the operations of the new Consortium were in effect part of her struggle to reserve for herself exclusive economic domination in the Far East much as the United States reserves to herself the exclusive right to dominate the Western Hemisphere. The pressure brought to bear by the Morgan group and the State Department for Japan to withdraw her claims were a challenge to Japanese imperial plans.

11. *The Near East Sphere of Influence*

American investments in the Near East, chiefly in tobacco and oil, have turned that section of the world into an American "sphere of influence." The extent to which the government at Washington has been willing to back up American investors in that region is described in the following statement issued by the United States Bureau of Naval Intelligence.

"We have extensive interests in the Near East, especially in tobacco and petroleum. Early in 1919 several American destroyers were ordered to Constantinople for duty in the Near East. . . . The possible development of the economic resources of this part of the world were very carefully investigated by representatives of American commercial interests. These representatives were given every assistance by the Navy, transportation furnished them to various places, and all information of commercial activities obtained by the naval officers in their frequent trips around the Black Sea given them. . . . The Navy not only assists our commercial firms to obtain business, but when business opportunities present themselves, American firms are notified and given full information on the subject. . . . One destroyer is kept continually at Samsun, Tur-

[1] Dewey, "China, Japan, and the U. S. A."

key, to look after the American tobacco interests at that port. . . .
The American tobacco companies represented there depend practically entirely on the moral effect of having a man-of-war in port
to have their tobacco released for shipment." [1]

One of the naval officers stationed in Turkish waters obtained
a concession which placed enormous sources of wealth at the
disposal of American investors. In 1909 this officer, Rear-
Admiral Colby M. Chester, obtained a preliminary agreement
from the Turkish Government for the building of a port and
railways and the exploitation of mines by American capital.
President Roosevelt fostered the enterprise. On its way home
from its trip around the world, the American fleet was directed
to stop at Smyrna and take a number of Turkish officers on
board "in the interest of the American concession." [2] The attempts of the Chester interests to have the agreement ratified
met with serious rivalry from the Bagdad Railway Company, a
group of German capitalists. Ratification was also delayed by
the Turkish revolution. In 1910 the grant was signed by the
new Minister of Public Works, and submitted to the Turkish
Parliament for ratification. This victory of American over
German capitalists was due in large measure to the assistance
of the State Department.

During the negotiations, Secretary Knox, ready to extend
"dollar diplomacy" to all spheres in which American finance
might be interested, informed Admiral Chester of his deep
interest in the concession; and Assistant Secretary of State
Huntington Wilson, who arrived in Constantinople in 1909
to attend the coronation ceremonies of the new Sultan, publicly
stated that the object of his visit was to aid the Chester Claim. [3]
Furthermore . . . "After the convention was submitted to the
Turkish Parliament, every Government in Europe, through
the Chancelleries in Constantinople, recognized the successful
termination of the contest by sending congratulations to John
Ridgely Carter, the Acting American Ambassador in Constan-

[1] Bierstadt, "Great Betrayal," p. 97.
[2] "Current History Magazine," v. 16, p. 955.
[3] Ibid., p. 957.

tinople, for his diplomatic efforts in securing the concession." [1]

But again the Chester interests were confronted by difficulties. In rapid succession Turkey was involved in a war with Italy (1911), in the two Balkan wars of 1912, and finally in the World War. These did not affect the plans of the Chester group, however. In 1912 the Ottoman American Development Company was organized to exploit the concession. The company was organized with the understanding that it "would receive the strong backing of the home Government," according to Henry Woodhouse, who adds that "no attempt to open up trade for American citizens in a foreign country ever received more cordial and helpful cooperation from the Federal Government than that accorded to the Chester group." [2]

During the World War, the Chester grant was in abeyance, but in 1922 it came to the front again. The Ottoman American Development Company was reorganized with General George W. Goethals as president. On April 11, 1923, the Turkish National Assembly extended the Chester concession and on April 30, a convention putting the concession into effect was signed at Angora by the Turkish Minister of Public Works and by the American company. The new concession was three times as large as the old and one of the richest in the world. [3]

By this agreement, the Chester group is to build three systems of railways aggregating 2,714 miles so laid as to interconnect with the present railroads. One section is to extend from Alexandretta Bay to Harput, then to Arghana, where the great copper mines are located, then to Bitlis; then on through Mosul to Kerkuk and to Suleimanieh. To this a section would be added to extend from Harput to Sivas by way of Chalty and from Harput to Van, crossing two great oil fields.

The second division is to run from Angora to Sivas to Samsun, which is destined to become the outlet and inlet for commerce on the Black Sea; and from Chalty to the Black Sea, with a parallel branch from Trebizond to Erzerum.

[1] "Current History Magazine," v. 16, p. 957.
[2] Ibid., p. 958.
[3] Ibid., v. 18, pp. 393-400.

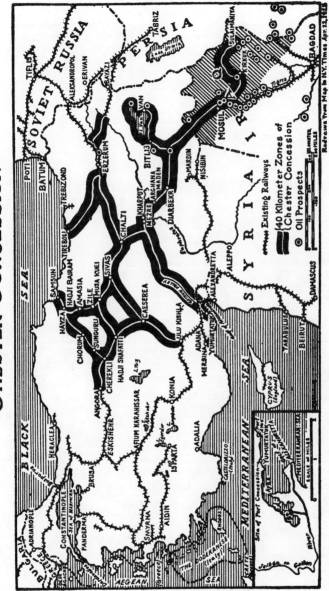

CHESTER CONCESSION

The third division is to connect Angora with Samsun by way of Yozgad, and the Angora-Sivas line with the Uhr Kishla terminal of the Bagdad Railway by way of Cesaria with a branch to Sivas and a section to extend from Erzerum to Bayezed on the Persian Border.[1] In this the American group would lay out a network of railways covering the country.

But more than that, the Chester interests obtained the mineral rights to the territory 20 kilometers on each side of the railroads. These mineral resources are valued at ten billion dollars. The oil fields of Erzerum, Bitlis and Van are estimated to have potentially over eight billion barrels of oil. The Arghana copper mines are estimated to have 200 million tons of high grade copper ore. These territories are also rich in oil, gold, platinum, silver, iron, lead, zinc, tin, mercury, cobalt, manganese, nickel, antimony, coal and salt.[2]

12. *The Struggle for Oil*

In its advance in the Far East American capital met the opposition chiefly of Japan; in its attempts to exploit the Near East it was bound to collide with Great Britain, which for years has had a sphere of influence there. The fate of the Chester grant was complicated by the conflict of the Standard Oil Company and the British oil interests for the enormously rich petroleum area in Mesopotamia. The villayet of Mosul, which was included in the Chester grant, was also included in a concession obtained before the war by the Turkish Petroleum Company, a British concern. In addition, this section was marked off as a British sphere of influence by an Anglo-French agreement signed during the war, and after the armistice when British troops occupied Mosul. By the Treaty of Sevres, drawn up by the San Remo Conference of 1920 to settle the Turkish question, Mesopotamia, which later became the Kingdom of Iraq, was made independent. Britain was given a mandate over it by the League of Nations. The Mosul area, included in the Chester grant, thus became British territory.

[1] For map see "Current History Magazine," v. 17, p. 395.
[2] Ibid., p. 393 ff.

Furthermore, at San Remo, France and England signed on April 25, 1920, an agreement by which the French were given a 25 per cent interest in the Turkish Petroleum Company, with a concession to the oil rights of Mosul.[1]

At this point, the Standard Oil Company put in its claim for a share in the exploitation of the Mosul field on the basis of the Open Door Policy. Behind the attempts of Standard Oil to penetrate into the fields of the Near East, the entire government machinery at Washington lined up. On March 12, 1920, the Senate requested information as to what restriction foreign countries were putting upon citizens of the United States "in the matter of prospecting for petroleum or in the acquisition and development of land containing the same" and what steps the Government was taking to secure the removal of these restrictions. During the summer of 1920 a vigorous correspondence over the question of oil was carried on between Washington and Downing Street. When the news of the San Remo agreement became public, Secretary of State Bainbridge Colby on November 20, 1920, dispatched a protest to Great Britain against the exclusion of American interests from mandates established under the League of Nations, even though the United States was not a member of the League.[2] Secretary Colby maintained that the San Remo oil agreement violated the Open Door principle, and constituted a premature recognition of the Turkish Petroleum Company's concessions to which the United States Government could not subscribe. Lord Curzon replied that the concession in Mesopotamia had been obtained by the Turkish Petroleum Company before the war; to which Colby countered that "such information as this government has received indicates that prior to the war the Turkish Petroleum Company . . . possessed in Mesopotamia no right to petroleum concessions or to the exploitation of oil."[3] The controversy became even sharper with the inauguration of the Harding

---

[1] Great Britain, "Miscellaneous," no. 11 (1920). "Political Science Quarterly," v. 39, pp. 265–279.

[2] "London Times," April 6, 1921, p. 9.

[3] Davenport and Cooke, "Oil Trusts," p. 103.

administration. The State Department also made strenuous
efforts to open up Palestine to the Standard Oil Company, which
had claims there, and also carried on a struggle with the British
Foreign Office over the oil fields in Djambi—again in behalf
of Standard Oil.[1] The Department even went so far as to demand on February 1, 1921, that the League of Nations Council
which was meeting in Paris reconsider the question of the mandates over former German colonies. Meantime, the Standard
Oil Company was carrying on private negotiations with the oil
magnates in London with the result that in July, 1922, the American trust was offered a share in the Turkish Petroleum Company.[2] Thus Mosul was now contested by the Turkish Petroleum Company, in which the Standard Oil Company had a
hand, and by Chester's Ottoman American Development Company. To cap the climax, the Turks demanded back the oil
fields not only of Mosul, but of two other fields comprised
in the Chester grant; while the French produced a pre-war
claim to a railway from Samouv to Sevas, also included in the
Chester grant. The validity of the Turkish Petroleum Company's claims depend, in part, on the final disposition of Mosul.[3]

The first Lausanne Conference, which met from November,
1922, to February, 1923, was devoted primarily to straightening
out conflicting oil claims in the Near East. On behalf of the
Standard Oil Company, the State Department had already invoked the Open Door Policy. Now, at the Lausanne Conference, Richard Washburn Child, the American ambassador at
Rome, who attended as an "unofficial observer," declared that
the American Government once more repudiated the San Remo
agreement and would "protect its rights and assure the Open
Door." The Conference settled very little and another conference was called at Lausanne lasting from April until July
1923. The convening of this Conference was marked by the
public announcement that the Chester grant had received its

[1] U. S. Congress, 68:1; "Sen. Doc." 97.
[2] L'Espagnol, "World Struggle for Oil," p. 170. "Political Science
Quarterly," v. 39, p. 275.
[3] Ibid., p. 276.

final approval by the Angora Government. Mosul again became the battleground of the Anglo-American-French interests united in the Turkish Petroleum Company and the Chester group. The State Department officially threw its support to the American interests by instructing its "unofficial" representative at the conference, Joseph C. Grew, to reaffirm that the United States did not recognize the validity of the Turkish Petroleum Company's concession.

Secretary Hughes at this time denied that the Chester group "had been promised moral or political endorsement or have received assurances that in the event of any dispute this Government would be bound to defend the validity of the concession." [1]

Recent reports indicate that after a two-year fight between American and British investors in the Ottoman American Development Company, control has been definitely vested in the hands of Americans headed by Admiral Chester and his sons. Of the Company's stock, 3,000 shares are in the hands of Americans as against 7,000 shares controlled by British interests. Negotiations are being conducted for taking over most of the 7,000 shares, giving the Chester group almost 100 per cent control of the company. The company's concession having been approved by the Angora Government, the Chester group is planning to carry out its plans for building the Bagdad Railway, and to work its oil and mineral claims. [2]

In March, 1925, it was officially announced that the cabinet of the Kingdom of Iraq had signed an agreement with the Turkish Petroleum Company granting it a concession to exploit the oil fields in Mosul and Bagdad for seventy-five years. The negotiations begun in 1922 to admit American groups into the Turkish Petroleum have been completed. As the company is organized at present it consists of the Anglo-Persian group with 25 per cent of the stock; the French groups, 25 per cent; the Royal and Shell, 25 per cent; The Standard Oil Co. and the Sinclair Consolidated Oil Corporation, 25 per cent. [3] Thus the

[1] "Current History Magazine," v. 19, p. 485.
[2] "New York Times," May 28, 1925, p. 29:2.
[3] "Investor's Review," v. 48, p. 273.

Chester group and the American Oil groups have definitely established a sphere of influence in the Near East.

13. *An International Trust*

The policy of cut-throat competition for "spheres of influence" in the Far East has been replaced by the American policy of an international trust for the exploitation of China. In this trust, known as the Chinese Consortium, the American group of bankers plays the leading rôle owing to America's dominant economic position in the world. This trust will handle all future loans and concessions in China. It has been backed up by the Nine Power treaties signed at the Washington Arms Conference. This attempt at the financial annexation of China by the Morgan group of banks will leave the United States and Japan dominant rivals in the Far East.

In the Near East, the State Department has succeeded in opening a sphere of influence for the Standard Oil Company. In addition American warships are stationed there to assist American traders and investors. Again an international trust of British, French and American interests has been formed, in the shape of the Turkish Petroleum Company, for the exploitation of Near Eastern oil fields.

"It is surely obvious," wrote Franklin K. Lane, former Secretary of the Interior, in 1920, "that if not only nationals, but States themselves, represented by Governments, take part in economic competition, and turn themselves into business houses or manufacturing firms, there is no hope of appeasing the conflicts which will constantly arise from commercial rivalry." [1]

[1] L'Espagnol, "World Struggle for Oil," p. 183.

IV

POLITICAL "REGULATION"

1. Economic and Strategic Bases

Investing nations seeking to protect economic interests frequently find themselves in a position where economic and strategic considerations lead them to interfere in the internal affairs of undeveloped and weak countries. This interference may be the work of private investors or government officials, or of both investors and officials. Relations between European empires and the continents of Asia and Africa during the past sixty years furnish numerous illustrations of the principle.[1] Within the past generation the same principle has been repeatedly demonstrated in the annals of United States diplomacy.

Interference with the internal politics of foreign states which does not extend to the point of military intervention and occupation can best be described by the term "regulation." [2]

Among the considerable number of instances in which the United States has "regulated" without resorting to military intervention and occupation, the Hawaiian Revolution of 1893, the Panama Revolution of 1903 and the Mexican revolutions following 1911 are outstanding cases.

2. The Hawaiian Revolution of 1893

Hawaii has long been an object of American enterprise. In 1875 a reciprocity treaty was drawn up under which certain grades of Hawaiian sugar were admitted free to the United States.[3] The results of this treaty were immediate. Before its signing, the imports of Hawaiian sugar had never amounted

[1] Woolf, "Economic Imperialism," pp. 40–88.
[2] Blakeslee, "Mexico and the Caribbean," p. 199 ff.
[3] U. S. "Treaties, Conventions, etc., 1776–1909," v. 1, pp. 915–917.

to 20 million pounds in any year. "They touched that figure
the first year. Thereafter the rate of increase was extraordinary. . . . By 1882, the imports exceeded 100 million
pounds; by 1887, 200 millions." [1] The effect of the reciprocity
treaty was to place the Hawaiian planters fiscally on a parity
with the planters of Louisiana, and as the land of Hawaii was
peculiarly adapted to the raising of sugar, the Hawaiians had
a constant advantage over their American competitors.

Business men were quick to seize this advantage. "The
planters who reaped the high profits were chiefly Americans." [2]
It was they who held the dominant place in the economic affairs
of Hawaii.

The McKinley Tariff Act of 1890 put sugar on the free list,
forcing Hawaiian planters to compete directly with Cuba,
Java and Brazil. Hard times for the islands immediately
followed. After the passage of the McKinley Act, the price
of raw sugar in Honolulu fell in one day from $100 to $60
per ton. The value of sugar lands and of sugar stocks dropped
correspondingly. United States Minister Stevens, reporting on
the situation, writes under date of November 20, 1892: "The
loss to the owners of the sugar plantations and mills . . . has
not been less than $12,000,000, a large portion of this loss fall-
ing on Americans residing here and in California. Unless
some positive measures of relief be granted, the depreciation
of sugar property here will continue to go on. Wise, bold
action by the United States will rescue the property holders
from great losses." [3]

Two moves were necessary for the restoration of Hawaiian
prosperity. One was the annexation of Hawaii to the United
States. The second was the imposition of a duty on the sugar
that was competing with the Hawaiians for the United States
market.

American commercial interests in Hawaii were ready for
joint action aiming to establish a United States protectorate or

[1] Taussig, "Some Aspects of the Tariff Question," p. 59.
[2] Ibid., p. 60.
[3] U. S. "Foreign Relations," 1894; "Appendix," II, pp. 382-3.

to secure recognition. It was therefore easy to mobilize American public opinion in Hawaii about a Committee of Public Safety, which was organized in January, 1893, under the chairmanship of Chief Justice Dole who had resigned his official post in order to act with the Committee.[1]

United States Minister Stevens, who had been in consultation with representatives of the Committee, requested the State Department to station a naval vessel at Honolulu to protect American life and property. On January 16, 1893, at the direction of Mr. Stevens, the commander of the *Boston* landed marines.[2] Immediately the Governor of the Island of Oahu and the Minister of Foreign Affairs addressed official communications to the United States Minister, protesting against the landing of troops "without permission from the proper authorities." In reply, Minister Stevens assumed full responsibility.

On the day following the landing of the marines, the Committee of Safety proceeded to the government building, and there, under cover of the guns of the United States marines, who were drawn up to protect the Committee against possible attack, a proclamation was read, abrogating the Hawaiian monarchy and declaring a provisional government to exist "until terms of union with the United States have been negotiated and agreed upon." Within an hour after the reading of this proclamation, and while the Queen and her government were still in authority, and in possession of the palace, the barracks, and the police station, the United States Minister accorded the Provisional Government his recognition.[3]

Commissioners came at once to the United States, found President Harrison and Secretary of State Foster friendly to the new government, drew up a treaty of annexation, signed it and presented it to the Senate on February 15—one month after the outbreak of the revolution. On March 4, the Cleveland Administration took office, withdrew the treaty from the

---

[1] U. S. "Foreign Relations," 1894; "Appendix," II, p. 387.
[2] Idem.
[3] Ibid., p. 388.

Senate, and made an investigation of the whole affair. While there was some dispute as to detail, there was agreement on the main facts.[1]

A long fight ensued between the "expansionists" and the "anti-expansionists." Hawaii was finally annexed by joint resolution during the heat of the Spanish-American War (July 7, 1898). But in the meantime, in 1894, the Wilson Tariff Act again imposed a duty on sugar, and as Hawaiian sugar was admitted free, prosperity was restored to the islands. "Sugar growing, which had barely held its own from 1890 to 1894, now resumed its upward march. New plantations were opened, old ones enlarged their output, more and more sugar was poured into the United States, and the islands again boomed." [2]

Historians treat this revolution quite frankly as an American enterprise. "In Hawaii the more influential and the propertied classes supported the revolution and desired annexation. In the United States the desire for expansion was stimulated by the fear that some other nation might seize the prize." [3] "A revolution, largely fomented by American interests there," writes Prof. C. A. Beard.[4] The revolutionists themselves, declare that "of the capital invested in the islands, two-thirds is owned by Americans," and that "the revolution was not the work of filibusters and adventurers, but of the most conservative and law-abiding citizens, of the principal tax-payers, the leaders of industrial enterprises, etc." [5] United States Minister Stevens confirmed this point of view by referring to the leaders of the revolution in this language: "four highly respectable men, with Judge Dole at the Head. . . . P. C. Jones is a native of Boston, Mass., wealthy, possessing property interests in the islands, and a resident here for many years." [6]

A well organized revolution, sponsored by American business

---

[1] U. S. Congress, 52:2; "Sen. Ex. Doc." 76.
[2] Taussig, supra, p. 63.
[3] Lingley, "Since the Civil War," p. 295.
[4] Beard, "Contemporary American History," p. 203.
[5] Hawaiian Branches of the Sons of the American Revolution, etc., "Address."
[6] U. S. "Foreign Relations," 1894; "Appendix," II, p. 387.

men, supported by the United States diplomatic representative and bulwarked by a new tariff act, were in their combination, sufficiently efficacious to prevent the heavy property losses which Mr. Stevens had foreseen.

3. *The Panama Revolution*

A second illustration of the principle of "regulation" may be found in the episodes surrounding the Panama Revolution of 1903. Efforts to build a canal across the Isthmus of Panama had covered centuries. The French who had made an ambitious attempt to compass the task were finally defeated by disease and by shortage of funds. After much negotiation with Colombia and after an arduous debate over the relative merits of the Panama and Nicaragua routes, Congress authorized the President to negotiate for a canal across the Isthmus of Panama. If this proved impossible, within a reasonable time the President was authorized to use the Nicaragua route. The treaty, prepared in accordance with this act, and ratified by the Senate, provided that the United States should pay Colombia ten millions of dollars for a perpetual lease on a six mile strip through which the canal was to be built.[1] The Colombian Congress, after a lengthy special session, called for the purpose of ratifying the treaty, adjourned without action on October 31, 1903.

Long before the adjournment it was quite evident that no action would be taken, and many of the people of Colombia, and particularly of the State of Panama were outspoken in their denunciation of the Congressional failure. Two of the foremost citizens of the Isthmus, José Agustin Arango and Dr. Manuel Amador Guerrero, conferred with Captain J. R. Beers, freight agent of the Panama Railroad, as to the desirability of organizing a revolution. After this conference Dr. Amador went to Washington and met Secretary Hay. At the same time Philippe Bunau-Varilla, former chief engineer of the French canal company, arrived in New York and agreed to the revolutionary project.[2] Amador then returned to Panama,

[1] Johnson, "Four Centuries of the Panama Canal," ch. IX.
[2] Ibid., pp. 162–171.

but his friends were evidently not yet convinced of the determination of the United States to see matters brought to a focus.

A. M. Beaupré, United States Minister at Bogota, notified Secretary Hay on October 31 that the Colombian Congress had adjourned without ratifying the treaty, adding: "The people here in great anxiety over conflicting reports of secession movements in the Cauca and Panama." Two days later in a letter, he reiterated his statement regarding the anxiety felt in Colombia over the possibility of an insurrection in Panama.[1]

Meanwhile events had moved with dramatic rapidity on the Isthmus. November 2 the Acting Secretary of the Navy wired to the Commander of the *Nashville* at Colon: "Prevent landing of any armed force, either Government or insurgent with hostile intent." At the same time messages were sent to three other war vessels: "Maintain free and uninterrupted transit. If interruption is threatened by armed force, occupy the line of railroad. Prevent landing of any armed force, either Government or insurgent, with hostile intent at any point within fifty miles of Panama. If doubtful as to the intention of any armed force, occupy Ancon Hill strongly with artillery. . . . Government force reported approaching the Isthmus in vessels. Prevent their landing if in your judgment landing would precipitate a conflict."[2] Thus on the day before the revolution was scheduled to take place, the United States Navy was fully instructed to prevent the Colombian Government forces from landing on the Isthmus.

Meanwhile preparations had been made for the revolution to take place at Panama. The prospective rebels seem to have hesitated at the last moment, however, and Acting Secretary of State Loomis wired from Washington to Ehrman at Panama: "Uprising on Isthmus reported. Keep Department promptly and fully informed." This message was sent at 3:40 P. M. That evening a reply was received from Ehrman at 8:15: "No uprising yet. Reported will be in the night. Situation is critical." Two hours later another telegram came from

[1] U. S. "Foreign Relations," 1903, p. 218, 221, 233 ff.
[2] Ibid., p. 247.

Ehrman: "Uprising occurred tonight, 6; no bloodshed. Army and navy officials taken prisoners. Government will be organized tonight." At 11:18 on the same night, Loomis directed Ehrman to "act promptly" in preventing Colombian troops from proceeding from Colon to Panama.[1]

On the same day 400 Colombian troops had disembarked at Colon. The officers, going at once to Panama, had fallen into the hands of the insurgents. Colon was in such complete ignorance of the situation at the other end of the railroad line that Commander Hubbard of the *Nashville* wired to the Secretary of the Navy on November 3: "No revolution has been declared on the Isthmus and no disturbances. . . . It is possible that movement may be made tonight at Panama." The next day he was able to report the establishment of the revolutionary government at Panama on the previous evening.[2]

The situation was indeed critical for the insurgents, who had neither army nor equipment. Colombian troops were at Colon in force, and the Colombian Government was making every effort to raise an emergency army to quell the rebellion. The United States Navy handled the matter with rare tact. They persuaded the troops at Colon to re-embark and sail for home, and a vessel, approaching Panama with additional troops, was prevented from landing and turned back to Cartahena.

Beaupré, United States Minister in Bogota, had an anxious time of it. On November 4 he had reported the insurrection to the State Department, and on November 6 he had notified the Department that General Reyes, clothed with special powers, wished to know whether the United States was prepared to assist Colombia to preserve her sovereignty on the Isthmus. If the United States would permit Colombia to land troops on the Isthmus, General Reyes offered either to declare martial law and ratify the treaty by a decree, or else to call another session of Congress, as the United States might desire. Again, on November 7 Beaupré telegraphs that Reyes has full powers, and is

---

[1] U. S. "Foreign Relations," 1903, p. 231.
[2] Ibid., pp. 249–250.

insistent on knowing whether the United States will co-operate with. him to maintain sovereignty on the Isthmus in accordance with the Treaty of 1846, Article 35.[1]

The offer came too late. Already the United States had made its decision. On November 6, three days after the outbreak of the revolution, Secretary Hay wired to Beaupré: "The people of Panama having, by an apparently unanimous movement, dissolved their political connection with the Republic of Colombia and resumed their independence, having adopted a government of their own, republican in form, with which the Government of the United States of America has entered into relations, the President of the United States, in accordance with the ties of friendship which have so long and so happily existed between the respective nations, most earnestly commends to the Governments of Colombia and of Panama the peaceable and equitable settlement of all questions at issue between them."[2]

Beaupré did not seem to understand. Again he wired to ask whether Reyes would be free to conduct operations in Panama. Hay replied on November 11 that General Reyes would get "a courteous reception and considerate hearing. It is not thought desirable to permit landing of Colombian troops on Isthmus, as such a course would precipitate war." Then, later, "I telegraphed you on November 6 that we had entered into relations with the provisional government." There was nothing left for Colombia to do but to lodge a protest and a threat to sever diplomatic relations.[3]

The process of recognizing the new Republic of Panama went through with astonishing smoothness and unparalleled expedition. On November 6, three days after the outbreak of the revolution, Acting Secretary Loomis notified Ehrman at Panama that: "When you are satisfied that a de facto government, republican in form, and without substantial opposition

---

[1] U. S. "Foreign Relations," 1903, pp. 224-6.
[2] Idem.
[3] Ibid., pp. 228-9.

from its own people, has been established in the State of Panama, you will enter into relations with it as the responsible government of the territory." [1]

On the same day, November 6, Ehrman advised the Secretary of State that Philippe Bunau-Varilla had been appointed Envoy Extraordinary and Minister Plenipotentiary to the United States. The following day, November 7, Bunau-Varilla, from New York, advised Secretary Hay of his appointment, and added: "In extending her generous hand so spontaneously to her latest born, the Mother of the American Nations is prosecuting her noble mission as the liberator and the educator of the peoples. In spreading her protecting wings over the territory of our Republic the American Eagle has sanctified it." Secretary Hay replied immediately, and on November 13, ten days after the outbreak of the revolution of November 3, 1903, President Roosevelt officially received Bunau-Varilla as a representative of Panama. [2]

The haste of the recognition, and the other circumstances surrounding the incident lent colour to the rumour that the whole affair had been arranged by the United States. President Roosevelt had added fuel to the flames of this controversy by writing to Dr. Albert Shaw on October 10, 1903: "I cast aside the proposition at this time to foment the secession of Panama. Whatever other governments can do, the United States cannot go into the securing, by such underhand means, the cession. Privately, I freely say to you that I should be delighted if Panama were an independent state, or if it made itself so at this moment." [3]

Seven years later, at Berkeley, Cal., in a speech dealing with his official acts, Mr. Roosevelt is reported to have described the Panama episode in these picturesque terms: "I am interested in the Panama Canal because I started it. If I had followed the traditional conservative methods, I would have submitted a dignified state paper of probably two hundred pages to

[1] U. S. "Foreign Relations," 1903, p. 233.
[2] Ibid., p. 234, 240, 245.
[3] "Literary Digest," v. 29, p. 551.

the Congress and the debate would have been going on yet.   But I took the Canal Zone and let the Congress debate, and while the debate goes on, the Canal does also." [1]

A storm of public discussion followed this speech and by way of clarifying the issue, President Roosevelt wrote: "I was prepared, if necessary, to submit to Congress a recommendation that we should proceed with the work in spite of Colombia's opposition, and indeed had prepared a rough draft of a Message to that effect."   Then came the rejection of the Treaty by the Colombian Congress.   "If I had observed a judicial inactivity about what was going on at the Isthmus, had let things take their course, and had then submitted an elaborate report thereon to Congress, I would have furnished the opportunity for much masterly debate in Congress, which would now be going on —and the Canal would still be fifty years in the future."   He then describes the events of the revolution, and adds: "We recognized the Republic of Panama.   Without firing a shot we prevented a civil war.   We promptly negotiated a treaty under which the Canal is now being dug. . . . Be it remembered that unless I had acted exactly as I did act there would now be no Panama Canal.   It is folly to assert devotion to an end, and at the same time to condemn the only means by which the end can be achieved." [2]   The doctrine that "the end justifies the means" never was more emphatically stated. [3]

"Our government hastened to take advantage of what the gods had brought," writes Prof. Paul L. Haworth. [4]   "Three days after the revolt began, Secretary Hay cabled the American consul at Panama to recognize the de facto government, and a week later President Roosevelt formally received M. Bunau-Varilla as envoy extraordinary and minister plenipotentiary of the Republic of Panama.   A few days later (November 18), Hay and Bunau-Varilla signed a treaty by which Panama promised to cede perpetual control of a zone ten miles wide

[1] "Washington Post," Mar. 24, 1911.
[2] "Outlook," v. 99, pp. 314–318.
[3] "I Took the Isthmus."
[4] Haworth, "United States in Our Own Times," p. 306.

across the Isthmus, while the United States agreed to pay therefor $10,000,000 down and an annuity of $250,000, beginning nine years thereafter."

Less than three weeks after the adjournment of the Colombian Congress, the Panama Revolution had occurred "with the sympathy if not the support of the American administration." [1] The revolutionary government had been recognized by cable; a treaty had been drawn up and signed. Most of these events occupied only fifteen days.[2]

4. *Mexico, Diaz and Oil*

The Hawaiian Revolution of 1893 and the Panama Revolution of 1903 lie so far in the past that they have become an accepted part of American history. So well authenticated are the facts in each of these cases that they might serve as a formidable precedent for the "regulation" of the internal politics of weak neighbours by American interests. However, the "regulation" of Mexican affairs between 1910 and 1917 furnishes ample and contemporary evidence of the manner in which both American economic interests and the officials of the Federal Government interfere with the internal life of a neighbouring state whose resources and capital are extensively held by United States investors.

The ambitions of Napoleon III for a Latin-American Empire collapsed in 1867. During the next forty years, relations between the United States and Mexico grew, both in friendliness and understanding, until they culminated in the general arbitration treaty of 1908.[3] In 1910 this good feeling took the form of a personal meeting at the international boundary between President Taft and President Diaz. The next year the "Mexican controversy" was precipitated by the Madero Revolution.

Under the administration of Diaz, Mexico enjoyed peace and a superficial prosperity, but the chief beneficiaries of this

---

[1] Beard, "Contemporary American History," p. 278.
[2] U. S. Congress, 63:2; "Sen. Doc." 471.
[3] U. S. "Treaties, Conventions, etc.," v. 1, p. 1204.

prosperity were wealthy Mexican and foreign corporations. "Mexico was rich, but the Mexicans were poor." [1] Diaz built the edifice of his power upon concessions which were granted to those who had the means to carry forward the development of Mexico's immense natural resources. As a matter of course, much of this surplus capital came from foreign investors. In 1911 capital investments in Mexico were estimated as follows: British, $321 million; French, $143 million; United States, $1,058 million; Mexican, $793 million; all others, $119 million. [2]

When Diaz came to power in 1876, Mexico was a feudal state in which single landowners held tracts that included hundreds of thousands or even millions of acres, upon which the peon or serf population did the work. The granting of concessions to railroad, mining and other business enterprises helped in the establishment of a class of business men in the north and east of Mexico where most of the industrial development was taking place. Francisco Madero, who was the titular leader of the Revolution of 1911, was a member of this business class, and it was from this business class that he secured his support in the earlier stages of the revolution.

However inevitable may have been the break between the great landowners and the business group, it might have been postponed for a time but for the discovery of oil along the Gulf Coast, in the neighbourhood of Tampico and of Tuxpan.

Edward L. Doheny and a group of American capitalists had secured the Hacienda del Tulillo in 1900. This estate covered 280,000 acres, and was bought for $325,000. Later, the same men obtained an adjoining 150,000 acres. "The first oil ever produced or used in Mexico in substantial quantities" came from a well at Ebano which began to flow on May 14, 1901. Most oilmen were skeptical as to the possibilities of this new field, but Mr. Doheny tells in detail how he believed, persevered, and finally won a fortune. [3]

[1] Ogg, "National Progress," p. 286.
[2] U. S. Congress, 66:2; "Sen. Doc." v. 10, p. 3322.
[3] Ibid., v. 9, pp. 209–214.

An idea of the value of the Mexican oil field is suggested by Clarence W. Barron. "The average California oil well will yield from 100 to 200 barrels per day, and 600 barrels is a big well."[1] The California yield is far above the average for the oil industry of the United States. Compared with these figures, the Mexican yields were staggering. Casiano No. 7 started with a production of about 70,000 barrels a day on September 10, 1910. The well was partially shut down under a pressure of 285 pounds per square inch, and then produced 25,000 barrels a day. "It was nine years old yesterday, and is flowing at the same rate that it did when it first came in. It has produced over 100,000,000 barrels of oil."[2] Wells in the United States are ordinarily pumped. Mexican oil flows out under pressure. Cerro Azul, which has been called the greatest oil well in the world, ran 1,400,000 barrels before it could be capped, and then, under a back pressure of 900 pounds, the well produced between 45,000 and 50,000 barrels per day.[3] At that time Cerro Azul had been flowing for more than three years. Mr. Doheny also testified that a well drilled in 1904 "is still capable of producing about 800 barrels of oil per day after 15 years of continuous flowing."[4]

A glance at the figures of oil production gives an excellent idea of the spectacular rise of petroleum from a position of insignificance to the first place among Mexican industries. The first official records show a production of 220,650 barrels in 1904. The next year's production increased only a little; in 1906, it passed the million barrel mark; in 1909 it stood at 3,332,807 barrels. The next year it quadrupled: 14,051,643 barrels in 1910. Year by year this increase continued until production touched 25,902,439 barrels in 1913. Within a decade Mexico had risen from a position of no importance in the oil world, to be, next to the United States, the largest producer of

[1] Barron, "Mexican Problem," p. 110.
[2] U. S. Congress, 66:2; "Sen. Doc." v. 9, p. 230.
[3] Ibid., pp. 293-4.
[4] Ibid., p. 216.

petroleum. By 1920 Mexican production exceeded the combined production of all oil fields in the world outside of the United States.[1] By 1910, therefore, it was evident that the oil fields of Mexico were one of the richest economic prizes in the world.

It was during these same years—1905–1915—that the development of the internal combustion engine and the use of fuel oil under marine boilers had led British statesmen and business men to undertake a worldwide quest for oil reserves.[2] The Doheny interests soon had powerful rivals. Doheny was first in the field, however, and by the time his important rivals were in a position to compete with him, he was in virtual control of the Mexican oil market.

Lord Cowdray had come to Mexico to carry out certain harbour improvements for the Mexican Government. In the course of this work, he became interested in oil concessions, and Diaz, who was personally friendly to Lord Cowdray, and who pursued a shrewd policy of balancing one foreign interest against another to prevent anyone from exercising a dominating influence over Mexican affairs, made it possible for Lord Cowdray to secure oil concessions that made him a serious competitor of the American interests.[3]

The favours that Diaz was showing Lord Cowdray boded ill for the American oil interests in Mexico, and when, in 1910, Diaz was elected President for the eighth time, it seemed certain that the British interests in the Mexican oil fields would win a decisive advantage over all of their rivals.

But Diaz had reckoned without the new class of business men that the industrial development of Mexico had called into being. One of these men, Francisco Madero, had contested the election of 1910 against Diaz; had been "counted out" by the Diaz machine, and had thereupon started a revolution against Diaz with the demand that Diaz either resign or permit a fair

---

[1] "Mineral Industry," 1923, pp. 494–95.
[2] Delaisi, "Oil," chs. II and III.
[3] U. S. Congress, 66:2; "Sen. Doc." v. 10, p. 2532 ff. "World's Work," v. 27, pp. 289–298.

election.[1] Since Diaz would do neither, Madero headed a revolution which had soon spread over the whole northern area of Mexico.

All of the forces were present to create a revolution against the Diaz regime: a discontented, exploited, landless peasantry; a newly developed and hampered business class seeking to take power from the hands of the aristocracy, and a serious clash of interests between the British and American oil companies. Then, too, Madero developed surprising strength. Ogg noted that he was "rich enough to bring his cause prominently before the people." [2]

There has been considerable discussion as to the source of this wealth. It seems to be agreed on all hands that the Madero family were well-to-do economically, but it is also true that the accounting presented by the Madero family to the Government, and paid out of the public treasury after Madero came into power, showed expenses of nearly three-quarters of a million dollars (Mexican) on behalf of the revolution. The Washington representative of the Maderistas places the amount at about $600,000.[3]

At the time of the revolution charges were freely made that the money came in part from American oil interests. These charges were repeated before the Senate Foreign Relations Committee by some of the men who had been close to Madero.

Juan Pedro Didapp testified [4] regarding accusations brought against Madero by the Diaz party and two of the men who fought with Madero testified as to their understanding of the source from which the funds for the revolution were coming. One of these men, Lawrence F. Converse of Los Angeles, a 23 year old captain in the Madero army, acting as courier, gave this testimony.[5]

[1] Ogg, "National Progress," p. 287.
[2] Idem.
[3] U. S. Sen. For. Rel. Com., "Revolutions in Mexico," 1913, p. 750.
[4] Ibid., p. 462.
[5] Ibid., pp. 104-5.

Senator Smith: Did you have any occasion to know whether he was receiving pecuniary assistance from here?

Mr. Converse: I know this,—that Abraham Gonzales——

Senator Smith: He is the present governor of Chihuahua?

Mr. Converse: Yes; and Braulio Hernandez, who was provisional secretary of state in Madero's revolution and later secretary of state of Chihuahua, and Mr. Madero himself, told me that as soon as the rebels made a good showing of strength several leading bankers in El Paso stood ready to advance him—I believe the sum was $100,000; and these same men told me also that the Standard Oil interests had bought bonds of the provisional government of Mexico.

Senator Smith: In large quantities?

Mr. Converse: I do not know the quantities, but I know they said that the Standard Oil interests were backing them in their revolution.

Senator Smith: Did you learn under what conditions?

Mr. Converse: I was taken into their confidence as an officer on their staff, and the matter came up in the course of conversation with them.

Senator Smith: Was anything said as to what the Standard Oil people were to have in return?

Mr. Converse: They were to have a high rate of interest and there was a tentative agreement as to an oil concession in the Southern States of Mexico.

Senator Smith: Were there any other companies that were associated with Madero in that enterprise?

Mr. Converse: Not that I know of. There were none of them mentioned. The Standard Oil was the only concern mentioned, and the bankers in El Paso.

Senator Smith: Do you know whether they did receive through these banks or other persons any pecuniary aid?

Mr. Converse: I know that Mr. Madero carried a great quantity of cash on his person, as did his officers, and that frequently money in large quantities came across the river.

On the other hand, Mexicans like Jose Vasconselos, who were intimately connected with Madero throughout the revolution, are emphatic in declaring that there was no American money placed at the disposal of the Madero Party.

Be that as it may, there is no question but that the sentiment in the United States was strongly in favour of Madero, and

that the United States Government took the earliest opportunity
of recognizing him. Just how far Madero went in restricting
British oil interests and in favouring those of the United States
is also open to some question.[1]

5. *Huerta and British Oil*

Madero's regime lasted two years. He was then deposed,
and subsequently executed by Victoriano Huerta.

Madero had been looked upon as a friend of the United
States. After his election in 1911 he had been recognized
promptly by the United States, although at no time "did the
Maderist regime command full support of the Mexican people."
On March 14, 1912, President Taft had prohibited the pur-
chase of arms and ammunition in the United States by factions
which were resisting the new government. Despite these good
offices Madero was overthrown in February, 1913, by Felix
Diaz, nephew of the ex-president, and Victoriano Huerta,
Commander-in-Chief of the Federal Army.[2]

On assuming office, President Wilson found himself facing
a Mexico torn by civil war, with Huerta in power as representative of the feudal landholders, ready to continue the old
policy of Diaz. Part of this policy was to favour the British
oil interests headed by Lord Cowdray's syndicate. "That the
Huerta forces have maintained the Diaz policy of antagonism
to American oil interests and friendship to Lord Cowdray is
apparent," one observer stated at that time. "On Lord Cowdray's own statements, the firm subscribed to three per cent of
the loan floated by Huerta. . . . It is a rich prize for which
these American and British capitalists are contending. . . ."[3]

The nature of the interest which the leading powers held
at this time in Mexican oil was described by Edward L. Doheny,
as follows: "Inasmuch as both Germany and Great Britain are
seeking and acquiring sources of supply for large quantities of
petroleum, it seems to me that there can be no question but

[1] U. S. Sen. For. Rel. Com., "Revolutions in Mexico," 1913, p. 273 ff.
[2] Ogg, "National Progress," p. 288.
[3] "World's Work," v. 27, p. 294.

that the United States must avail itself of the enterprise and ability and pioneer spirit of its citizens to acquire and to have and to hold a reasonable portion of the world's petroleum supplies. If it does not it will find that the supplies of petroleum not within the boundaries of United States territory will be rapidly acquired by citizens and Governments of other nations. . . . There are somewhere between 50 and 100 American companies, large and small, that have holdings of supposed oil lands in Mexico, acquired either by purchase or lease. . . . This oil field, discovered by Americans . . . having a potential daily productive capacity nearly, if not quite, equal to that of the United States, having a reasonable oil valuation of some billions of barrels, is the source to which the United States must look for the supply of petroleum which will justify the building of a commercial fleet that can compete for cost of operation with any other fleet which the great nations of the world may have or construct. . . . Mexico is not the only source for petroleum in large quantities, but it has the greatest developed and demonstrated supply, and all other probable sources of great supply are politically, nationally, and geographically less favourably situated than are the American oil holdings in Mexico." [1]

At the same time, the British Government had acquired an interest in oil [2] and consequently an interest in Mexico. During 1913 and 1914 the press of both countries freely discussed the oil struggle behind the diplomacy of President Wilson and Earl Grey. American oil put Madero in as president of Mexico, the London Mail declared, but British oil interests kept Huerta in power. [3] Discussions of the Mexican situation turned into discussions of oil supplies. "Actually," one American review stated in 1913, "the situation is vitally affected by the arrival of the oil-driven battleship in the King's navy. The position of Britain as mistress of the seas is at stake. Oil

---

[1] U. S. Congress, 66:2; "Sen. Doc." v. 9, pp. 255–258.
[2] L'Espagnol, "World Struggle for Oil." Davenport and Cook, "Oil Trusts."
[3] "Current Opinion," v. 55, p. 396.

is king now as cotton was in our civil war. The American people may not have realized this new importance of oil. Europe is awake to it." [1]

6. *Washington Backs American Oil*

Among those who were firmly convinced that Huerta was favouring British oil interests and opposing American oil interests were President Wilson and Secretary of State Bryan. They believed, according to so intimate an observer as Colonel E. M. House, that British oil men "had not only already obtained concessions from the Huerta government, but expected to obtain others." [2] Lord Cowdray, head of the Pearson syndicate, and Sir Lionel Carden, the British minister in Mexico, were believed by the State Department and President Wilson to be intriguing with Huerta for domination of the Mexican oil fields. The British have one interest in Mexico, Secretary Bryan told a British diplomat, and that's oil. "That's just what the Standard Oil people told me in New York," the diplomat replied. "The ideas that you hold are the ones which the Standard Oil is disseminating. You are pursuing the policy which they have decided on. Without knowing it you are promoting the interest of the Standard Oil." [3] Later, describing a personal talk with President Wilson about the Mexican situation and Lord Cowdray's oil interests, Colonel House wrote, "We do not love him, for we think that between Cowdray and Carden a large part of our troubles in Mexico has been made." [4]

7. *Woodrow Wilson versus Huerta*

The conviction that Huerta was friendly to British oil interests led to a long-drawn-out policy of political intrigue, financial strangulation, moral eloquence, and finally armed intervention, the consistent aim of which was to drive Huerta from Mexican

---

[1] "Current Opinion," v. 55, p. 394.
[2] Hendrick, "Life of Page," v. 1, p. 206.
[3] Ibid., p. 203.
[4] Ibid., p. 218.

politics. Latin Americans who were led by President Wilson's pre-election speeches and writings to believe that during his administration they would be free to govern themselves without North American interference, were quickly disillusioned. Huerta overthrew the government of Madero in February 1913. On March 11, seven days after taking office, President Wilson declared: "We can have no sympathy with those who seek to seize the power of government to advance their own personal interests or ambition. We are friends of peace, but we know that there can be no lasting or stable peace in such circumstances." These words were an intimation that the United States was to break for the first time with its policy of recognizing de facto governments. While all the leading governments of the world recognized Huerta, President Wilson established a "moral empire" in America by refusing to recognize a provisional president who had come into power through revolution.[1]

"Thus was marked a new phase of our relations with Mexico. It began a period of direct intervention."[2] This refusal to recognize Huerta involved "an innovation in our dealings with Latin-American states. Hitherto the question of recognition was settled on grounds of the new government's strength and probable permanence."[3] However, this "moral" Monroe Doctrine, by which the United States was to regulate Latin-American politics through the withholding of recognition, was by no means absolute. During the controversy over the recognition of Huerta, the United States recognized the government of Colonel Benavides in Peru, although this government, like that of Huerta, had achieved power through violent revolution.[4]

8. *President Wilson Intervenes*

Within three months of his accession to the presidency, Huerta was face to face with a formidable Constitutionalist up-

[1] "World's Work," v. 28, pp. 52–58.
[2] "University of California Chronicle," v. 22, p. 51.
[3] Ogg, "National Progress," p. 290.
[4] U. S. "Foreign Relations," 1914, p. 1066.

rising headed by Carranza, Villa and other powerful chieftains. The attitude that President Wilson was taking had convinced these men that it was impossible for Huerta to survive, hence they hastened to prosecute a cause that seemed destined to sure success.

Having decided to remove Huerta and support the cause of the Constitutionalists, President Wilson recalled the American ambassador, who had been urging the recognition of Huerta in the interests of peace and order, and in his stead sent John Lind as confidential agent of the President of the United States in the City of Mexico. In presenting this matter to Congress, President Wilson said: "The present situation in Mexico is incompatible with the fulfilment of international obligations on the part of Mexico, with the civilized development of Mexico herself, and with the maintenance of tolerable political and economic conditions in Central America."

Lind was therefore instructed to make the following offer to Huerta:

"(a) An immediate cessation of fighting throughout Mexico, a definite armistice solemnly entered into and scrupulously observed;

"(b) Security given for an early and free election in which all will agree to take part;

"(c) The consent of General Huerta to bind himself not to be a candidate for election as President of the Republic at this election; and

"(d) The agreement of all parties to abide by the results of the election and co-operate in the most loyal way in organizing and supporting the new administration." [1]

In addition, President Wilson's confidential agent proposed that if the Huerta Government acted on these suggestions, the government of the United States would recommend to American bankers "the immediate extension of a loan." [2] These proposals were rejected by the Huerta regime as a humiliating and unnecessary interference in Mexican affairs.

[1] U. S. "Congressional Record," v. 50, pp. 3803-4.
[2] U. S. "Foreign Relations," 1913, p. 835.

But President Wilson was prepared to interfere even further. On August 27, in a message delivered at a joint session of both houses of Congress, he announced that he would "follow the best practice of nations in the matter of neutrality by forbidding the exportation of arms or munitions of war of any kind from the United States to any part of the Republic of Mexico."[1] The message implied that the United States was ready to intervene at the proper time, and hinted at the reasons for intervention, declaring that "Mexico lies at last where all the world looks on. Central America is about to be touched by the great routes of the world's trade and intercourse running free from ocean to ocean at the Isthmus. The future has much in store for Mexico, as for all the states of Central America; but the best gifts can come to her only if she be ready and free to receive them and to enjoy them honourably. . . . Mexico has a great and enviable future before her, if only she choose and attain the paths of honest constitutional government. . . . While we wait, the contest of the rival forces will undoubtedly for a little while be sharper than ever, just because it will be plain that an end must be made of the existing situation, and that very promptly." On the same day instructions dictated by the President were cabled to American consuls in Mexico ordering them to "convey to the authorities an intimation that any maltreatment of Americans is likely to raise the question of intervention."[2]

The determination of the United States to coerce Mexico was thus clearly stated; it was now merely a question of time and means. The capture of Torreon by Villa on October 1, was a severe blow to the Huerta government. Demands for intervention by the United States became more insistent in the American press. One of the chief obstacles, however, was Great Britain's recognition, if not support, of the Huerta regime. According to one close observer, "Mr. Wilson had many tempestuous conflicts with the British Foreign Office over the apparent support given to the Huerta regime by Sir Lionel

[1] U. S. "Foreign Relations," 1913, p. 823; see p. 820 for full text.
[2] Ibid., p. 896.

Carden, the British Minister to Mexico, a support intensified to no small extent by the large British oil companies in Mexico whose influence in London official circles was appreciable." [1] Ambassador Page was doing his best to initiate Earl Grey into the doctrines of the new "moral" diplomacy, explaining that in case of "continued and utter failure" to settle Mexico's affairs peacefully, "the United States might feel obliged to repeat its dealings with Cuba." [2]

9. *United States and British Co-operate*

On October 26 elections were held in Mexico "without any violence" as far as Mexico City was concerned [3] and, by manipulations not unknown outside of Mexico, Huerta was elected as interim constitutional president, although he had announced that he would not be a candidate. Shortly following the election, the Department of State announced, in unmistakable language, its intention of destroying the Huerta regime.

"While the President feels that he cannot yet announce in detail his policy with regard to Mexico," Secretary Bryan cabled to American diplomatic officers on November 7, "nevertheless he believes that he ought, in advance thereof, to make known to the Government to which you are accredited his clear judgment that it is his immediate duty to require Huerta's retirement from the Mexican Government, and that the Government of the United States must now proceed to employ such means as may be necessary to secure this result." [4] First among the necessary means to remove Huerta was to get Great Britain to desert him. At this time Downing Street was negotiating with the United States for the abolition of the Panama Canal tolls, which worked to the disadvantage of British commerce. In November, Sir William Tyrell, formerly secretary to Earl Grey, the British Foreign Minister, arrived in

---

[1] Lawrence, "True Story of Wilson," p. 100.
[2] U. S. "Foreign Relations," 1913, p. 852 ff.
[3] Ibid., p. 850.
[4] Ibid., p. 856.

Washington to discuss an arrangement by which, in return for lifting the Panama tolls, Great Britain would give the United States a free hand in Mexico. On November 14, Colonel House was able to report a conversation involving himself, Sir William, and President Wilson during which the President "elaborated upon the toll question much to the satisfaction of Sir William," who in turn "assured the President that his government would work cordially with ours and that they would do all that they could to bring about joint pressure through Germany and France for the elimination of Huerta." [1] The conversation between Sir William and President Wilson brought out a statement of policy toward Latin America which is not often found in official documents.

"When I go back to England," said the Englishman, as the interview was approaching an end, "I shall be asked to explain your Mexican policy. Can you tell me what it is?"

President Wilson looked at him earnestly and said, in his most decisive manner:

"I am going to teach the South American Republics to elect good men!"

. . ."Yes," replied Sir William, "but, Mr. President, I shall have to explain this to Englishmen, who, as you know, lack imagination. They cannot see what is the difference between Huerta, Carranza, and Villa."

The only answer that he could obtain was that Carranza was the best of the three and that Villa was not so bad as he had been painted.[2]

Fortified by Sir William's assurance that the British Government would countenance the removal of Huerta, President Wilson was ready to state his aims a shade more emphatically than before, and to threaten intervention more openly. "The present policy of the Government of the United States is to isolate General Huerta entirely," Secretary Bryan cabled the American diplomatic representatives on November 24, "to cut him off from foreign sympathy and aid and from domestic

[1] Hendrick, "Life of Page," v. I, pp. 207–208.
[2] Ibid., pp. 204–5.

credit, whether moral or material, and to force him out. It hopes and believes that isolation will accomplish this end and shall await the results without irritation or impatience. If General Huerta does not retire by force of circumstances it will become the duty of the United States to use less peaceful means to put him out. . .

"It will give other Governments notice in advance of each affirmative or aggressive step it has in contemplation should it unhappily become necessary to move actively against the usurper; but no such step seems immediately necessary." [1]

For the time being, the United States had to content itself with a financial blockade of Mexico. Ambassador Page, however, had already notified the State Department that the British Government regarded Huerta's collapse as "certain, imminent and desirable," but they also regarded that "as the task of the United States." [2] Pressure brought to bear by the United States prevented Huerta from obtaining a loan in Europe, with the result that in January, 1914, Huerta issued a decree suspending payment of interest on all government bonds foreign and domestic for six months. This national bankruptcy was attributed by the Wall Street Journal to President Wilson's financial blockade. [3]

Meantime the forces of Carranza and Villa, whom the United States now openly favoured, were winning military victories in the North. [4] Accordingly, Secretary of State Bryan notified other governments that the United States would remove the embargo on arms, so that the triumphant Constitutionalists might seize power by force. The State Department also implied that not only would the United States dictate to Mexico as to who shall not be its president, but that it would also dictate as to who shall, and that this regulation of Mexico's affairs it would not share with any of the European Powers. In reply to an offer by Great Britain that "European Governments might

[1] U. S. "Foreign Relations," 1914, p. 444.
[2] Ibid., 1913, p. 861.
[3] "Wall Street Journal," Jan. 15, 1914, p. 5.
[4] O'Shaughnessy, "Diplomat's Wife in Mexico," pp. 245-250.

be willing to request Huerta to resign" so that Huerta would "feel that he could save his face by yielding to the request of several strong powers" Secretary Bryan replied:

"The President warmly appreciates the suggestion of Sir Edward Grey but fears that the .revolution in Mexico has reached such a stage that the sort of settlement proposed, namely the elimination of General Huerta and the substitution of others in authority at Mexico City, would be without the desired effect of bringing peace and order. . . . From many sources which it deems trustworthy the Government of the United States has received information which convinces it that there is a more hopeful prospect of peace, of the security of property and of the early payment of foreign obligations if Mexico is left to the forces now reckoning with one another there. . . . The President is so fully convinced of this, after months of the most careful study of the situation at close range, that he no longer feels justified in maintaining an irregular position as regards the contending parties in the matter of neutrality. He intends therefore, almost immediately, to remove the inhibition on the exportation of arms and ammunition from the United States. . . ." [1]

The forces which the United States favoured were winning, and it was cheaper to let Mexicans kill each other than to attempt an invasion; the United States was ready, therefore, to surrender the "moral" policy, and to supply arms for one of the sides in the civil war of a nominally independent country. The embargo on arms was lifted on February 3. A statement issued by President Wilson on that day admitted that the United States was not neutral when the embargo was declared. At that time the President had declared that the embargo was in accord with "the best practice of nations in the matter of neutrality." In removing the embargo he declared that "the executive order under which the exportation of arms and ammunition into Mexico is forbidden was a departure from the accepted practices of neutrality—a deliberate departure from these practices under a well considered joint resolution of Congress . . . the existence of this order hinders and delays the very thing the Government of the United States is now

[1] U. S. "Foreign Relations," 1914, p. 444.

insisting upon, namely, that Mexico shall be left free to settle her own affairs and as soon as possible put them upon a constitutional footing by her own force and counsel. The order is, therefore, rescinded." [1]

American investors in Mexico continued to press the administration to intervene. Senator Albert B. Fall, for many years the intimate of Edward L. Doheny, and himself an investor in Mexico, explained to the United States Senate on March 9 the subtle differences between "interposition, or non-political intervention, upon the one hand, and political intervention in the domestic affairs of Mexico upon the other." He advocated that the administration should "immediately direct the use of the land and naval forces of this Government for the protection of our citizens and other foreigners in Mexico wherever found, and lend their assistance to the restoration of order and the maintenance of peace in that unhappy country and the placing of the administrative functions in the hands of capable and patriotic citizens of Mexico." [2] This policy outlined by a Republican senator was followed by the Democratic administration, which was watchfully waiting for an opportunity to "restore order in Mexico."

10. *The Tampico Flag Incident*

For almost a year the United States Government had been actively interfering with Mexican affairs for the purpose of ousting Huerta and placing in power forces which it thought would be more favourable to American investors in Mexico. Those who had land, mineral, industrial and oil investments in Mexico were crying so loudly for intervention that President Wilson declared: "I have to pause and remind myself that I am President of the United States and not of a small group of Americans with vested interests in Mexico." [3] A financial blockade deprived Huerta of money; one confidential agent of President Wilson was issuing ultimatums in Mexico City,

[1] U. S. "Foreign Relations," 1914, pp. 447–8.
[2] U. S. "Congressional Record," v. 51, p. 4527.
[3] Tumulty, "Wilson as I Know Him," p. 146.

another had been sent to negotiate with Carranza, a third was conferring with Villa. Foreign governments had been repeatedly advised that Huerta must go and that the United States would support the Constitutionalists. In the light of these facts, the events of April 1914 are instructive illustrations of modern American statecraft.

On April 9 Admiral Mayo, in command of the United States warships stationed at Tampico cabled to Washington: "This forenoon Mexican soldiers arrested paymaster and whaleboat's crew of *Dolphin,* part of whom were in boat with flag flying, marched them two blocks through streets, then back to boat, and there released them. General Zaragoza expressed regret verbally. In view of publicity of event, I have called for formal disavowal and apology, punishment of officer in charge Mexican squad, and salute to American flag within 24 hours from 6 P. M. Thursday." [1] On the same day, Admiral Mayo informed the Mexican commander of the Huerta forces at Tampico, General Zaragoza, that the salute was to consist of 21 guns, which would be duly returned by the American ships.[2] The Huerta Government protested that the "American marines disembarked at a place subject to military authority where military operations were being conducted and where a hostile attack had just been made," that they disembarked "without previous advice and without permission from the military authorities of Mexico"; and that "a military commander who sees the arrival of men in uniform at the post he is guarding should proceed to arrest them pending an investigation as to whether the presence of these men is or is not justifiable." [3] Furthermore, the marines had been immediately released, the officer who arrested them had been punished, and Huerta in a written statement expressed regret for the incident and ordered an investigation. A written report by Admiral Fletcher on April 11, showed that apologies were made by the Huertista commander immediately after the inci-

[1] U. S. "Foreign Relations," 1914, p. 449.
[2] Ibid., p. 448.
[3] Ibid., p. 454, 462.

dent and it was explained, in extenuation, that the arresting officer was "ignorant of the first laws of war and was carrying out his instructions to allow no boats whatever at that warehouse dock" where the American marines had landed.[1]

Under ordinary circumstances the incident might have been dropped, but it furnished too good an opportunity to "move actively against the usurper."[2] Although the government of the United States appreciated "the courteous and conciliatory attitude of General Huerta" it nevertheless insisted that in addition to apologies he salute an American flag on Mexican territory.[3] Before the negotiations with Mexico City had proceeded very far, ten American battleships were hurried to Tampico on April 14, carrying a regiment of marines.[4] Upon hearing the news that the whole North Atlantic fleet was being rushed to the Gulf, Huerta remarked "Is it a calamity? No, it is the best thing that could happen to us!"[5] At the same time he offered to place the whole Tampico affair before the Hague Tribunal for arbitration.[6] When this offer failed, he agreed to fire the twenty-one guns provided that a salute of twenty-one guns was fired by an American battery simultaneously. He explained that he did not "desire to salute first because he believed that the United States Government would not return the salute and would thereby humiliate his government."[7] Despite the urgent cable by the American Chargé d'Affaires in Mexico City, Nelson O'Shaughnessy, that "an absolute coincidence in time" in the salutes was "the best arrangement that can be made," Secretary of State Bryan insisted on the technicality of having Huerta, whose government the United States had not recognized, fire the twenty-one guns first. "I have all the time a sickening

---

[1] U. S. "Foreign Relations," 1914, pp. 450–451.
[2] See Bryan's cable on p. 99.
[3] U. S. "Foreign Relations," 1914, p. 459.
[4] Idem.
[5] O'Shaughnessy, "Diplomat's Wife in Mexico," p. 266.
[6] U. S. "Foreign Relations," 1914, p. 461.
[7] Ibid., p. 464.

sensation," Mrs. O'Shaughnessy wrote at the American Embassy at Mexico City on April 25, "that we are destroying these people and that there is no way out. We seem to have taken advantage of their every distress." [1] That the flag incident at Tampico and the controversy over the twenty-one gun salute was a pretext for intervening in Mexico was clear to many observers. It was actually admitted by the State Department on April 16 in a communication to American newspaper men in Mexico City for their "private information, not yet for publication," declaring that the Tampico incident "was quite in the background, but reciting two recent and heinous crimes of Mexico. First, a cable for the Embassy was held over by a too-zealous partisan of the *censura* at the cable office. . . . The incident was less than nothing, until mentioned in the open cable from Washington. The other incident, also well enough known, happened a short time ago in Vera Cruz, where another too-zealous official arrested an orderly in uniform, carrying the mails between the ships and the Vera Cruz post office. That matter was dismissed after an apology, a nominal punishment of the offending official, and the immediate release of the carrier. Admiral Fletcher attached no importance to the affair." [2]

On April 18 a last desperate attempt to prevent these trivial incidents from being used as an excuse for intervention were made both by the Huerta Government and Chargé O'Shaughnessy. Huerta acceded to the demand of the United States that he fire the salutes first, provided that Chargé O'Shaughnessy "would sign a protocol . . . stating that upon the salute being rendered by the Mexican battery it would be returned according to international usage by the American warship." The American Chargé was prepared to sign such a document [3] but was ordered not to do so by Secretary Bryan, who declared that the United States would return the salute without a written promise, which might be construed as a recognition of Huerta's

---

[1] O'Shaughnessy, supra, p. 268.
[2] Ibid., p. 269.
[3] U. S. "Foreign Relations," 1914, p. 469.

government, "whereas the President has no intention of recognizing the Huerta Government." [1]   The unbending attitude
of Washington confirmed Huerta in his belief that the United
States was determined to humiliate him and Mexico; besides,
he counted on uniting all Mexican factions in resistance to
intervention by a foreign nation.   The unconditional demands
of the United States were turned down.   Having manœuvred
Huerta into a position where the long-standing plan of ousting
him could effectively be carried out, President Wilson on
April 20 once more addressed a joint session of both houses
of Congress on Mexican affairs.

After describing the Tampico flag incident in terms not
justified by the Mayo report, the President declared that "had
it stood by itself it might have been attributed to the ignorance
or arrogance of a single officer.   Unfortunately, it was not an
isolated case.   A series of incidents have recently occurred
which cannot but create the impression that the representatives
of General Huerta were willing to go out of their way to show
disregard for the dignity and rights of this Government and
felt perfectly safe in doing what they pleased. . . . A few
days after the incident at Tampico an orderly from the U. S. S.
Minnesota was arrested at Vera Cruz while ashore in uniform
to obtain the ship's mail, and was for a time thrown into jail.
An official dispatch from this Government to its embassy at
Mexico City was withheld by the authorities of the telegraphic
service until peremptorily demanded by our Chargé d'Affaires
in person." [2]   As Secretary Bryan had predicted, the Tampico
affair had been supplemented by two other pretexts.   The
incidents referred to by the President as showing that Huerta
was going out of the way to show disregard for the dignity of
the United States, was reported four days before by Admiral
Fletcher as follows:

"About 10 A. M. on April 11, while in the post office at Vera
Cruz, a mail orderly from the *Minnesota* got into a discussion
with a Mexican mail orderly of the 18th battalion.   They could

[1] U. S. "Foreign Relations," 1914, p. 471.
[2] Ibid., p. 475.

not understand each other and the policeman, in order to avoid a possible disturbance, directed them both to come with him to the station. The police judge, upon hearing the statement of the police officer, at once told our mail orderly he was not at fault and would not be detained. The Mexican mail orderly was found at fault by the judge and was detained and turned over to the military authorities and was given proper punishment. The attitude of the Mexican authorities was correct; there is no cause for complaint against them and the incident is without significance." [1]

Similarly, on April 12, when the cable referred to in the President's message was held up in Mexico City, Chargé O'Shaughnessy, in two separate cables, explained to the State Department that the incident was "really due to ignorance of censor." [2] President Wilson was kept in touch with every official communication from Mexico; nevertheless, he misstated the facts surrounding three trivial incidents in such a way as to rouse national excitement and asked Congress to approve his using "the armed forces of the United States in such ways and to such an extent as may be necessary to obtain from General Huerta and his adherents the fullest recognition of the rights and dignity of the United States." [3] It may be stated at once that the salute of twenty-one guns was never obtained and the entire flag incident at Tampico was dropped. The use of armed forces in Mexico was the outcome of the policy announced the previous year that the administration would "seek the retirement of Huerta from the Mexican Government, and that the Government of the United States must now proceed to employ such means as may be necessary to procure the result."

11. *The Capture of Vera Cruz*

The President's message called forth a flood of patriotic oratory in Congress. The administration leader in the House, Oscar Underwood, connected the American flag with property

---

[1] U. S. "Foreign Relations," 1914, p. 465.
[2] Ibid., pp. 453–4.
[3] Ibid., p. 476.

interests in Mexico, referred to the impending invasion of Mexico as war, and admitted that it had been coming for a long time. "War," he declared, "never comes from one incident, and never has. For more than a year we have been facing a state of turmoil, a state of disorder—I may not go too far if I say a state of anarchy—in the Republic of Mexico, that has threatened the lives and property of the citizens of the United States. . . . We have hoped from day to day that a peaceful settlement might be reached, but I will say to you . . . that peace without strife never comes to that nation that is not willing to protect its citizenship, sustain its property interests in a foreign country, and, above all other things, compel a decent respect to the flag of the Nation . . . the flag that makes it safe for an American to put his foot on foreign soil." [1] Before Congress could act on the President's message, however, matters quite remote from the three incidents mentioned in it induced him to order the immediate seizure of Vera Cruz.

At 2:30 in the morning of April 21 the President was awakened by a telephone call from Secretary of State Bryan who informed him that the German steamship *Ypirango,* carrying munitions, would arrive at Vera Cruz that morning about ten o'clock. Secretary of the Navy Daniels also got on the wire, and after consulting his two cabinet officers and his private secretary, President Wilson said: "Take Vera Cruz at once." [2] The *Ypirango* was carrying arms for the Huerta forces. On Febuary 3, the embargo on arms to Mexico had been lifted so as to treat Mexico "as any other country would be which was torn by civil war." [3] On April 21, by order of the President, the *Ypirango,* carrying arms for the de facto government of Mexico, was stopped. Marines and bluejackets landed at Vera Cruz, seized the cable office, post office, telegraph office, customs house, and railroad station, and on the following day American forces "commenced advance to take the entire city at eight o'clock under guns of war vessels."

[1] U. S. "Congressional Record," v. 51, p. 6937.
[2] Tumulty, "Wilson as I Know Him," p. 152.
[3] U. S. "Foreign Relations," 1914, p. 447.

Mexicans in Vera Cruz resisted what they termed "the unlawful landing of American marines," for no war had been declared. Many of these were civilians defending their homes, as indicated by an order issued by Admiral Fletcher declaring that "such firing by irregulars not members of an organized military force is contrary to the laws of war; if persisted in it will call for severe measures." [1] At the same time the Huerta general at Vera Cruz announced he did not intend to fight, but would leave with all his soldiers, tearing up the track behind him.

The capture of Vera Cruz cost the United States the lives of seventeen marines and bluejackets. It cost Mexico the lives of two hundred men, women and children. Its ostensible object was to obtain satisfaction for the affront to the American flag at Tampico. The satisfaction was never again requested. Its actual object was the removal of Huerta and the installation of the Constitutionalists. It was President Wilson's way of teaching Mexico "to elect good men." While the firing was still going on at Vera Cruz, John Lind, the President's confidential agent in Mexico, declared in a public statement: "We have no quarrel with the revolutionists, therefore, while Huerta is blocked away from supplies, the revolutionists will push forward steadily and irresistibly. The end should not be far off, so far as Huerta is concerned." [2] On the same day the wife of the American Chargé d'Affaires at Mexico City wrote that "With the taking of Vera Cruz, through whose customs a full fourth of the total imports come, Huerta is out a million pesos a month, more or less. We are certainly isolating and weakening him at a great rate. 'Might is right.' We can begin to teach it in the schools." [3]

Despite the aid which the American Government gave to the Constitutionalists by seizing Vera Cruz, Carranza considered the act a violation of Mexico's sovereignty. He had already notified William Bayard Hale, another of President Wilson's confidential agents, that "No foreign nation can be permitted

---

[1] U. S. "Foreign Relations," 1914, pp. 477-81.
[2] "New York Sun," April 23, 1914.
[3] O'Shaughnessy, supra, p. 290.

to interfere in the interior matters of Mexico." [1] Now, on
April 22, he notified the State Department that although "the
individual acts of Victoriano Huerta will never be sufficient to
involve the Mexican nation in a disastrous war with the United
States," yet "the invasion of our territory and the stay of your
forces in the port of Vera Cruz, violating the rights that constitute our existence as a free and independent sovereign entity,
may indeed drag us into an unequal war. . . . I interpret the
sentiment of the great majority of the Mexican people, so
jealous of its rights and so respectful of the rights of foreigners,
and invite you only to suspend the hostile acts already begun, to
order your forces to evacuate all places that they hold in the
port of Vera Cruz, and to present to the Constitutionalist
Government . . . the demand on the part of the United States
in regard to acts recently committed at the port of Tampico."
In the face of Carranza's nationalist stand, the United
States did everything in its power to prevent the Constitutionalists from supporting Huerta. Special agent Carothers
worked on Villa, and through him the Constitutionalists were
notified by the State Department that the object of the extensive
military activity of the United States on the border would be
"governed entirely by the attitude of General Carranza, General
Villa and their associates." As a result, Villa was prevailed
upon to apologize to the State Department for Carranza's
protest. It seemed as if the United States was to have a free
hand in regulating Mexico's affairs by force.[2]

12. Ordering a Government for Mexico

Interference by the United States in the affairs of one
Latin-American state always tends to unite all of Latin America in a common fear. It was with this in mind that Huerta
declared that "Mexico is defending not only her national
sovereignty but that of all Latin America as well." [3] On April
25 the representatives of Argentina, Brazil and Chile offered

[1] O'Shaughnessy, supra, p. 55.
[2] U. S. "Foreign Relations," 1914, pp. 484-8.
[3] "World's Work," v. 28, p. 130.

to mediate the conflict between the United States and Mexico in order "to prevent any further bloodshed." [1]   This offer was accepted by Huerta and the United States, and representatives of both governments met the mediators at Niagara. However, while the negotiations toward the conference were still in progress, General Funston, commanding United States army forces, formally took over Vera Cruz from the navy on April 30, and declared himself military governor of the city. American troops took control of the general treasury, the customs house, the civil courts, and the post office, in compliance with instructions from the Secretary of War and by direction of the President. [2]

The conference which met at Niagara did not attempt to settle the three incidents which President Wilson used as a pretext for invading Vera Cruz. At the very beginning of the conference President Wilson stated his object, which was the elimination of Huerta and the placing in power of the Constitutionalists.   A message to the American delegates stated that "the elimination of Huerta by one process or another, is now clearly inevitable, the only question remaining being the method, the occasion and the circumstances of his elimination. . . . The object of our conferences now is to find a method by which the inevitable can be accomplished without further bloodshed. By the inevitable we mean not only the elimination of Huerta but the completion of the revolution by the transfer of political power from Huerta to those who represent the interests and aspirations of the people whose forces are now in the ascendency." [3]   In a number of messages to the American delegates, President Wilson made it clear that the United States would insist on a complete acceptance of its programme by Mexico. "It would . . . be futile," his message of May 27 said, "to set up a provisional authority which would be neutral.   It must, to be successful, be actually, avowedly and sincerely in favour of the necessary agrarian

[1] U. S. "Foreign Relations," 1914, p. 489.
[2] Ibid., pp. 496-7.
[3] Ibid., pp 505-6.

and political reforms, and it must be pledged to their immediate formulation. . . . And it will be impossible for the United States to withdraw her hand until this Government is finally satisfied that the programme contemplated will be carried out in all respects.

"We are putting these conclusions bluntly, not in the form, of course, in which we wish you to present them to the Mediators, but flatly for the sake of clearness.

"The case lies in our mind thus: the success of the Constitutionalists is now inevitable. The only question we can now answer without armed intervention on the part of the United States is this: Can the result be moderated; how can it be brought about without further bloodshed; what provisional arrangement can be made which will temper the whole process and lead to the elections in a way that will be hopeful of peace and permanent accommodation? If we do not successfully answer these questions, then the settlement must come by arms, either ours or those of the Constitutionalists." [1]

Backed by this threat—that unless Mexico accepted the programme of the United States peacefully, it would be forced upon her by arms—the American delegation at Niagara proposed to the mediators and the Huerta representatives (1) that a Constitutionalist be made provisional president of Mexico, (2) that the election board shall contain a Constitutionalist majority, (3) that the land and naval forces of the United States shall remain in Mexico for an indefinite time, and extend to the elections. This was tantamount to controlling Mexico's elections through armed force, as the United States had done in Santo Domingo and Nicaragua. Not only did the Huerta delegates turn the proposal down, but representatives of Carranza who met the American delegates at Buffalo declared that the mediators "ought to stop attempting to settle internal affairs of Mexico . . . that they would not accept as a gift anything which the Mediators could give them, even though it was what they were otherwise seeking . . . that no one would be satisfactory that was appointed by the Medi-

[1] U. S. "Foreign Relations," 1914, p. 510.

ators, even if it was Carranza himself, because anything that came from the Mediators would not be accepted by their party or by the Mexican people." [1]

The Niagara conference accomplished nothing. With American troops in control of Vera Cruz, Huerta's strategic base, the forces of Carranza and Villa seized Tampico, through which they received arms and ammunition. As they continued their advance southward, Huerta was forced out. He resigned on July 15 and left Mexico, without ever having been called upon again to make amends for "insulting the dignity of the United States flag." Within a few weeks, Carranza was installed as first chief of Mexico at the capital, and both parts of President Wilson's avowed programme of teaching Mexico to elect good men seemed to have been carried out.

13. *American Oil Backs Carranza*

Huerta was opposed and Carranza was assisted, not only by the United States Government, but by the United States oil interests as well. Mr. Doheny made this quite clear in his testimony before the Senate Committee in 1919.

The British oil interests and the British Government were lined up on one side and the American oil interests and the American Government were on the other. "It was a well known fact that the British assisted in the sale of a large amount of Huerta bonds and they were distinctly favourable to the Huerta Government at that time. Our Government had shown its animosity to Huerta and its desire to support his opponents. So that our action was in line with our own Government and that of the British was in line with the supposed sympathies of the British Government." [2]

In the course of his testimony Mr. Doheny made good his assertion, at least in so far as the American oil interests were concerned. When President Wilson refused to recognize Huerta, the Doheny interests stopped paying him taxes, thus depriving him of an important source of revenue.

[1] U. S. "Foreign Relations," 1914, p. 538.
[2] U. S. Congress, 66:2; "Sen. Doc." v. 9, p. 284.

The Chairman. At that time were you paying taxes to the Huerta Government on your oil shipments?

Mr. Doheny. Up to that time we had been paying; but . . . as soon as our Government turned its back on Huerta and refused to recognize him, we refused to pay him any more taxes." [1]

Mr. Doheny's company went further, however, and when the Constitutionalists under General Aguilar came into the Tuxpan field with a demand for $10,000, this amount was paid, under protest, but "with the knowledge and consent and after consulting John Lind, the United States presidential representative in Mexico." [2] This transaction might be explained on the ground of duress, were it not for the fact that on at least three other occasions the Doheny interests contributed to the support of the Constitutionalists.

On the first of these occasions Mr. Doheny met a Constitutionalist representative (Felicitas Villareal) in the Hotel Belmont, New York, and gave him $100,000 in cash "for the purpose of helping to finance their needs." [3]

On the second occasion Mr. Doheny sent a representative to see Carranza and told him "to assure General Carranza of our friendship toward the cause of the Constitutionalists and of our refusal to pay taxes to Huerta . . . and to tell him that if they needed fuel oil of any sort we would be glad to furnish them the fuel, keeping an account of it." [4] The oil furnished on this basis totalled $685,000. While this amount was ultimately set off against the taxes which the Doheny interests were paying Carranza, the open oil credit proved of great importance to the Constitutionalists at a critical period in their operations.

The third instance in which Mr. Doheny's group assisted Carranza is shrouded in mystery. A check for $3,466.86, drawn by the Huastica Petroleum Co., was paid to Dr. Henry Allen Tupper at a time when Dr. Tupper was actively advocating the recognition of Carranza. Mr. Doheny admitted these

[1] U. S. Congress, 66:2; "Sen. Doc." v. 9, pp. 276-7.
[2] Ibid., p. 277.
[3] Ibid., p. 278,
[4] Idem.

facts, but did not know the use to which the money had been put.[1]

By way of summarizing the results of these excursions into Mexican politics, Mr. Doheny said: "This is merely one of a hundred or more incidents which show the checkered career of a company doing business outside of the boundaries of its own country, and is given merely for the reason that it shows the attitude of our Company toward the Constitutionalist forces when they were in need of help. So far as we know, every American corporation doing business in Mexico extended sympathy or aid, or both—and we extended both—to Carranza from the time that President Wilson turned his back on Huerta." [2]

Here is no equivocation and no effort to side-step the issue. Mr. Doheny tells frankly and specifically how and when he put both cash and credit behind Carranza   He says, furthermore, that in his opinion, many other American firms did the same thing. Whether, as Mr. Doheny asserts, the American interests in Mexico followed the lead of the United States Government, or whether, as Mr. Wilson, Mr. Bryan and others asserted, the United States Government was subject to constant pressure from the vested interests seems to be a matter of opinion.   Both sides find no difficulty in agreeing that they were co-operating to control the internal political life of Mexico.

14. *"Confiscation" and the Constitution of 1917*

Carranza received active assistance from the American Government and from the United States oil interests in his effort to take the Mexican Government out of the hands of British-supported Huerta. But there was an element in the situation which neither Mr. Wilson nor Mr. Doheny seem to have understood—the Mexican Revolution.

In its earlier phases, the Mexican Revolution appeared merely as a struggle between Mexican political leaders who had, as their objective, an increase in their personal power. By the

---

[1] U. S Congress, 66:2; "Sen. Doc." v. 9, pp. 292–3.
[2] Ibid., p. 279.

time that Carranza appeared on the scene, however, the Revolution had entered a different phase. It was no longer a case of Carranza versus Huerta, but Carranza, Zapata, Villa and other advocates of land reform, versus Huerta, the landlords, the Federal Army and the machinery of the Federal Government. Although Carranza was himself a landowner, he adopted the slogan of land reform. The peons who supported the revolution wanted land and peace. The Constitutionalists promised both. By 1914, therefore, in so far as the masses in Mexico were concerned the revolution had ceased to be purely personal and political, and had entered a social stage. It is impossible here to discuss the Mexican Revolution [1] but it is necessary to note that a Constitutional Convention met on December 2, 1916, and that, on February 5, 1917, the new constitution was promulgated.[2] From the standpoint of foreign investors, the most important doctrine embodied in this constitution was that the sub-soil rights of Mexico (minerals, fuels, etc.) belonged to the Mexican people. The essential elements in this doctrine are stated in Article 27.

"The ownership of lands and waters within the limits of the national territory is vested originally in the Nation." These are the opening words of Article 27. The right of the Nation to transmit title to private persons is then asserted, but "the nation shall have at all times the right to impose on private property such limitations as the public interest may demand as well as the right to regulate the development of natural resources. . . . In the Nation is vested direct ownership of all minerals or substances which in veins, masses, or beds constitute deposits whose nature is different from the components of the land." A later section of the same article vests the title to water rights in the Nation.

While this assertion of the title of the nation or state to the land of the state is a commonplace in the laws of most modern countries, who embody it in the doctrine of the right of eminent domain, the application of the principle to silver, copper,

[1] Ross, "Social Revolution in Mexico." Beals, "Mexico," p. 53 ff.
[2] U. S. Congress, 66:2; "Sen. Doc." v. 10, pp. 3123-52.

gold, and especially to oil created consternation among the foreign investors in Mexico. Abstractly the people of Mexico are sovereign. That is, they have the right to regulate their own affairs free from outside interference. Practically the essential resources of Mexico are in the hands of foreign capitalists (principally Americans) whose business it is to make what they can out of the resources and people of Mexico. Therefore, when the Constitutionalists, who had won the economic and diplomatic support of the United States, proposed the passage of Article 27, Secretary Lansing addressed a communication to Charles Parker, representative of American interests, containing a protest against the proposed Article 27, which was then before the Constitutional Convention.[1] The Lansing note pointed out that the article was, in effect, confiscatory, and urged the necessity of its modification.

This note was one of a long series of communications in which the United States State Department opposed, first the passage of Article 27 by the Constitutional Convention, and then its enforcement by the Carranza Government. On February 19, 1918, Carranza issued a decree imposing a petroleum tax under Article 27, and the United States State Department replied on April 2 with a "formal and solemn protest of the Government of the United States against the violation or infringement of legitimately acquired American property rights involved in the enforcement of the said decree." [2] The controversy dragged on until, on August 12, 1918, Secretary Lansing asked Carranza to "suspend all operation of said decrees in order that the American Government may examine carefully and consider their provisions, purpose, and results as affecting rights and properties of American citizens." [3] To this protest Carranza replied on August 13 that the enforcement of the decrees did not admit of further delay. He also called the attention of the State Department to the fact that the decrees were a part of the fiscal legislation of the Mexican Government, and as

[1] U. S. Congress, 66:2; "Sen. Doc." v. 10, p. 3121.
[2] Ibid., p. 3155.
[3] Ibid., p. 3158.

such were not the legitimate subject of diplomatic representations. Following this, on August 17, the Acting Secretary of State for Mexico pointed out, in a carefully prepared note, that any sovereign state has the right to decide its own fiscal policy, and that so long as this policy does not discriminate against the property rights of the citizens of any particular nation, it is not the legitimate subject of diplomatic representations. Furthermore, that the nationals of any state must expect to abide by the laws of the country in which they invest. The Acting Secretary wrote:

"The criterion of the Mexican Government in this matter is not an innovation in international law, but the simple application of the principle of the equality of nations, frequently forgotten by strong governments in their relations with weak countries." [1]

Carranza evidently had these and similar negotiations in mind when he said to the Mexican Congress on September 1, 1919: "Unfortunately the Mexican Government has received suggestions more or less vehement from the United States Government when it has tried to make reforms that may injure American citizens. These suggestions deliberately destroy our liberty for legislation, and nullify the rights we have to progress in accordance with our ideas. The argument used by the American State Department, as well as by the American press has been that our duties are confiscatory. The Mexican Government hopes the Northern Republic will respect the sovereignty and independence of Mexico. . . . The revolution has implanted reforms making for the welfare and progress of the Mexican people. The Government is attempting to respect and consolidate existing rights, but absolutely cannot accept the principle that the liberty of Mexicans to govern according to their own necessities should be limited." [2]

Throughout this correspondence, the American State Department was frankly defending the American investors in Mexico,

[1] U. S. Congress, 66:2; "Sen. Doc." v. 10, p. 3161.
[2] DeBekker, "Plot Against Mexico," pp. 235-272.

and as most of the correspondence had to do specifically with the oil tax decrees, the correspondence centres around oil. The Mexicans, on the other hand, were insisting upon the right to levy taxes in accordance with the provisions of their own constitution. The diplomatic power of the United States was therefore being brought to bear against the enforcement, in Mexico, of the Mexican constitution and of Mexican law.

15. *Oil Producers versus Mexico*

The United States State Department was not left to fight the battle alone. Mr. Doheny, in the course of his testimony, stated the situation in these cogent words: "I will skip over this matter of the direct dispute between the oil men and our Government on the one hand with the Mexican Government on the other." [1] At the same point in his testimony Mr. Doheny declares that the oil companies refused to comply with the decrees of the Mexican Government "with the consent and approval and at the suggestion of our own State Department."

Nor did the oil companies stop with a mere refusal to obey the laws of Mexico. They organized and began a campaign to overthrow the Mexican Government. There were three phases of this campaign: first, subsidizing counter-revolution in the Mexican oil fields; second, a publicity campaign against Mexico, carried out in the United States; and third, a formal demand upon the Peace Conference, then sitting in Paris, that Mexico be denied a place among the nations that were entitled to join the League of Nations.

16. *Counter-Revolution in the Oil Fields*

After the promulgation of the Constitution of 1917 the oil producers began the payment of regular monthly sums to a local landowner named Pelaez, who held title to properties leased to the Mexican Eagle Oil Co. Pelaez "has an organized force of some numbers, and has held possession of a large

[1] U. S. Congress, 66:2; "Sen. Doc." v. 9, p. 267.

portion of the country for the last two years. I think his force was organized at about the promulgation of the Constitution in 1917 and in opposition to that constitution." [1]

L. J. DeBekker notes that he was told at the American Embassy in Mexico City that "the oil men paid Pelaez, for guarding their interests, $200,000 a month. . . . I was surprised to learn from the spokesman for the oil interests next day that they would like to see Pelaez President of Mexico, because he was their friend." [2]

The Association of Oil Producers in Mexico made a vigorous reply to this article in which they declared that "Pelaez's troops are operating in the oil fields only . . . for the reason that the Government is attempting to confiscate their oil values." In the same letter, the Oil Producers state that in 1916 Pelaez had made a demand for monthly payments, and that these were finally made with the full knowledge and with the advice of the State Department. [3]

At the Senate hearings on September 11, 1919, Mr. Doheny testified as follows: [4]

The Chairman. Has our State Department been aware of the fact that you have been making payments to Pelaez?
Mr. Doheny. Yes; not only aware of it, but so far as they could, without giving it in writing, they have approved of it.

At another point in the testimony:

Senator Brandegee. Are you now having to pay tribute to anybody for protection at the present time?
Mr. Doheny. We are paying tribute to Pelaez.
Senator Brandegee. At what rate now?
Mr. Doheny. I do not know the rate.
Senator Brandegee. Do you know the total payment to all of the companies?
Mr. Doheny. The total payment to all of the companies is less than $30,000.

[1] U. S. Congress, 66:2; "Sen. Doc." v. 9, pp. 279–280.
[2] "Nation," v. 109, p. 37.
[3] Ibid., pp. 108–109.
[4] U. S. Congress, 66:2; "Sen. Doc." v. 9. p. 289.

For more than two years, therefore, according to their own testimony, the oil producers had been maintaining a private army under Pelaez, at a cost running into hundreds of thousands per year, because the Mexican Government, in its enforcement of the laws, was "attempting to confiscate their oil values."

17. *Mexican Policy from 1910 to 1919*

During the years from 1910 to 1919—that is, after the importance of the Mexican oil fields had been established beyond the possibility of doubt, Mexico was in constant turmoil. The Mexican Revolution cannot be laid to the discovery of oil, but the attitude of the United States toward the various revolutionary governments was profoundly affected by the presence of American investors in the Mexican oil fields. From the earliest days, when Diaz was showing his friendship to the Cowdray interests, through the exclusion of Mexico from initial membership in the League of Nations, responsible officials of the United States Government as well as representatives of the American oil companies were playing an active part in Mexican politics.

The officials of the United States Government, from the President down, were at times openly partisan in the favouritism which they showed to those factions that were willing to promote American interests in the oil fields. This partisanship took various forms, all the way from diplomatic protests against the violation of American property rights in the oil fields to the military seizure of Vera Cruz, in an openly avowed effort to destroy the power of one of the Mexican factions that was known to favour the British oil claims.

The American investors, on the other hand, played an even more active part in Mexican politics; refusing to pay taxes to one faction, and providing open oil credits for the rival faction; subscribing large amounts of money to the cause of the Constitutionalists as against the Huertistas; paying a monthly stipend to the leader of a band of brigands as a means of protecting the oil companies against the necessity of paying taxes

to the constituted authorities; carrying on a publicity campaign
in the United States looking to intervention in Mexico; following the President of the United States to the Peace Conference and there persuading him that Mexico must not be given
an equal footing with other nations in the League. Mr. Doheny, the leader of the American investors in Mexico, testified
to these exploits with an adventurer's love of good sport, and
speaks as though it were a matter of course that the Federal
Government should give its aid to foreign investors.

The State Department has placed itself on record, again and
again, as the avowed partisan of the American oil interests
in Mexico, going so far as to insist that the Constitution of
Mexico be modified in such a way as to allow American investors an extended opportunity for making profits out of the
exploitation of Mexican resources.

Evidence might be cited in far greater detail. Enough has
been presented, however, to prove that the United States Government and the United States investors have both taken a part
in the "regulation" of Mexico's internal politics during the
decade ending with 1919.

18. *Political Domination of Weak Nations*

The political regulation employed by the American interests,
private and public, in the control of Latin-American internal
affairs, is in reality political domination and the denial of the
right of self-government. This fact is now admitted by standard historians. For example, Prof. Wm. R. Shepherd in a
recent article makes an ironical reference to the erstwhile liber-
tarian ideals professed by the United States.

"Moreover there are certain pleasant terms in international
parlance the use of which an honest consistency would have to
make us forego. 'The twenty-one independent republics of the
New World,' the 'equality of sovereign states in this hemisphere,'
the 'self-determination of small nations,' even 'Pan-Americanism'
and similar expressions, would have to fall somewhat into desue-

UNITED STATES CARIBBEAN INTERESTS

Possessions
Protectorates
+ Naval Stations

Cuba
Dominican Republic
Virgin Islands
Haiti
Porto Rico
Corn Islands
Canal Zone
Nicaragua
Costa Rica
Panama

Reproduced from Lingley's "Since the Civil War" p. 524.

tude, except as ornate trappings for state occasions. And yet, if it be true that several of the Caribbean countries are in fact no longer independent and belong almost, if not quite, in the category of the British crown colonies, so far as their relationship to the United States is concerned, the inconsistency in employing misnomers would seem already obvious." [1]

Prof. Albert Bushnell Hart is more outspoken.

"In addition the United States between 1906 and 1916 obtained a protectorate over the neighboring Latin American states of Cuba, Haiti, Panama, Santo Domingo and Nicaragua. Altogether, those five states included 157,000 sq. miles and 6,600,000 people." [2]

At least one modern American history presents a map of the Caribbean with American protectorates (including the above countries) indicated by a special marking. [3]

The Cuban treaty of 1904 contained the germ of the idea which has since been applied to considerable portions of the Caribbean area. Under this treaty it is impossible for Cuba to enter into any foreign alliance or to make any important changes in internal policy without the acquiescence of the United States.

If the principle of political regulation may be stated in a sentence, it is that:

Weak neighbouring countries in which there are important American investments must expect to have their internal affairs dominated by the United States Government whenever such a domination seems advantageous to American interests. This principle is "the present form of Monroeism," evolved and supported by "the authors and representatives of the imperialist movement: McKinley, Roosevelt and Lodge; by the representative of dollar diplomacy: Taft; by the representative of the tutelary, imperialist, financial and biblical mission: Wilson." [4]

---

[1] Blakeslee, "Mexico and the Caribbean," p. 202.
[2] Hart, "New American History," p. 635.
[3] See reproduction, facing p. 120.
[4] Pereyra, "El Mito de Monroe," p. 12.

V

ARMED INTERVENTION

1. *The Strategic Importance of the Caribbean Area to the United States*

Between spheres of influence like China and the Near East, and outright colonial possessions like the Philippines and Porto Rico, stand the protectorates, which, though not owned by the United States, are under its political and economic control. Three of these protectorates—Santo Domingo, Haiti, and Nicaragua—have been acquired through armed intervention. All three are in the area around the Caribbean Sea, whose strategic and economic importance doomed it as an inevitable prey to American expansion.

The importance of the Caribbean region to the United States lies in its proximity, its commercial advantages as a source of raw materials and a market for manufactured goods, and as a strategic military addition to the Panama Canal. The opening of the Panama Canal raised the Caribbean "to a commanding position among the trade routes of the world." [1] Central America, President Woodrow Wilson declared, "is about to be touched by the great routes of the world's trade and intercourse running from ocean to ocean at the Isthmus." [2] In addition the Caribbean is the gateway to the Panama Canal, and expansionists have advocated turning it into an "American lake." [3]

The strategic importance of the Caribbean has impelled the United States to acquire naval footholds in that region. In addition to several good harbours on the Gulf of Mexico and the naval base at Key West, Florida, in its own territory, it

[1] Academy of Political Science, "Proceedings," v. 7, p. 383.
[2] U. S. "Congressional Record," v. 50, pp. 3803-4.
[3] Academy of Political Science, "Proceedings," v. 7, p. 393.

has acquired ports belonging to the little republics to the south.[1] From Guantanamo, Cuba, the United States commands the Windward Passage between Cuba and Santo Domingo; from Porto Rico it controls the Mona passage; by turning Haiti and Santo Domingo into protectorates, the United States has acquired the Mole St. Nicholas in the former, and Samana Bay in the latter, as first class naval bases. A treaty with Nicaragua gives the United States possession of the Great Corn and Little Corn Islands and the right to build a naval station on the Gulf of Fonseca. The Virgin Islands, acquired from Denmark in 1917, also offer facilities for an excellent naval base; while the Panama Canal itself forms the centre of American naval power.[2]

In addition to these strategic considerations, the outbreak of the World War forced the Caribbean countries to turn to the United States for economic relationships, not only in matters of trade but also for loans. "In several cases, our government has already taken a guiding hand in the negotiations. Conferences for the adjustment of the debt of Nicaragua, Haiti and Santo Domingo have taken place, not in those countries, nor in the offices of New York bankers, but in the Department of State and the Bureau of Insular Affairs."[3]

One American authority has summarized the matter by describing the Caribbean area as "a tropic belt similar to that which European nations have acquired long ago in other parts of the world. . . . They are so many natural markets lying upon one of the greatest commercial highways of the present and future—to and from the Panama Canal. From them come raw materials and secondary foodstuffs requisite for our factories and exchangeable for our basic foodstuffs and manufactured articles. They have become localities, also, for the investment of American capital under circumstances that may invite the exercise of political influence to a greater or less degree."[4]

[1] Blakeslee, "Mexico and the Caribbean," p. 320.
[2] Ibid., pp. 303-4.
[3] Academy of Political Science, "Proceedings," v. 7, p. 390.
[4] Blakeslee, supra, p. 187.

The importance of the Caribbean economically and strategically has caused it to be called "the Mediterranean of the New World," and the countries around it "the American tropics." The necessity for expansion on the part of the United States, and the need for the rapidly accumulating capital of its financiers to find the nearest and easiest possible outlet, gave rise to a diplomacy which in one form or another has brought a number of the Caribbean countries under the direct control of the United States. As one historian has put it, "Cuba is no more independent than Long Island. The island of San Domingo, with its two Negro republics, is no more independent than the State of New York. Nicaragua and Panama are only nominal republics, and nominal sovereignties. . . . If we are to have a Caribbean empire, we must get it by destroying the republican independence of the powers concerned. . . . We must make up our minds that if we acquire these islands we shall eventually have practically to annex the whole of Central America." [1]

The Caribbean policy of the United States has touched directly or indirectly all of the republics bordering on the Caribbean and the Gulf. Its character can best be described by considering its application to three countries, Santo Domingo, Haiti, and Nicaragua.

2. *The Financial Conquest of Santo Domingo*

The first of the Caribbean countries to suffer American military intervention and the practical establishment of a protectorate was Santo Domingo.

Armed intervention in Santo Domingo and its domination as an American protectorate becomes clearer when its position in the American empire is fully realized. When President Grant proposed the annexation of the republic he declared:

"The acquisition of Santo Domingo is desirable because of its geographical position. It commands the entrance to the Caribbean Sea and the Isthmus transit of commerce. It possesses the richest soil, the most capacious harbours, most salubrious climate

[1] Academy of Political Science, "Proceedings," v. 7, p. 423.

and the most valuable products of the forests, mines and soil of all the West Indian islands. Its possession by us will in a few years build up a coastwise commerce of immense magnitude. . . . In case of foreign war it will give us command of all the islands referred to and thus prevent an enemy from ever possessing herself of rendezvous on our very coast." [1]

In 1893 the San Domingo Improvement Company, an American concern with offices in New York, bought the debt of 170,000 pounds sterling which a Dutch company had loaned to the Dominican Government, and with it the right to collect all customs revenues to satisfy this claim. [2] In 1909 President Jiminez of the Dominican Republic appointed a board of his own to collect customs. The American company thereupon appealed to the State Department at Washington to protect its interests, and after negotiations the Dominican Government was induced to offer to buy the company's debt for $4,500,000. On January 1, 1903, representatives of both governments signed a protocol providing for this settlement and for a board of arbitrators to fix the details of payment. It was also agreed that in case Santo Domingo failed to pay, the United States was to appoint a financial agent to take over certain customs houses. This was the first economic hold on the little republic. [3]

Financial difficulties prevented Santo Domingo from paying its debts and reports were circulated that French and Italian vessels were on their way to the island to collect the debts by force. [4] Taking advantage of this opportunity, Secretary of State Hay instructed the American Minister, Thomas C. Dawson, to suggest to the Dominican Government that it "request" the United States to take over its customs houses. [5] Pressed on all sides by foreign investors, President Morales had no choice but to make "the appeal."

On February 4, 1905, a protocol was drawn up between the two governments by which the United States was to act as

---

[1] Inman, "Problems in Pan Americanism," p. 273.
[2] Jones, "Caribbean Interests of the U. S.," p. 110 ff.
[3] U. S. "Treaties, Conventions, etc.," v. 1, p. 414.
[4] U. S. "Foreign Relations," 1905, p. 334.
[5] Ibid., p. 298, 334, 342.

bankrupt's receiver for Santo Domingo, taking over all its customs houses, administering its finances, and settling the claims of foreign and domestic creditors. Of the revenues which the United States should collect, 55 per cent were to be used for paying bondholders and the remainder was to be turned over to the Dominican Government for administrative expenses.[1] The Senate at Washington refused to ratify this drastic protocol, but President Roosevelt entered into an "executive agreement" with the president of the Dominican Republic which achieved the same results. Under this agreement the customs collectors were to be American and to have the support of American warships.[2] In that same year an American receiver-general named by President Roosevelt proceeded to collect customs "under the protection of the United States Navy,"[3] and to issue bonds for the purpose of paying foreign creditors. Roosevelt's tactics were severely criticized in and out of Congress, but finally the Senate decided to give the arrangement a coat of legality. On February 25, 1907, it ratified a revised treaty which provided: (1) that the President of the United States should appoint a customs collector for Santo Domingo and assistants; (2) that the United States government should afford them such protection as might be necessary; (3) that the Dominican Government could not increase its debts or lower its taxes without the consent of the United States.[4] By the provisions of this treaty the American receiver-general was to issue twenty million dollars gold bonds for paying off Santo Domingo's public debt. The sum total of revenues collected was to be applied as follows: First, to paying the expenses of the receivership; second, to paying the interest on the bonds; third, to the payment of the annual sums provided for the amortization of the bonds; fourth, to the purchase, cancellation and retirement of the bonds; fifth, what was left was to be given to the Dominican Government. The

---

[1] U. S. "Foreign Relations," 1905, p. 342.
[2] Jones, supra, p. 110 ff.
[3] Latané, "U. S. and Latin America," p. 279.
[4] U. S. "Foreign Relations," 1907, pp. 307-9.

loan of twenty million dollars provided in the treaty was made by Kuhn, Loeb & Co. The treaty is still in force, and under its provisions the United States Government is "to collect customs for fifty years" in order to pay interest to the New York bankers.[1]

American financial control of Santo Domingo was soon followed by interference with its political life. In 1911 the Dominican president was shot and a provisional government established. In the fall of the following year President Taft sent two special commissioners to investigate the situation. They were to make the trip in a gunboat accompanied by 750 marines.[2] At the suggestion of the American commissioners the provisional president resigned. This interference by the United States led only to further revolutionary outbreaks.

An example of the workings of the Dominican treaty may be seen in the loan contract made in 1914 by the National City Bank of New York with the approval of the State Department by which the bank loaned Santo Domingo $1,500,000 at six per cent. The contract[3] specifically stated that the loan was made "in conformity to the Convention between the United States of America and the Dominican Republic ratified July 8, 1907, the payment of the principal and interest of which notes is secured by the pledge by the Republic of its customs revenues subject to an existing charge thereon securing the $20,000,000 Five per cent Customs Administration Sinking Fund Gold Loan of the Republic under and pursuant to the terms of the said convention," etc.[4] The $20,000,000 loan which had first claim on the customs was the one issued by Kuhn, Loeb & Co.

The inauguration of Woodrow Wilson in 1913 did not change the attitude of Washington regarding government interference on behalf of American finance. On September 9, Secretary of State Bryan notified Santo Domingo that the influence of

[1] U. S. "Foreign Relations," 1907, pp. 307-9. Jones, supra, p. 118.
[2] U. S. "Foreign Relations," 1912, p. 367.
[3] Ibid., 1913, pp. 459-60, 465-6.
[4] Idem.

the United States would be exerted to discourage revolutions and to support the "lawful authorities." As revolutionary activities continued, the United States sent a warship, and Secretary Bryan notified the revolutionary elements that if they succeeded the State Department would not recognize them and would "withhold the portion of the customs collections belonging to Santo Domingo." [1] The American minister in Santo Domingo proceeded to arrange for new elections, and over the vigorous protests of the Dominican Government, three American commissioners arrived on warships to watch the elections. [2] The following year the elections were again supervised by American commissioners.

3. Armed Political Control

American financial and political interference in Santo Domingo finally led to armed intervention. In April 1916 another insurrection took place in Santo Domingo, and this time, on May 4, 1916, United States marines were landed. "Stealthily American battleships entered the roadstead of Santo Domingo City, and under cover of a score or more long-range, big-caliber guns the American admiral, with a large force of marines, landed on Dominican territory." [3]

President Jiminez resigned and the Dominican Congress elected Dr. Henriquez y Carvajal temporary president. The State Department refused to recognize this legally chosen president unless he signed a treaty with the United States which Washington had been pressing on Santo Domingo since 1915. [4] This treaty was even more drastic than the one forced on the republic in 1907, and was similar in nature and intent to the one forced by the Wilson administration on Haiti. It called for the control by American officials of the Dominican customs, treasury, army and police. President Henriquez refused recognition by the State Department on such terms; whereupon,

[1] U. S. "Foreign Relations," 1912, pp. 425-7.
[2] Ibid., pp. 441-53.
[3] U. S. "Haiti Hearings," p. 49. "Current History Magazine," v. 15, p. 893.
[4] Ibid., p. 894. U. S. "Haiti Hearings," p. 93.

on October 17, following instructions from Washington, the American customs collector refused to pay the duly elected Dominican Government the revenues to which it was entitled.[1] A deadlock ensued. The entire country rallied around the president; political differences were forgotten, and officials performed their duty without pay as far as they could, owing to the refusal of the American officials to turn their salaries over to them until the treaty was signed. "The resistance to the American demands, though passive, was general." [2] This deadlock was finally broken by the flourish of American rifles. Captain H. S. Knapp, in command of the marines, declared martial law on November 29, 1916. He ousted the Dominican officials, dissolved the national legislature, forbade elections and declared himself "supreme legislator, supreme judge, and supreme executor," [3] established a regime of military force and courts martial, set up a rigid censorship, levied taxes and increased the public debt. This military dictatorship was, according to the official proclamation of martial law, set up under instructions from Washington because the "United States government . . . has urged upon Santo Domingo certain necessary measures which that government has been unwilling or unable to adopt." [4] Thus the United States frankly set up a military dictatorship for the purpose of forcing Santo Domingo to sign a treaty giving American investors complete control over the finances and administration of the republic.

The military dictatorship lasted until 1924. "A rear-admiral of the American navy is military governor and exercises full executive and legislative functions, the Dominican congress being suspended. The posts of cabinet ministers are filled by officers of the American navy and marine corps." [5] There is an American minister in Santo Domingo but naturally his duties are nominal. The military regime was to last until Santo Domingo was willing to sign the proposed treaty, thus

[1] U. S. "Haiti Hearings," p. 93.
[2] Blakeslee, "Mexico and the Caribbean," p. 208.
[3] U. S. "Haiti Hearings," pp. 51-2.
[4] Ibid., pp. 93-4.
[5] Blakeslee, supra, p. 208.

allowing the United States to do "legally" what it had been doing by force. "The result of the operations of this arrangement," Secretary of State Knox declared in 1912, when he tried to obtain the Senate's assistance in forcing a similar arrangement on Nicaragua and Honduras, "has been that the creditors now punctually receive their interest." [1]

As a result of the American occupation, the Dominican Government was expelled, "The Government treasury was seized; the national congress was dismissed; elections were prohibited; thousands of marines were spread over the country and with unlimited authority over the natives; public meetings were not permitted; . . . destructive bombs were dropped from airplanes upon towns and hamlets; every home was searched for arms, weapons, and implements; homes were burned; natives were killed; tortures and cruelties committed; and 'Butcher' Weyler's horrible concentration camps were established. . . . Repressions and oppressions followed in succession. When protests were made the protestants were fined heavily and also imprisoned, and when resistance or defense attempted bullets and bayonets were used. Criticism of the acts of the military government were not permitted . . . and those who violated the order were severely punished by fines and imprisonment. . . . The Dominican people have been 'taxed without representation' and the money so raised expended recklessly and without in any way consulting them. . . . For five years this policy of suppression, repression, oppression and maladministration has continued." [2]

4. *American Bankers and Armed Intervention*

The direct connection between American investments and the military regime is indicated in a circular issued by Speyer & Co. and the Equitable Trust Co. of New York on June 20, 1921:

"The United States Military Government of Santo Domingo issues in behalf of the Dominican Republic $2,500,000 Four

[1] U. S. "Foreign Relations," 1912, p. 1089.
[2] U. S. "Haiti Hearings," pp. 50–1.

Years Customs Administration 8% Sinking Fund gold bonds."
The bonds, this circular said, will contain the following clause:
"With the consent of the United States there is secured the
acceptance of and validation of this bond issue by any government of the Dominican Republic as a legal, binding, and ir-
revocable obligation of the Dominican Republic, and the duties
of the General Receiver of Dominican Customs as provided under the American-Dominican Convention of 1907, are extended
to this Bond issue." The circular adds this sentence: "Until all these bonds shall have been redeemed the Dominican Republic agrees not to increase its public debt, nor to modify its
customs duties without the previous consent of the United States
Government; and its customs revenues shall continue to be collected by a General Receiver of Customs appointed by and responsible to the President of the United States."

This circular, explaining the reasons for an American customs
receiver, also quotes a letter from Lieutenant Commander
Arthur H. Mayo, U. S. Navy officer in charge of the Department of Finance and Commerce of the military government of
Santo Domingo, which explains the purposes of the military
regime. This letter is dated June 16, 1921, and is addressed
to the Equitable Trust Co. and Speyer & Co.

"The Military Government will be withdrawn only upon the
consummation of a treaty of evacuation between the Dominican Republic and the United States Government which shall contain
among other provisions (a) ratifying all acts of the Military
Government; (b) validating the above loan of $2,500,000 and (c)
extending the duties and powers of the General Receiver of Dominican Customs until said Bonds shall have been paid."
"The Bonds are secured by a charge upon the customs and other
revenues of the Dominican Republic."

Under the caption *Purpose of Loan*, the bankers' circular
states: "The proceeds of this loan are to be used mainly for
the completion of essential public works . . . and in part for the
retirement of certificates of indebtedness. This work will be
done under the supervision of American engineers, and such

portion of the loan as is used for the purchase of supplies and equipment will be spent in the United States." [1]

A similar circular was issued in 1922 by Lee, Higginson & Co., declaring that: "Acting under Authority of the United States Government the Military Government of Santo Domingo issues on behalf of the Dominican Republic $6,700,000 Twenty-Year Customs Administration 5½% Sinking Fund Gold Bonds. . . ." With the approval of the State Department the bonds stated that the Military Government of Santo Domingo guaranteed "the acceptance and validation of this Bond issue by any Government of the Dominican Republic as a legal, binding, and irrevocable obligation of the Dominican Republic." In a letter to Lee, Higginson & Co. reproduced in the bankers' circular, Lieutenant-Commander D. W. Rose, U. S. naval officer in charge of the Department of Finance and Commerce of the Military Government of Santo Domingo again assured the bankers that during the life of the loan—which was to extend to March, 1942—the Dominican customs duties "shall be collected and applied by an official appointed by the President of the United States and that the loan now authorized shall have a first lien upon such customs revenues." [2]

A plan for the withdrawal of American marines from Santo Domingo was proposed by the Wilson administration in December, 1920, and a similar plan by the Harding administration on June 14, 1921. The plan made the military governor the provisional Dominican executive, and gave him the power to call elections. The Dominicans were to have this slight measure of autonomy provided they drew up an agreement with representatives of the American Government ratifying all acts of the American military occupation, and entrusting the command and organization of Dominican forces to American officials.[3] These proposals were turned down by the people of Santo Domingo, who protested especially against the loans floated in their name by the American Military Government with American bankers,

---

[1] Speyer & Co., and Equitable Trust Co., "Circular," June 20, 1921.
[2] Lee, Higginson & Co., "Circular," March, 1922.
[3] "Current History Magazine," v. 15, p. 895.

for which Santo Domingo paid interest varying from 9 to 19
per cent.[1] On June 26, 1924, the Dominican Republic "ratified
the treaty with the United States providing for the evacuation of
the Dominican Republic by American military forces which have
been stationed there since 1916. Simultaneously, it was
announced from Washington that the withdrawal of the 1,800
marines in the Dominican Republic would be begun as soon as
possible after July 10."[2] Later it was announced in the press
that "General Horacio Vasquez and Frederico Velásquez were
formally inaugurated as President and Vice President, respectively, of the Dominican Republic on July 12. At the same
time, the American flag was lowered from the fort and the
Dominican emblem was hoisted. These acts brought to an end
the military administration of the United States in the Dominican Republic."[3] Santo Domingo has thus been given a formal
kind of partial independence in return for signing a treaty
which makes it an actual protectorate.

5. *The Military Conquest of Haiti*

The military invasion of Haiti by the United States and the
establishment of a virtual protectorate is the result of two
parallel lines of policy, one political and one financial, which
converged and became amalgamated in one unified policy carried
out jointly by American financiers and the State Department.

A report of twenty-four distinguished American lawyers[4] on
Haiti points out that Haiti was a sovereign state under a

---

[1] "Current History Magazine," v. 15, p. 895.

[2] Ibid., v. 20, p. 845.   [3] Ibid., p. 1011.

[4] The twenty-four lawyers were Frederick Bausman, Seattle; Al-
fred Bettman, Cincinnati; William H. Brynes, New Orleans; Charles
C. Burlingham, New York; Zechariah Chafee, Jr., Cambridge;
Michael Francis Doyle, Philadelphia; Walter L. Flory, Cleveland;
Raymond B. Fosdick, New York; Felix Frankfurter, Cambridge;
Herbert J. Friedman, Chicago; John P. Grace, Charleston, S. C.;
Richard W. Hale, Boston; Frederick A. Henry, Cleveland; Jerome S.
Hess, New York; William H. Holly, Chicago; Charles P. Howland,
New York; Francis Fisher Kane, Philadelphia; George W. Kirchwey,
New York; Louis Marshall, New York; Adelbert Moot, Buffalo;
Jackson H. Ralston, Washington, D. C.; Nelson S. Spencer, New
York; Moorfield Storey, Boston; Tyrrell Williams, St. Louis.

republican form of government from 1804, when she won her independence from France, until 1915, when the United States forced her to sign a treaty even more drastic than that foisted on Santo Domingo. Haiti has a population of three million people living under more or less primitive economic conditions and subject to occasional political disturbances. Despite these disturbances, the report declares, no American citizen has ever been injured in person or property, and even during revolutionary outbreaks no foreigner was molested. Foreign investments were at all times respected and the interest on Haiti's foreign debt scrupulously paid. "Her relations with other governments have been free from adverse criticism. She has never manifested hostility to the United States and has given no occasion for our intervention in her affairs." [1]

America's earlier interest in Haiti was naval. In 1847 the United States attempted to obtain control of the harbours of Samana Bay, on the eastern coast of Santo Domingo, and of Mole St. Nicholas, on the northwest coast of Haiti, for avowed use as naval bases. In 1891 the United States sent Admiral Gharardi with a considerable fleet to Port au Prince, capital of Haiti, to negotiate for the cession of Mole St. Nicholas, but the Haitian government refused to discuss the matter and the fleet was recalled.

6. *Enter the National City Bank*

It was with the entrance of the National City Bank into Haiti that State Department interference became a definite policy. In 1881 the National Bank of Haiti, founded with French capital, was entrusted with the administration of the Haitian treasury. In 1910 this bank was reorganized in connection with a new government loan taken by French bankers, and replaced by the National Bank of the Republic of Haiti, which, like the old institution, was entrusted with the administration of the Haitian treasury. Under the contract with the

[1] Foreign Policy Association, "Seizure of Haiti."

French bankers the bank was to make certain annual loans to the Haitian government.[1]

At this juncture the National City Bank became interested, and Secretary of State Knox, pursuing his policy of "dollar diplomacy," intervened in the matter and objected to the contract saying that "some American banking interests ought to be represented." He called a conference of the New York bankers, with the result that in 1911 the National City Bank, Speyer & Co., Hallgarten & Co., and Ladenburg, Thalman & Co. each became subscribers to 2000 shares of the new bank.[2]

Shortly after the European War broke out, Secretary of State Bryan in several interviews with the American bankers "suggested the advisability of the American interests acquiring the French shares in the bank, and making it an American bank. That suggestion was repeated from time to time, and after some extended conferences, . . . the National City Bank purchased the stock held by the other three American parties." This was in 1917. Two years later, "after several suggestions from the State Department . . . the National City Bank purchased all the assets of the French institution" for $1,400,000.[3] Thus the National Bank of Haiti became the property of the National City Bank of New York.

The State Department began to take steps to insure the bankers' investment. On six occasions during 1914 and 1915 the Department made direct overtures to Haiti to obtain control of the customs, internal political disturbances furnishing the pretext. In October, 1914, Secretary of State Bryan wrote to President Wilson:

"It seemed to me of the first importance that the naval force in Haitian waters should be at once increased, not only for the purpose of protecting foreign interests, but also as evidence of the earnest intention of this Government to settle the unsatisfactory state of affairs which exists." [4]

[1] U. S. "Haiti Hearings," p. 105.
[2] Idem.
[3] Ibid., p. 106.
[4] Foreign Policy Association, supra, p. 4.

The State Department took advantage of a revolutionary outbreak in the north province to propose to President Zamor that he be kept in power provided he would sign a convention turning over the customs houses to American control. The President refused to compromise the independence of Haiti and resigned. On December 10 the newly chosen president was formally presented with a similar proposal by the American minister in Haiti, and again the proposal was turned down.[1]

One week later a contingent of United States marines landed in Port au Prince,[2] proceeded to the vaults of the National Bank of Haiti, and in broad daylight forcibly seized $500,000 and carried it aboard the gunboat *Machias*. The money was transported to New York and deposited in the vaults of the National City Bank. This money was the property of the Haitian Government and had been deposited for the redemption of paper currency. Haiti at once protested against this violation of her sovereignty and her property rights and requested an explanation from the United States. None was ever given.[3]

According to the testimony of Roger L. Farnham, Vice President of the National City Bank, before a Senate Committee in 1921, this raid of the marines was arranged by the State Department and the National City Bank.[4] The chief object of the State Department and the bankers at this time seems to have been to force the Haitian Government, by depriving it of ready money, to sign a treaty turning over the customs houses to American control. On January 28, 1915, Secretary of State Bryan wired via the Navy Department to Admiral Caperton, in command of American forces in Haitian waters, as follows:

"You will issue to that Government a warning that any attempt that might be made to remove the funds of the bank will compel you to take into consideration means to prevent such violation of foreign stockholders' rights."[5]

[1] U. S. "Haiti Hearings," pp. 5–6.
[2] U. S. "Foreign Relations," 1915, p. 476.
[3] "Current History Magazine," v. 15, p. 886. U. S. "Haiti Hearings," p. 6. U. S. "Foreign Relations," 1915, pp. 499–500.
[4] U. S. "Haiti Hearings," p. 123.
[5] Ibid., p. 292.

In· March, 1915, the United States sent the Ford mission to negotiate with the Haitian government for American control of the customs, and again Haiti turned the proposal.down. In May another commission arrived and presented the draft of an agreement providing for (1) military protection and intervention by the United States, (2) arbitration of claims made by foreigners, (3) prohibition of the cession of Mole St. Nicholas or its use to any other government. The last clause would indicate that the political aims of Washington and the financial aims of the National City Bank were now fused into one project.[1]

7. The Marines Take Possession

This proposal was being negotiated when on July 27 a revolution broke out in Port au Prince. President Guillaume fled to the French legation, and on the same day a number of political prisoners were massacred in the prison of Port au Prince. On the morning of July 28 President Guillaume was dragged out of hiding and killed. During all these disturbances not a single American or other foreigner was molested.[2] Nevertheless, on the afternoon of July 28 an American warship dropped anchor in the harbour of Port au Prince and marines were landed by Admiral Caperton.[3] The revolution was not the cause for landing marines but merely the "awaited opportunity," for the marines were landed "at the request of the State Department." [4]

The Haitian legislature met to elect a new president to fill the vacancy caused by the assassination of Guillaume. Under orders from the State Department, Admiral Caperton forced the legislature to postpone the election until the American naval officers could canvass the situation. The purpose of this interference with the elections of a nominally independent

---

[1] Foreign Policy Association, supra, p. 5.

[2] Foreign Policy Association, "Seizure of Haiti." Johnson, "Self-Determining Haiti," p. 7.

[3] U. S. Marine Corps, "Report on Haiti," p. 3. U. S. "Haiti Hearings," p. 306.

[4] Johnson, supra, p. 7. U. S. Marine Corps, supra, p. 4.

republic is shown in the message sent by Admiral Caperton to the Navy Department on August 2, 1915:

"Large number Haitian revolutions, largely due existing professional soldiers called Cacos. . . . They have demanded election Bobo President. . . . Stable government not possible in Haiti unless Cacos are disbanded and power broken.

"Such action now imperative at Port au Prince if United States desires to negotiate treaty for financial control of Haiti. To accomplish this must have regiment of marines in addition to that on Connecticut. . . . As future relations between United States and Haiti depend largely on course of action taken at this time, earnestly request to be fully informed of policy of United States." [1]

Admiral Caperton now attempted to force, at the point of marine bayonets, the treaty which the State Department and the National City Bank had failed to obtain through negotiation and through financial pressure. The first step was to obtain a candidate who would be willing to serve American purposes. Such a candidate was found in the person of Sudre Dartiguenave, who offered, if elected president of Haiti, to accede to any terms made by the United States, including the surrender of customs control and the cession of Mole St. Nicholas.[2] Regarding this candidate Admiral Caperton wired the Navy Department at Washington on August 5, that he "has never been connected with any revolution" and "realizes Haiti must agree to any terms laid down by the United States. . . . If elected must be sustained by American protection." [3] Dartiguenave was acting not out of choice, but out of a realization that before the rifles of American marines Haiti was helpless. He begged only "as far as possible to avoid humiliation." [4]

Admiral Caperton, frankly protecting the interests of the National City Bank, ordered the government of Haiti to restore the treasury service to the National Bank of Haiti, which the

[1] U. S. "Haiti Hearings," p. 313.
[2] Foreign Policy Association, supra, p. 6. U. S. "Haiti Hearings," p. 315.
[3] Ibid., p. 312.
[4] Ibid., p. 325. U. S. "Foreign Relations," 1915, p. 431.

government had withdrawn in January when it discovered that it could not draw money at its own discretion.[1]

Having found a candidate willing to accept Washington's terms, the Navy Department wired on August 10 that Admiral Caperton might "allow election of president to take place whenever Haitians wish. The United States prefers election of Dartiguenave . . . United States will insist that the Haitian government will grant no territorial concessions to any foreign governments. The Government of the United States will take up the question of the cession of Mole St. Nicholas later along with the other questions to be submitted to the reorganized Government."[2] These other questions referred to the control of customs and the protection of the National City Bank's investments. "In order that no misunderstanding can possibly occur after election," the Secretary of State wired on the same day to the American Minister at Port au Prince, "it should be made perfectly clear to candidates, as soon as possible, and in advance of their election, that the United States expects to be entrusted with the practical control of the customs and such financial control over the affairs of the republic of Haiti as the United States may deem necessary for efficient administration." The message added, significantly, that the United States would support a government elected under these terms "as long as necessity may require."[3]

On the day on which the Haitian legislature voted for the new president, marines guarded the doors of the chamber and Admiral Caperton's chief of staff circulated among the congressmen.[4] Dartiguenave was elected.

8. *Martial Law in Haiti*

Two days after the election, Robert Beale Davis, American Chargé d'Affaires at Port au Prince, submitted to the new Haitian Government the draft of a treaty, accompanied by a

---

[1] U. S. "Haiti Hearings," p. 323.
[2] Ibid., p. 315. U. S. Marine Corps, supra, p. 16.
[3] U. S. "Haiti Hearings," p. 315. U. S. "Foreign Relations," 1915, pp. 479-480.
[4] Foreign Policy Association, supra, p. 6.

memorandum stating that "the State Department at Washington expected that the Haitian National Assembly . . . would immediately pass a resolution authorizing the President of Haiti to accept the proposed treaty without modification." [1]   This new draft, resting as it now did on armed force, went much further than previous drafts. Not only did it provide for American control of customs and finances, but in addition called for a native constabulary to be "organized and officered by Americans" and forbade Haiti to sell or lease any of its territory to a foreign government. With these terms, Secretary Lansing observed in his cablegram of August 24, the Haitian Government had been familiar for more than a year.[2]

But Haiti was no more willing than before to give up its life as an independent republic. The State Department seemed to have been aware of this; to insure the acceptance of the treaty by the Haitian Government, Admiral Caperton was ordered to seize ten of the principal customs houses, to collect the customs dues, to organize a constabulary and temporary public works, and to support the new Haitian administration.[3] Admiral Caperton realized the full significance of this order. On August 19 he cabled to Washington:

"United States has now actually accomplished a military intervention in affairs of another nation. Hostility exists now in Haiti and has existed for number of years against such action. Serious hostile contacts have only been avoided by prompt and rapid military action which has given United States control before resistance has had time to organize. We now hold capital of country and two other important sea-ports." [4]

Between August 21 and September 2 the American forces took over the customs houses at the ten leading ports of Haiti.[5] For several months American naval officers collected all customs

[1] U. S. "Haiti Hearings," p. 8.
[2] Ibid., p. 328.
[3] Foreign Policy Association, supra, p. 8. U. S. Marine Corps, "Report on Haiti," p. 19.
[4] U. S. "Haiti Hearings," p. 335.
[5] "Current History Magazine," v. 15, p. 887. U. S. Marine Corps, supra, pp. 19-23.

dues and made all disbursements. Since the customs houses were the only source of national income, this deprived the Haitian Government of all income and added to the already existing pressure for the ratification of the proposed treaty. Opposition to the acts of the United States and to the treaty spread throughout the country. President Dartiguenave and his cabinet threatened to resign. Caperton wired Washington that in case they did resign a military government should be established with an American officer at the head. "Present is most critical time in relations with Haiti," he cabled, "and our decision now will, to a great extent, determine future course. If military government is established, we would be bound not to abandon Haitian situation until affairs of country are set at right and predominant interests of the United States of America secured." [1] These predominant interests which were to be secured by a military dictatorship were embodied in the proposed treaty. To one of his captains in Haitian waters Admiral Caperton explained: "We are having our own troubles in Port au Prince endeavoring to get the treaty through. Things are not entirely satisfactory, and I may be forced to establish a military government here." [2]

By September the forces under Admiral Caperton were in complete control of Haiti, guarding all the principle towns, collecting and spending all revenues, and turning none of the money over to the Haitian Government. "Public order and the public purse were altogether in the mastery of the Navy Department." [3] On September 3, martial law was formally declared. [4] The object was, of course, to push the treaty through. "Successful negotiation of treaty is predominant part of the present mission," Admiral Caperton wired to the commanding officer of the battleship *Connecticut* in northern Haitian waters. "After encountering many difficulties treaty situation at present looks more favorable than usual. This has been effected by exercising military pressure at propitious moments in negotia-

[1] U. S. "Haiti Hearings," p. 338.
[2] Ibid., p. 343.
[3] Foreign Policy Association, "Report on Haiti," p. 9.
[4] U. S. "Foreign Relations," 1915, p. 522.

tions. Yesterday two members of cabinet who have blocked negotiations heretofore resigned. President himself believed to
be anxious to conclude treaty. At present am holding up offensive operations and allowing President time to complete cabinet
and try again. Am therefore not yet ready to begin offensive operations at Cape Haitien but will hold them in abeyance
as additional pressure." [1]

As a result of this "additional pressure" the Haitian Government signed the treaty without modification on September 16,
1915, and a modus vivendi was drawn up for its immediate application. But the work of Washington was not yet done.
Under the Haitian constitution, as under that of the United
States, no treaty is binding unless ratified by the Senate. The
opposition there seemed to be irreconcilable to American conquest. Thereupon Admiral Caperton, acting under instructions from Washington, seized a consignment of unsigned bank
notes intended for the Haitian Government and declared that
they would be turned over to the Haitian authorities immediately after ratification of the convention.[2] On October 3, Secretary of the Navy Daniels authorized Admiral Caperton to
arrange for the payment of a weekly amount to the Haitian
Government for current expenses, adding that "question payment back salary will be settled by department immediately after
ratification of treaty." [3]

On November 10, Secretary Daniels cabled Admiral Caperton a message which is the epitome of government support of
American investments.

"Arrange with President Dartiguenave," the cable read,
"that he call a cabinet meeting before the session of senate
which will pass upon ratification of treaty and request that you
be permitted to appear before that meeting to make a statement
to President and to members of cabinet. On your own authority state the following before these officers: 'I have the honor
to inform the President of Haiti and the members of his cabi-

[1] U. S. "Haiti Hearings," p. 353.
[2] Ibid., pp. 379-383.
[3] Ibid., p. 383.

net that I am personally gratified that public sentiment continues favorable to the treaty; that there is a strong demand from all classes for immediate ratification and that treaty will be ratified Thursday. I am sure that you gentlemen will understand my sentiment in this matter, and I am confident if the treaty fails of ratification that my Government has the intention to retain control in Haiti until the desired end is accomplished, and that it will forthwith proceed to the complete pacification of Haiti so as to insure internal tranquillity necessary to such development of the country and its industry as will afford relief to the starving populace now unemployed. Meanwhile the present Government will be supported in the effort to secure stable conditions and lasting peace in Haiti, whereas those offering opposition can only expect such treatment as their conduct merits. The United States Government is particularly anxious for immediate ratification by the present senate of this treaty.' . . . It is expected that you will be able to make this sufficiently clear to remove all opposition and to secure immediate ratification." [1]

Admiral Caperton made the situation so clear that the treaty was ratified by the Haitian Senate on the very next day, November 11, 1915.

9. *The Treaty*

Article Two of the treaty, forced upon Haiti by the combined efforts of the State and Navy Departments and Admiral Caperton's marines, provided that "the President of Haiti shall appoint, upon nomination by the President of the United States, a general receiver . . . who shall collect, receive, and apply all customs duties on imports and exports accruing at the several customshouses and ports of entry of the Republic of Haiti." It also provided that "the President of Haiti shall appoint, upon nomination by the President of the United States, financial adviser, who shall be an officer attached to the ministry of finance, to give effect to whose proposals and labors the minister will lend efficient aid."

[1] U. S. "Haiti Hearings" p. 394. U. S. "Foreign Relations," 1915, p. 458.

Article Five provided that "all sums collected and received by the general receiver shall be applied, first, to the payment of the salaries and allowances of the general receiver, his assistants, and employees, and expenses of the receivership, including the salary and expenses of the financial adviser . . . second, to the interest and sinking fund of the public debt of the Republic of Haiti; and, third, to the maintenance of the constabulary . . . and then the remainder to the Haitian Government for the purposes of current expenses."

Under Articles Eight and Nine, Haiti was forbidden to increase its public debt or modify its customs duties without the consent of the United States. Article Ten called for "an efficient constabulary, . . . composed of native Haitians," which shall be "organized and officered by Americans," which shall, among other things, supervise and control arms and ammunition and military supplies. By Article Eleven Haiti was forbidden to surrender "by sale, lease or otherwise" any of its territory. The treaty was to remain in force for ten years, and "further for another term of ten years if . . . either of the high contracting parties" should find that its purpose "has not been fully accomplished." [1]

The treaty was ratified by the United States Senate in May, 1916. It is still in force and American marines still occupy Haiti. Credit for its acceptance by Haiti is not entirely due to the efforts of the Secretary of State, the Secretary of the Navy, and Admiral Caperton. Roger L. Farnham, Vice President of the National City Bank, was "effectively instrumental in bringing about American intervention in Haiti," being transported in his goings and comings between New York and Port au Prince aboard vessels of the United States Navy. [2]

10. The Military Occupation

At the suggestion of Mr. Farnham of the National City Bank, and upon nomination of President Woodrow Wilson of the United States, the Haitian government appointed John

[1] U. S. "Haiti Hearings" pp. 204–7.
[2] Johnson, "Self-Determining Haiti," p. 20.

Avery McIlheny of Louisiana as Financial Adviser under
Article II of the new treaty. The Financial Adviser, nominally
a Haitian official, proceeded to complete the conquest of Haiti
by the National City Bank. In July, 1920, he notified the Haitian Government that he had "instructions from the Department
of State" that Haiti must give "its immediate and formal approval" to an agreement providing for:

"(1) A modification of the Bank Contract agreed upon by the
Department of State and the National City Bank of New York.

"(2) Transfer of the National Bank of the Republic of Haiti
to a new bank registered under the laws of Haiti to be known as
the National Bank of the Republic of Haiti.

"(3) The execution of Article 15 of the Contract of Withdrawal,
prohibiting the importation and exportation of non-Haitian money
except that which might be necessary for the needs of commerce
in the opinion of the Financial Adviser." [1]

The purpose of this new agreement arranged by the State
Department and the National City Bank was to give the latter
a monopoly on the financial life of Haiti. Haitians, Europeans,
and even American business concerns protested against this arrangement on the ground that such an arrangement would
"make all other bankers and merchants the humble tributaries"
of the National City Bank. But the American Financial Adviser continued to press for the acceptance of this agreement
by Haiti by withholding the salaries of Haitian officials "by order of the American minister." [2] Haiti protested to Washington
against this action, but was informed by the State Department
that salaries would be withheld until Haiti accepted the Financial
Adviser's terms.[3]

While the Financial Adviser was riveting the economic control of the National City Bank over Haiti, the military authorities were fastening political control. Under the eyes of American marines Haiti adopted a new constitution on June 18,
1918, by which "all acts of the Government of the United States

[1] "Nation," v. 111, p. 308.
[2] Johnson, supra, p. 44 ff.
[3] "New York Times," Sept. 20, 1920.

during its military occupation in Haiti are ratified and confirmed." The new constitution also abolished one of Haiti's oldest safeguards, which provided that foreigners could not hold land.

Charges of brutality have been made against the American occupation in Haiti. Over 3,000 "practically unarmed Haitians" have been killed by American marines, according to one observer.[1] The U. S. Marine Corps Report gives the number of Haitians killed as 3,250—"killed either by marines or by the person of the gendarmerie of Haiti."[2] The work of building a highway from Port au Prince to Cape Haitien was in charge of an officer of marines, "who stands out even in that organization for his 'treat 'em rough' methods. He discovered the obsolete Haitian *corvée* and decided to enforce it with the most modern Marine efficiency. The *corvée*, or road law, in Haiti provided that each citizen should work a certain number of days on the public roads to keep them in condition, or pay a certain sum of money. . . . The Occupation seized men whereever it could find them, and no able-bodied Haitian was safe from such raids, which most closely resembled the African slave raids of past centuries. And slavery it was, though temporary. By day or by night, from the bosom of their families, from their little farms or while trudging peacefully on the country roads, Haitians were seized and forcibly taken to toil for months in far sections of the country. Those who protested or resisted were beaten into submission. . . . Those attempting to escape were shot. . . ."[3]

These atrocities resulted in a brief revolt led by an educated and cultured Haitian, Charlemagne Peralte, who had been forced to work in convict clothes on the streets of Cape Haitien. The revolt was crushed and Charlemagne Peralte was killed. "Not in open fight, not in an attempt at his capture," but "while standing over his camp fire, he was shot in cold blood

---

[1] Johnson, supra, p. 12.
[2] U. S. Marine Corps, "Report on Haiti," p. 108.
[3] Johnson, supra, p. 13.

by an American Marine officer who stood concealed by the
darkness, and who had reached the camp through bribery and
trickery." [1]   A protest lodged by prominent Haitians with the
Senate Committee of Inquiry into the occupation of Haiti in
1921 declares that the American Occupation "is the most
terrible régime of military autocracy which has ever been
carried on in the name of the great American democracy.

"The Haitian people, during these past five years, has passed
through such sacrifices, tortures, destructions, humiliations, and
misery as have never before been known in the course of its
unhappy history." [2]   According to an American recently returning from a visit to Haiti in 1920, "if the United States should
leave Haiti today, it would leave more than a thousand widows
and orphans of its own making, more banditry than has existed
for a century, resentment, hatred and despair in the heart of a
whole people, to say nothing of the irreparable injury to its
own tradition as the defender of the rights of man." [8]

While these atrocities were going on, American business and
finance were profiting by the Occupation. The advantages of
the treaty were thus described to the Senate Committee which
investigated the Occupation in 1921, by H. M. Pilkington,
vice-president and manager of the American Development
Company of Haiti:

"I next made it my business to come in contact with what we
might call the ruling or political class of the country (Haiti),
because, at basis, every industrial or other enterprise is fundamentally dependent upon the laws and the execution of those laws
in whatever country may be concerned. The original financing of
this Haitian-American Corporation was brought about and put
to the public directly and definitely upon assurance in Washington,
by competent people and competent officials, that the treaty between
the United States and Haiti was, in fact, to be a living thing.
The largest feature in the floating of the securities of this company . . . was predicted, one might say, wholly as to security,

[1] Johnson, supra, p. 14. U. S. Marine Corps, supra, pp. 70–2.
[2] U. S. "Haiti Hearings," pp. 10–33.
[8] Johnson, supra, p. 19.

upon the implied bona fides of the United States in carrying out this treaty,—the basing of which was security for foreign capital." [1]

The National City Bank continued to tighten its "economic stranglehold" on the little republic. On June 22, 1920, the National Railroad of Haiti, comprising almost the entire railway system of the island, went into bankruptcy as a result of the failure of the Haitian Government to pay the interest and sinking fund charges on outstanding bonds. The concession was held by a syndicate of which Roger L. Farnham was president and which was financed by the National City Bank. When the road failed, the United States federal courts appointed Roger L. Farnham receiver. [2]

On March 28, 1917, Haiti and the United States signed a protocol extending the 1915 treaty for twenty years, and stating that there was "urgent necessity for a loan for a period of more than ten years." [3] Two years later, by a protocol signed on October 3, 1919, Haiti agreed to seek a national loan of $40,-000,000 for thirty years. The revenues to secure this loan were to be collected by officers nominated by the United States even after the expiration of the 1915 treaty. [4] Early in 1922 the American financial adviser in Haiti, the National City Bank, the Haitian-American Sugar Corporation and the West Indies Trading Company began negotiations for a loan to Haiti. In March the financial adviser, McIlheny, informed the Senate Committee investigating Haitian affairs that three companies were bidding to float this loan, specifying the National City Bank, Speyer & Co., and Lee, Higginson & Co. [5] This throws an interesting sidelight on the technique of diplomacy, in view of the facts that the National City Bank had a monopoly on Haitian financing, and that McIlheny had been appointed by President Wilson at the suggestion of a National

[1] U. S. "Haiti Hearings," p. 789.
[2] "New York World," Feb. 19, 1924, p. 3. U. S. "Haiti Hearings," p. 121.
[3] U. S. "Treaties, Conventions, etc.," v. 3, p. 2678.
[4] Ibid., pp. 2678–82.
[5] "New York Times," March 17, 1922, p. 30:5.

City Bank official. The appearance of throwing the proposed Haitian loan open to competition was continued in September, when Acting Secretary of State William Phillips formally invited American bankers to bid for a $16,000,000 loan. The loan was being floated, technically, by Haiti, and Haiti was to be responsible for it; nevertheless the bankers were asked to send their bids not to the Haitian Government, but to the American financial adviser through the Division of Latin-American Affairs of the State Department at Washington.[1] The bonds were to be secured by a first lien on Haiti's internal revenue and a second lien on its customs—both sources of income controlled by Americans. The loan was the first bloc of the $40,000,000 loan provided for by the 1919 protocol. Whatever bids may have been offered, needless to say the concession to float the loan was obtained by the National City Company—a subsidiary of the National City Bank.[2]

The bonds were offered in the New York market in October, and among the sales literature was a letter from McIlheny. The letter emphasized that the bonds would be secured by Haiti's internal revenues and customs; that the 1915 treaty, running to 1936, gives the United States the power to nominate the customs receiver and the financial adviser; that the 1919 protocol gives the United States the power to appoint the collector of the revenues securing the 1922 loan even after the treaty of 1915 expires; and that the United States controls the increase of Haitian debts and the reduction of its customs.[3] On October 11, when the contract for the $16,000,000 loan was signed, McIlheny resigned as Haiti's financial adviser. President Harding appointed another American—John L. Hord —as his successor.[4] In addition to an American minister, an American financial adviser, an American receiver-general of customs and American marines, Haiti was saddled from time to time with special military envoys to force through important

[1] "New York Times," Sept. 13, 1922, p. 30:2.
[2] Ibid., Sept. 29, 1922.
[3] Ibid., Oct. 9, 1922.
[4] Ibid., Apr. 18, 1923.

plans for the State Department and the American bankers. In September, 1920, when Haiti objected to National City Bank control of the Haitian National Bank, Washington sent Admiral Knapp to liquidate the conflict. His mission was intended to be secret; it became public only as a result of Senator Harding's pre-election attacks on the Wilson administration. Admiral Knapp was vested with powers superior to those of the American minister in Haiti.[1]

In the spring of the following year, when Harding became president, the supreme American official in Haiti was a high commissioner—a title used frequently for proconsuls of the British Empire. This high commissioner was Brigadier-General John H. Russell of the United States Marine Corps. His mission, Secretary of State Hughes explained, was to put the 1915 treaty into effect.[2] General Russell, acting under instructions from Secretary of the Navy Denby, established court martial for civilians and promulgated a law of lese-majesty. On May 26 he issued an order to Haitians which declared that speeches and writings which "reflect adversely upon the United State forces in Haiti, or tend to stir up agitation against the United States officials, or the president of Haiti or the Haitian government" are "prohibited, and offenders against this order will be brought to trial before a military tribunal." [3] In August, 1921, three Haitian journalists were arrested and court martialed for criticising the American occupation in violation of General Russell's order.[4]

Further steps to bring Haiti under American economic control were taken in 1924, when the Haitian Council of State created an Internal Bureau of Revenue to collect all taxes except customs duties. This bureau is to be under the supervision of the American receiver-general appointed under the treaty of 1915, who is to appoint another American as head of

[1] "New York Times," Sept. 21, 1920.
[2] Ibid., Apr. 25, 1921, p. 16:7.
[3] Ibid., June 14, 1921.
[4] Ibid., Aug. 29, 1921, p. 25:3.

the new bureau. On June 18, 1924, the State Department at Washington announced the appointment of Dr. William E. Dunn, acting commercial attaché of the American Embassy at Lima, as director of the Bureau of Revenue.[1]

11. *The Nicaraguan Protectorate*

In Nicaragua, as in Santo Domingo and Haiti, the strategic interests of American diplomats and the financial interests of American bankers combined to produce first diplomatic and later military intervention. The strategic considerations centered around plans for a United States naval base at Fonseca Bay, and, more important still, a canal route across Nicaragua to supplement the advantages of the Panama Canal. The search for a canal route in Nicaragua is of long standing.[2]

The Clayton-Bulwer treaty of 1850 between the United States and England provided for a neutral canal across Nicaragua; later such a canal was seriously considered as an alternative to Panama. It will probably be built by the United States.[3] The route over which the United States proposed to build the canal was, however, contested by other Central American states, with the result that a series of revolutions and wars broke out in 1906, until in the late summer of 1907 a general war involving all five of the Central American republics seemed imminent. President Roosevelt and President Diaz of Mexico brought pressure to bear on the several governments to cease hostilities and offered to mediate the claims.[4] Under the guidance of the United States, delegates of the five republics met in Washington in 1907 and signed a series of eight conventions designed to promote the unity of Central America. The most important of these agreements provided for a Central American Court of Justice, composed of five members, one from each state, to which all disputes would be referred for final judgment. Although the United States signed not a single one of the

[1] "Current History Magazine," v. 20, p. 845.
[2] U. S. Congress, 57:1; "Sen. Doc." 357.
[3] Academy of Political Science, "Proceedings," v. 7, p. 426.
[4] Munro, "Five Republics of Central America," p. 208 ff.

agreements, it nevertheless proceeded to exercise the dominant rôle under the provisions. Thus President Taft, in his annual message to Congress in December, 1909, stated that "since the Washington Conventions in 1907 were communicated to the Government of the United States as a consulting and advising party, this Government has been almost continuously called upon by one or another, and in turn by all of the five Central American Republics, to exert itself for the maintenance of the conventions. Nearly every complaint has been against the Zelaya government of Nicaragua which has kept Central America in constant tension and turmoil."[1]

The government of President José Santos Zelaya opposed attempts on the part of the United States to extend its control over Nicaragua by obtaining Fonseca Bay and a canal route, as well as attempts of American business interests to establish themselves in the republic.

In 1909 a revolution against Zelaya broke out. It was financed by Adolfo Diaz, a local official at Bluefields of La Luz y Los Angeles Mining Company, an American corporation. Diaz was receving a salary of $1,000 a year. Though he is not known to have had other resources, he was able to advance the revolution $600,000, which he eventually repaid himself.[2]

The American consul at Bluefields, Thomas C. Moffat, knew about the revolution in advance, wiring the State Department on October 7 that it would break out the next day and that the new government would appeal "to Washington immediately for recognition." He was also apparently informed about the secret troop movements of the revolutionists and their plans.[3] Five days later Moffat was able to report to Washington that a provisional government had been established with General Juan Estrada at the head, that this government was "friendly to American interests," and that it guaranteed "annulment of all concessions not owned by foreigners."[4] As the fighting between

[1] U. S. "Foreign Relations," 1909, p. xvii.
[2] U. S. Sen. For. Rel. Com., "Convention Between U. S. and Nicaragua," 1914, Part I, p. 32, Part II, p. 88.
[3] U. S. "Foreign Relations," 1909, p. 452.
[4] Idem.

the Zelaya government and the rebels grew sharper the United States showed its hand more openly. Steamers of the United Fruit Company and other American vessels bearing the Nicaraguan flag transported men and munitions for the revolutionists with the knowledge and assistance of the State Department representatives in Central America.[1]

The pretext for an open break with the Zelaya government came late in 1909, when two American filibusterers, who had been caught trying to dynamite a vessel loaded with Zelaya's men, were court-martialed and executed after a confession.[2] Though these filibusterers had enlisted in the revolutionary forces and had thus assumed all the responsibilities of war, Secretary of State Knox on December 1 sent the Nicaraguan Chargé d'Affaires at Washington a harsh note giving him his passports and openly declaring that the United States was on the side of the revolutionists.[3] The note added: "Although your diplomatic quality is terminated, I shall be happy to receive you as I shall be happy to receive the representative of the revolution each as the unofficial channel of communication between the Government of the United States and the de facto authorities to whom I look for the protection of American interests." [4]

12. Protecting American Interests

Zelaya was forced to resign and flee the country. As his successor the Nicaraguan Congress elected Dr. José Madriz. Nevertheless the United States continued to support the Estrada revolution against the Madriz government. President Madriz protested to President Taft against American interference in the domestic affairs of the republic, but the United States insisted that American ships carrying arms and ammunition for the rebels be permitted to pass through the blockade established by the authorized government, and insisted furthermore that

---

[1] Zelaya, "Revolucion de Nicaragua," pp. 26–40.
[2] U. S. "Foreign Relations," 1909, p. 447.
[3] Ibid., p. 455.
[4] Ibid., p. 457.

customs duties be paid to the revolutionists.[1] Incidentally, the customs revenues at Bluefields had been pledged as a guaranty to a group of American bankers for a loan made in 1904.[2]

The government troops, however, defeated the insurgents and forced Estrada to retreat to Bluefields, where they attempted to blockade him. At once American marines landed. They prevented the government forces from blockading or attacking Bluefields. This gave the insurgents a chance to reorganize their forces, and with the support of American bayonets they were able to seize power. On August 20, after his forces had been defeated by Estrada's army, Madriz resigned. A week later Estrada and General Emiliano Chamorro entered Managua, the capital of Nicaragua.[3]

On October 11, 1910, the State Department appointed Thomas G. Dawson, American minister to Panama and the expert who had arranged for American control of the customs of Santo Domingo, as special agent to Nicaragua. He was instructed that to "rehabilitate the finances and pay the legitimate foreign and domestic claims it would be advisable to negotiate a loan secured by a percentage of the customs revenues to be collected according to agreement between the two Governments, but in such a way as will certainly secure the loan and assure its object." Dawson was also instructed to seek a constitution providing "suitable guarantees for foreigners," and compensation for the deaths of Cannon and Groce. He was to obtain liquidation of fixed claims, such as the Emery claim, and the adjudication of unliquidated claims. The State Department promised that when a plan for a loan to Nicaragua would be drawn up, it would "use its good offices to secure the conclusion of a contract based upon its terms between Nicaragua and some American financiers of high standing." [4]

When Brown Brothers and Company learned of these plans they offered to the State Department to float the Nicaraguan

---

[1] U. S. "Foreign Relations," 1910, p. 752.
[2] U. S. Sen. For. Rel. Com., supra, p. 227.
[3] U. S. "Foreign Relations," 1910, pp. 738–60.
[4] Ibid., pp. 763–4.

loan. These bankers had entered into an agreement with the George D. Emery Company to collect their claim from Nicaragua, which had been settled for $600,000 in September, 1909, just before Zelaya fell. On February 2, 1911, Brown Brothers and Company wrote to Secretary of State Knox:

"We understand that the Government of Nicaragua is considering the advisability of obtaining a new loan for the purpose of refunding her present indebtedness and of providing for other governmental needs. We also understand that, in order to secure such loan upon advantageous terms, the Government of Nicaragua is desirous of enlisting the good offices of our own Government and of entering into engagements with it which shall furnish a satisfactory basis for such security as may be required. Should this information be substantially correct, we beg to say that, as bankers, we shall be glad to have the opportunity of negotiating for such a loan. Apart from our general interest in a matter of this kind, we beg to add that we are interested in the George D. Emery Co.'s claim against Nicaragua, under the protocol of September 18, 1909 and that we have, therefore, a peculiar interest in the readjustment of that country's finances." [1]

Secretary Knox replied that Brown Brothers would have an equal opportunity with other American bankers to bid for any loan Nicaragua might desire to secure.[2]

Meanwhile Thomas C. Dawson proceeded to carry out his instructions. On October 27, 1910, aboard an American battleship, the principal leaders of the Estrada revolution signed a series of agreements later known as the Dawson Pact. These stipulated that the United States would recognize the revolutionary government which it had assisted to seize power on the following conditions:

1. That a constituent assembly be chosen at once which would elect Estrada president and Adolfo Diaz vice-president, for two years. Estrada could not succeed himself and no Zelayists could enter the administration.

2. That a mixed commission, satisfactory to the United States Department of State, be appointed to settle claims, including the Cannon-Groce indemnity.

[1] U. S. Sen. For. Rel. Com., supra, Part VI, pp. 170–171.
[2] Idem.

3. That Nicaragua would solicit the good offices of the American Government to secure a loan to be guaranteed by a certain per cent of the customs receipts collected in accordance with an agreement "satisfactory to both governments." [1]

Dawson cabled these agreements to the State Department. He added that Nicaragua would embody them in a formal communication in which it would also request the United States to send a financial expert to work out a financial plan. The formal communication arrived in Washington soon afterward.[2]

Dawson's dispatch of October 28 informed the State Department that "a popular presidential election is at present impracticable and dangerous to peace." Therefore, as provided by the Dawson Pact, the Conservative Assembly elected November 27–28 unanimously chose Estrada president and Diaz vice-president. On January 1, 1911, President Taft formally recognized the Estrada Government; three weeks later Secretary Knox instructed the new American minister to Nicaragua to carry out the provisions of the Dawson Pact. The dispatch added that Ernest H. Wands had been appointed by the United States Government as financial expert. Secretary Knox forwarded copies of the Santo Domingo loan convention and of the proposed loan conventions with Honduras and Liberia, saying the Honduras convention would "answer all the requirements of the present case." He further instructed the American minister that "the Government of Nicaragua is to proceed at the earliest possible date to the signature of a convention with the United States which shall authorize the contemplated bankers' loan contract" to be secured by a percentage of the customs receipts. Knox also mentioned that the Nicaraguan minister to the United States, Salvador Castrillo, Jr., had requested his government to authorize him to sign the desired convention.[3]

For a time the Dawson Pact was kept secret, but the defeated

[1] U. S. "Foreign Relations," 1910, pp. 763–4.
[2] Ibid., pp. 765–7. Ibid., 1911, pp. 625–7, 652–4.
[3] Ibid., 1910, pp. 765–7. Ibid., 1911, pp. 649–52.

Liberals in Nicaragua obtained a copy and published it.[1] The terms upon which General Estrada was supported by the United States aroused a storm of opposition in Nicaragua. Many patriotic elements saw in the Dawson Pact, with its provisions for a loan and American control of customs, the establishment of a virtual protectorate. American control of elections aggravated the situation. In February, 1911, the American minister in Nicaragua cabled to Secretary Knox that "the natural sentiment of an overwhelming majority of Nicaraguans is antagonistic to the United States, and even with some members of Estrada's cabinet I find a decided suspicion, if not distrust, of our motives." President Estrada, he added in another wire, dated March 27, was "being sustained solely by the moral effect of our support and the belief that he would unquestionably have that support in case of trouble." [2]

13. *The Knox-Castrillo Convention of 1911*

The chief object of supporting Estrada against the opposition of the Nicaraguan people was the floating of the loan and the control of customs to secure the loan. In April the Nicaraguan National Assembly determined to adopt a constitution guaranteeing the independence of the republic and directed against foreign control through loans. This constitution was opposed by the American representatives, and when it was adopted against their opposition, Estrada dissolved the assembly and called for new elections. The step was approved by the State Department at Washington. These proceedings resulted in protests which led to the resignation of Estrada in favour of vice-president Adolfo Diaz.[3]

But Diaz was no more popular than Estrada, and American support was necessary to keep him in office. "I am assured," the American minister wired the State Department on May 11,

---

[1] U. S. Sen. For. Rel. Com., "Hearings on Nicaraguan Affairs," 1913, p. 15.

[2] U. S. "Foreign Relations," 1911, pp. 655–6.

[3] Ibid., pp. 657–8, 660.

"the Assembly will confirm Diaz in the presidency according
to any one of the . . . plans which the Department may indicate. . . . A war vessel is necessary for the moral effect." [1]
On May 25 he wired that "rumours have been current that the
Liberals are organizing a concerted uprising all over the country
with the declared object of defeating the loan." The Liberals,
he added, were "in such a majority over the Conservatives"
that he hastened to repeat the suggestion "as to the advisability
of stationing permanently, at least until the loan has been put
through, a war vessel at Corinto." Secretary Knox replied
that Diaz should not be permitted to resign and that a warship
had been ordered to Nicaragua.[2]

While the struggle between the people of Nicaragua and the
American representatives was in progress, Secretary Knox
signed a convention with the Nicaraguan representative of the
American-controlled government, at Washington. The Knox-
Castrillo agreement of June 6, 1911, provided for the floating
of a $15,000,000 loan [3] to Nicaragua by American bankers and
the control of Nicaraguan customs houses by the United States.
Nicaragua also pledged itself not to alter the customs duties
without Washington's consent and to submit financial reports to
the State Department.[4] At the same time, the State Department negotiated with the banking houses of Brown Brothers and
Company, and J. and W. Seligman and Company for floating
the loan, stipulating that the Knox-Castrillo convention should
be made an integral part of the contract to be signed by the
Nicaraguan Government and the bankers.

The draft of an agreement for the $15,000,000 loan was sub-
mitted by the bankers to Nicaragua on June 21. The loan was
to be paid out by Brown Brothers and J. and W. Seligman, as
bankers, to themselves as creditors of Nicaragua in the following
way: to liquidate claims against Nicaragua; to establish a bank
which the American bankers should administer; to improve

---

[1] U. S. "Foreign Relations," 1911, p. 661.
[2] Ibid., 1911, pp. 661-2.
[3] Ibid., 1913, p. 1040.
[4] Ibid., 1912, pp. 1074-5. Blakeslee, "Latin America," p. 246.

the national railway, which they should control; and to build a new railway upon their own terms, a concession for which they were to obtain from Nicaragua and which they were to build with Nicaragua's money.[1]

The United States Senate refused to ratify the Knox-Castrillo convention, turning it down three separate times despite the special urging of President Taft.[2] Consequently, the loan agreement submitted by the bankers on June 21 could not go through. The following month, however, the bankers submitted another agreement which the American-controlled government of Nicaragua signed on September 1. Under this agreement Brown Brothers and J. and W. Seligman were to make a temporary loan of $1,500,000 to Nicaragua.[3] The bankers agreed to reorganize the National Bank, taking over 51 per cent of the stock, and allowing Nicaragua to keep 49 per cent.

The loan convention (known as the "Treasury Bills Agreement") stipulated the following terms: (1) $100,000 of the loan was to be used as initial capital for the proposed bank. (2) The balance was to be used for reforming the currency of Nicaragua. (3) The bankers were to hire monetary experts to reform the currency, but Nicaragua was to pay for them. (4) The bankers were to deposit the sum used for reforming the currency—$1,400,000—with the United States Mortgage and Trust Company. (5) The loan was to be secured by a lien on the customs. (6) The customs were to be collected by an American nominated by the bankers, approved by the Secretary of State, and "appointed" by Nicaragua. (7) The customs were not to be changed without the bankers' consent.[4] The contract also gave the bankers a lien on the liquor tax, and reserved to the bankers the right "to solicit of the United States of America protection against violation of the present

[1] U. S. Sen. For. Rel. Com., "Hearings on Nicaraguan Affairs," 1913, Part VI, pp. 174-202.
[2] U. S. "Foreign Relations," 1912, p. 1076.
[3] Ibid., pp. 1078-9.
[4] U. S. Sen. For. Rel. Com., "Convention Between the U. S. and Nicaragua," Part VI, pp. 205-6.

contract, and aid in enforcing its execution." The bankers and Nicaragua were to submit disputes to arbitration by the Secretary of State of the United States. Secretary Knox ordered the American chargé d'affaires to keep the Nicaraguan legislature in session until the loan agreement of September 1 was approved.

Correspondence between American agents in Nicaragua and the State Department at Washington continued to show that the United States was prepared to force political and financial control upon the little republic in the face of almost nation-wide opposition. On July 12 the American chargé d'affaires notified Secretary Knox that "opinion generally expressed is that the United States Government has repudiated its policy of protecting Nicaragua against foreigners holding rights in ruinous concessions or contracts. . . . I strongly urge that no further action be taken until the assembly approves the loan contract." A month later he cabled that the "opposition to these loan contracts and concessions is becoming more determined." [1]

The State Department replied on September 30: "You are instructed that of the Nicaraguan matters under consideration by the Department, the ratification of the pending loan contract and the amendment of the decree establishing a claims commission are of the first importance and should be disposed of before attention is directed to other subjects." On October 5 the State Department again instructed Gunther that "attention should be steadily directed to the loan and the claims commission matters; they are of the first importance and should be disposed of before consideration of political subjects, which should not be discussed unnecessarily." The Nicaraguan assembly approved the loan contracts on October 9. [2]

Under this agreement Secretary of State Knox appointed Colonel Clifford D. Ham as customs collector of Nicaragua. Colonel Ham was recommended by Brown Brothers and Com-

---

[1] U. S. Sen. For. Rel. Com., "Convention Between the U. S. and Nicaragua," Part VI, p. 636, 639.
[2] Ibid., pp. 667-70.

pany and J. and W. Seligman and Company as a person "worthy of our confidence." [1] From December 11 on, Colonel Ham collected the entire customs duties of Nicaragua. In December there also arrived in Managua Mr. Charles A. Connant of New York and Mr. Francis C. Harrison, formerly of the British Civil Service in India, to act as monetary experts for the bankers.

14. A Network of Loans

Juan Estrada was forced to resign because he sought to prevent the adoption of a constitution protecting Nicaragua's independence. His successor, Adolfo Diaz, supported by the "moral force" of an American battleship, continued Estrada's policy. While the loan contracts were being forced on Nicaragua, the assembly completed a new constitution. Chargé d'Affaires Gunther notified the State Department that this constitution provided that all government employees must be Nicaraguans except those on the Claims Commission, and that after adoption the constitution could be amended only by approval of two successive congresses. Gunther asked that the signing of the constitution be postponed: he had "in mind the customs authorities who are not Nicaraguans," but Americans. President Diaz and General Mena, who controlled the assembly, promised that the constitution would not be promulgated until January 31. Secretary Knox insisted that the promulgation of the constitution be postponed until the arrival of the new American minister, Mr. Weizel, on about January 18.[2]

The Nicaraguan assembly resented American interference. On January 12 it ordered the promulgation of the new constitution in a decree declaring that the "interposition of the Chargé d'Affaires of the United States carries with it, in effect, an insult to the national autonomy and the honor of the assembly." [3]

The new American minister's first act on arriving in Nic-

[1] U. S. "Foreign Relations," 1912, p. 1079.
[2] Ibid., pp. 993-6.
[3] Idem.

aragua was to study the new constitution and to notify the State Department of the provisions which he considered objectionable. He called the Department's attention to Article 2, which provided that "no compacts or treaties shall be concluded which are contrary to the independence and integrity of the Nation, or which in any wise affect its sovereignty." Article 55 provided that "Congress alone may authorize loans and levy contract by indirect measures." [1] The constitution also provided that foreigners must present their claims against the government in the same ways as Nicaraguans, and prohibited monopolies for the benefit of private individuals.

Minister Weizel called the State Department's attention to paragraph 14 of Article 85 as "most susceptible of adverse criticism." This section vested in the assembly the power to alienate or lease national property and to authorize the executive to do so "on conditions suitable to the Republic." It added that "the public revenues or taxes shall not be alienated or leased out." [2]

The constitution was promulgated with these clauses in it but the American bankers disregarded them in subsequent contracts and agreements. On March 26, 1912, they entered into an agreement with Nicaragua for a supplementary loan. Part of this loan—$500,000—was to be used by the monetary experts in stabilizing the exchange; the rest—$225,000—was to be used by the Nicaraguan Government for current expenses. The loan was for six months at six per cent, with an additional bankers' commission of one per cent. It was to be secured by the customs revenues, second only to the 1911 loan; by a lien on all government railway and steamship lines; and by the claims of Nicaragua against the Ethelburga syndicate of London. Proceeds of any sale of railways or steamships or any agreement with the Ethelburga syndicate were to be used for the repayment of the loans under this agreement. Anything left over was to be used for repaying the 1911 loan. This agreement also provided that Nicaragua should transfer all its

[1] U. S. "Foreign Relations," p. 997.
[2] Ibid., p. 997, 1003.

railway and steamship lines to a corporation to be organized in the United States and to be tax free. The bankers were to have a one-year option to buy 51 per cent of the capital stock of this new corporation for $1,000,000. If the bankers exercised this option they were to lend the company $500,000 for extensions and improvements. The bankers were also to have an option on the other 49 per cent; Nicaragua could not sell its share to anyone except the bankers until all the loans were paid up. Pending repayment the American bankers were to manage and control the railways and steamship lines exclusively and to choose the board of directors.[1] These loan negotiations were carried on jointly by the State Department and the bankers.[2]

Two months after this agreement was signed the American bankers signed an agreement with the Ethelburga syndicate of London. The Ethelburga bonds represented a loan contracted by the Zelaya government in 1909 for 1,250,000 pounds. By the agreement signed on May 25, 1912, the London balance, after interest and sinking fund had been paid off on the bonds, was transferred to the American bankers for account of Nicaragua. This balance amounted to about $1,195,000. The May 25 agreement was negotiated by the bankers in the name of Nicaragua. Under its terms the republic was to recognize the right of the American bankers and the London interests to "apply to the United States for protection against violation of the provisions of this agreement and for aid in the enforcement thereof." Among the provisions was that the bonds were to be secured by the Nicaraguan customs to be collected by Americans. The American bankers communicated with the State Department throughout the negotiations.[3]

On the same day that this agreement was signed with the Ethelburga bondholders the American bankers signed another agreement with Nicaragua supplementing the loan agreement of March 26. The March 26 loan was secured, in part, by the

[1] U. S. Sen. For. Rel. Com., "Convention Between U. S. and Nicaragua," Part VI, pp. 210-16.
[2] U. S. "Foreign Relations," 1912, pp. 1093-1100.
[3] Ibid., pp. 1081-2, 1100-1. U. S. Sen. For. Rel. Com., supra, Part VI, pp. 234-5; 239-49.

Ethelburga bonds. The supplementary agreement of May 25 provided that after interest and sinking funds on the bonds had been paid the balance should be used to repay loans made by the American bankers to Nicaragua.[1]

15. Bullet Diplomacy

Meantime the unpopularity of President Diaz increased. He was able to stay in power only because of American support. His opponents in the legislature were calling for an election. The American minister, with the approval of the State Department, informed them that before settling the political affairs of Nicaragua they should establish the proposed national bank and place the republic on a sound financial basis.

The Liberals refused to wait. On July 29 they proclaimed a revolution, seizing a large store of war materials, a part of the railway and steamers, and several customs houses. The American manager of the Bank of Nicaragua, Mr. Bundy Cole, wired to James Brown of Brown Brothers and Company, in New York, for protection. Brown Brothers and Company replied that the State Department advised them that Major Butler would arrive from Panama with American marines. On August 15 Major Butler landed with 412 marines, half of whom were quartered at the bank.[2] On September 4, 1912, the State Department notified the American minister at Managua that "the American bankers who have made investments in relation to railroads and steamships in Nicaragua, in connection with a plan for the relief of the financial distress of that country, have applied for protection." [3] The American marines at once took drastic action against the revolutionists. According to the report of the United States Secretary of the Navy for 1913, the following naval vessels with approximately 125 officers and 2,600 men participated in the subjugation of the revolution: *California, Colorado, Cleveland, Annapolis, Tacoma, Glacier,*

---

[1] U. S. Sen. For. Rel. Com., supra, Part IX, pp. 400–1.
[2] Ibid., Part XIII, pp. 504–10.
[3] U. S. "Foreign Relations," 1912, p. 1043.

Denver, and *Buffalo.* "The officers and men participated in the bombardment of Managua, a night ambuscade in Masaya, the surrender of General Mena and his rebel army at Granada, the surrender of the rebel gunboats of *Victoria* and *Ninety-Three,* the assault and capture of Coyotepe, the defense of Paso Caballos Bridge, including garrison and other duty at Corinto, Chinandego, and elsewhere." [1] The most notable event during the campaign was the assault and capture of Coyotepe which resulted in entirely crushing the revolution. The leader of the revolutionary forces surrendered to Rear Admiral Sutherland and was exiled to Panama aboard the U. S. S. *Cleveland.*[2] The part of the American minister in crushing the revolution consisted in sending notes to its leader, General Mena, to surrender the railroads which belonged to the American bankers. In this line of action he was assisted by the bankers' representatives.[3] Following the defeat of the revolutionists an election was held in which the American marines guarded the polls. On November 2 Diaz was re-elected for a term of four years.

16. *Exploiting Nicaragua*

The expenses incurred during the revolution forced Diaz to apply to the American bankers for another loan. The terms on which the bankers offered to make the loan were protested by Diaz as harsh, but they were backed up by the State Department, and were incorporated in the loan agreement on November 4, 1912.[4] Under this agreement the bankers were to lend Nicaragua $500,000 to be secured by the tobacco and liquor taxes, which were to be collected by the American-controlled Bank of Nicaragua. In addition the bankers were to get an option for the purchase of Nicaragua's 49 per cent of the railroad stock for $1,000,000. The $500,000 loan was to be made from the funds realized by the Nicaraguan customs (collected

[1] U. S. Navy, "Annual Report," 1912–13, p. 38.
[2] U. S. "Foreign Relations," 1912, pp. 1053–4.
[3] U. S. Sen. For. Rel. Com., supra, Part X, pp. 424–6.
[4] Ibid., Part VI, pp. 255–6.

by ·Americans) and the Ethelburga funds.[1] The Nicaraguan congress refused to approve this agreement. After paying $350,000 on account under this agreement, the bankers stopped payments.

While the bankers were negotiating for an option on the entire railroad of Nicaragua, Wilson was elected president of the United States. On February 2, 1913, the American minister at Managua informed the State Department that the bankers would not "advance another dollar n)r entertain a new proposition until they are certain that the incoming administration at Washington will continue the present policy. This is deeply disappointing to President Diaz, who desires to reach a definite settlement of the financial question while the present Washington administration is still in office, as it thoroughly understands that question. Nevertheless President Diaz assures me he will not enter into a final loan contract, without previous consultation with the Department."[2] To this Secretary Knox replied that "there is no foundation for the rumor that the incoming administration will change the present policy of the United States toward Central America," and instructed the American minister to confer with Mr. Bundy Cole, American manager of the National Bank of Nicaragua and representative of Brown Brothers and Company.[3]

With this assurance from the State Department, the bankers entered into a new agreement with Nicaragua on October 8, 1913.[4] The agreement stipulated the following:

1. The bankers were to exercise their option to buy 51 per cent of the railroad stock for $1,000,000.

2. They agreed to lend Nicaragua $1,000,000.

3. They agreed to lend the railroad of which they would own 51 per cent $500,000 for improvements and extensions.

[1] U. S. Sen. For. Rel. Com., supra, Part VI, pp. 258–61; Part VIII, 400–7.
[2] U. S. "Foreign Relations," 1913, p. 1035.
[3] Ibid., pp. 1036–67.
[4] U. S. Sen. For. Rel. Com., supra, Part VI, pp. 261–4.

4. The bankers also purchased 51 per cent of the stock of the National Bank for $153,000.

5. They obtained a preferential right to buy the remaining 49 per cent of both bank and railroad. Meantime they were to have custody of all the stock.

6. If Nicaragua defaulted, the bankers had the right to sell the bank and railroad stock six months thereafter.

7. The bankers' option on the concession for the Atlantic railroad granted in the 1911 loan agreement was cancelled.

8. The bank and railroad were each to have nine directors. Six were to be named by the bankers, one by the Secretary of State of the United States, two by Nicaragua.

9. The collection of internal revenues was to be resumed by Nicaragua.

Of the $2,000,000 advanced by the American bankers to Nicaragua in payment for the railroad stock and as a loan, the republic was actually to receive only $772,424. The balance was used to pay off in full all previous loans, for replenishing the exchange fund, buying shares in the National Bank, and paying various charges to the bankers.[1] As a result of this transaction, not only had the American bankers collected all previous loans, but Nicaragua owed them $1,000,000, her Ethelburga balance was gone, and the bankers controlled and managed her railroad and bank.

During the negotiation of the October 8 agreement, the State Department was negotiating for a canal route through Nicaragua for which the republic was to receive $3,000,000. This sum was intended to make it possible for Nicaragua to repay her debts to bankers. The October 8 loan was made with the approval of the State Department.[2] A statement by Brown Brothers and Company and J. and W. Seligman and Company indicates that they had the pending canal treaty in mind. The statement reads, in part:

[1] U. S. Sen. For. Rel. Com., supra, Part VI, p. 280. U. S. "Foreign Relations," 1912, pp. 1094–1102.
[2] Ibid., 1913, p. 1057, 1052.

"Should the United States Senate . . . ratify the pending treaty with Nicaragua, providing for the establishment of a naval station on the Gulf of Fonseca and granting a perpetual right to build the Nicaragua Canal, the proposed payment to Nicaragua of $3,000,000 provided in the treaty as compensation, would put that Government in a position where it could liquidate the greater part of the local debt and claims." [1]

17. Buying the Canal Route

The treaty giving the United States the right to construct a canal across Nicaragua was signed on February 18, 1916. It is known as the Bryan-Chamorro Treaty. Under its terms the United States paid Nicaragua $3,000,000 in return for the following concessions:

(1) The right to construct a trans-isthmian canal by San Juan and the Great Lake route or any other route in the territory of Nicaragua.

(2) The control by lease for 99 years of the Great Corn and Little Corn islands and of a naval base in the Gulf of Fonseca.

(3) The United States has the option of renewing the lease on the naval base for another 99 years. [2]

The advantages of this treaty to the United States Government have been explained by Colonel Clifford D. Ham, American customs collector in Nicaragua, to be that it forever eliminates "the danger of a foreign power seeking and obtaining those concessions"; that it promotes "better diplomatic and commercial relations" with Latin America; and that it would be "an important link in the chain, which we are attempting to forge, of preparedness and national defense, and the protection of our investment in the Panama Canal." [3]

That the Bryan-Chamorro Treaty was nothing less than a "proposed protectorate of Nicaragua by the United States" was clearly indicated in the official correspondence on the matter. [4]

One clause in the Bryan-Chamorro Treaty declared that

[1] U. S. "Foreign Relations," 1912, p. 1063.
[2] Blakeslee, "Mexico and the Caribbean," p. 306.
[3] "Review of Reviews," v. 53, p. 185.
[4] U. S. "Foreign Relations," 1913, p. 1027.

nothing in it was intended "to affect any existing rights" of Costa Rica, Salvador, and Honduras. It will be remembered that in 1906 and 1907 the conflicting claims of several Central American republics to the territory comprised in the proposed Nicaraguan canal led to war, and subsequently to the establishment under the direction of the United States of the Central American Court of Justice. The Court was hailed, at the time of its organization, as an inspiring example of international justice. The Court was also invoked again and again by the Taft administration to settle Central American disputes.

During the negotiation of the Bryan-Chamorro pact Costa Rica and Salvador protested.[1] The naval base on the Gulf of Fonseca caused particular alarm.[2] When the treaty was ratified they appealed to the Central American Court of Justice, declaring that the treaty violated their rights. The Court ruled that Nicaragua should maintain the status quo existing prior to the signing of her treaty with the United States; but both Nicaragua and the United States refused to abide by the decision of the Court. Subsequently Nicaragua refused to re-join the Court, and in 1918 the Court was formally dissolved. The United States destroyed its own creation to suit its purpose by instructing Nicaragua to refuse to execute the award.

Since completing the financial and military conquest of Nicaragua in 1913, the American bankers and the State Department have maintained effective control. In 1918 the High Commission of the Republic of Nicaragua was appointed to supervise the expenditures of the republic. The Commission consists of one Nicaraguan and two Americans, the latter chosen by the United States Secretary of State.[3] The Commission's reports are submitted to the Nicaraguan Government and to the State Department.

In 1920 repairs were needed on the Nicaragua railroad, controlled by Brown Brothers and J. and W. Seligman. The American bankers proceeded to float a $9,000,000 loan to Nic-

[1] U. S. "Foreign Relations," 1913, pp. 1022, 1025.
[2] Ibid., p. 1027.
[3] Moody's "Analyses of Investments; Governments," 1925, p. 538.

aragua. The purpose of this loan, they announced, was (1) to refund Nicaragua's external debt, including the Ethelburga bonds; (2) to enable Nicaragua to buy "such stock of the Pacific Railways of Nicaragua as is held by interests other than the Government"; (3) to build a railway to the Atlantic coast.[1] The American bankers, of course, controlled the Ethelburga bonds, and were the only interests "other than the Government" holding stock in the Pacific Railways. The loan largely came back to them with interest paid by Nicaragua.

In July, 1924, Nicaragua finished paying off its debt to Brown Brothers and J. and W. Seligman. As a result the Pacific Railways reverted to the republic. However, two Americans were appointed on the railroad's new board of directors. They were Joseph K. Choate and Jeremiah W. Jenks, who had been appointed to the High Commission.[2] In September of the same year Nicaragua bought the American bankers' share in the National Bank for over $300,000.[3] However, as in the case of the railroad, this formal transfer of the bank did not mean the end of American control. After President Martinez assured Colonel Clifford D. Ham, American customs collector since 1912, that Nicaragua would maintain the gold standard, an American commission was appointed to revise Nicaragua's banking and financial laws. The commission consisted of Abraham F. Lindberg, formerly deputy customs collector in Nicaragua; and Jeremiah W. Jenks, already on the High Commission and the railroad's board of directors.

While the bankers exercised control over Nicaragua's economic life, the State Department and the American marines supervised Nicaraguan politics. Opposition to the American-controlled Conservative government, particularly the Chamorro faction, had not abated since 1913. An uprising took place in the summer of 1921, and the government declared martial law. Washington shipped 10,000 rifles, a number of machine guns

[1] "Commercial and Financial Chronicle," New York, Dec. 18, 1920, p. 2372.
[2] Wall Street Journal, July 14, 1924.
[3] "Commercial and Financial Chronicle," New York, Sept. 13, 1924, p. 1236.

and several million rounds of ammunition. These enabled the Conservative government to retain control.[1] The Chamorro government was threatened by another uprising in the spring of 1922. The government arrested 300 Liberals and declared martial law. The American marines threatened action and the Chamorro government was safe.[2]

As in Haiti, the presence of marines led to conflicts with the natives. In February, 1921, marines wrecked the offices of the Nicaraguan paper *Tribuna,* alleged to have criticised the American troops. The marines were not subject to martial law, but were tried by a United States naval court which sentenced them to two years' imprisonment.[3] In December of the same year marines and native police clashed in the streets; and in January, 1922, a fight between marines and native police resulted in the death of four Nicaraguans, and the wounding of five. The United States Navy indemnified the families involved, and court-martialled the guilty marines.[4] They were sentenced to ten years, but the sentences were later reduced. In August, 1925, the marines were entirely withdrawn from Nicaragua. They have been replaced, however, by a native constabulary trained and officered by Americans.

18. *Militarism as an Imperial Asset*

Regulation, such as that described in this chapter, does not necessarily involve the use of armed force, although in all of the cases described the military machine of the United States played a part, even though it was as incidental as that connected with the Hawaiian Revolution. The military machine is close at hand, however, and when the necessity arises, as it did in the cases of Haiti, Santo Domingo and Nicaragua, it is employed without serious question.

Rich, well armed, equipped with a splendid navy, developing its investments in the Caribbean region at a rapid rate, the

---

[1] "New York Times," Dec. 2, 1921.
[2] Ibid., Apr. 7 and 25, May 23, 1921.
[3] Ibid., Feb. 10 and 27, 1921.
[4] U. S. Congress, 68:1; "Sen. Doc." 24.

United States turns, as a matter of course, to some of its weaker neighbours with the demand that they recognize the economic and strategic interests of the Giant of the North. Refusals greet these demands. The weak nations are still convinced of their right to independence and the exercise of sovereignty. They protest in the name of their "rights." Apparently, a small, weak nation has no rights that a great strong nation is bound to respect. Protests are ignored. Opposition is over-ruled. At length, pressed by political or economic necessity, the strong nation stretches out its military arm.

This is the story of France in Northern Africa, of the Japanese in Korea, of the British in India and Egypt. It is the general experience of great empires in their dealings with undeveloped countries. During the past twenty years the United States has added several important chapters to this experience by her armed intervention in the Caribbean.

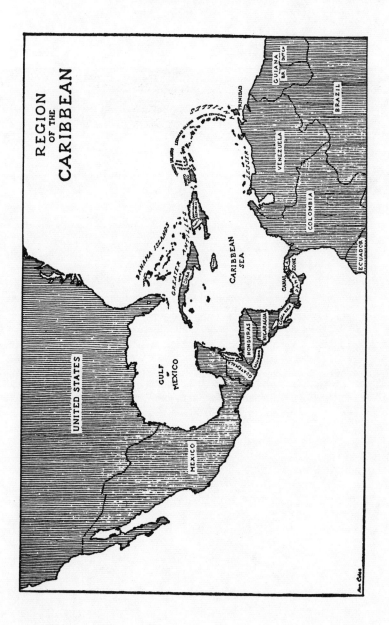

REGION OF THE CARIBBEAN

UNITED STATES

GULF OF MEXICO

MEXICO

BAHAMA ISLANDS

GREATER ANTILLES

CUBA

CARIBBEAN SEA

GUATEMALA

HONDURAS

NICARAGUA

COSTA RICA

PANAMA

CANAL ZONE

TRINIDAD

COLOMBIA

VENEZUELA

ECUADOR

GUIANA

BR. DUTCH

BRAZIL

VI

ACQUISITION WITHOUT ANNEXATION

1. *The Sugar Bowl of the World*

When the United States declared war on Spain in 1898, American investments in Cuba amounted to $50 million; up to 1909 they had increased to $141 million;[1] today they have reached a total of $1,250 million.[2] In 1902 the volume of exports from the United States to Cuba was $25 million; at the end of 1923, exports had reached $193 million a year.[3] In the past twenty-two years imports into the United States from Cuba have risen from $34 million to $359 million. In 1923 the United States bought 83 per cent of Cuba's total exports; in the same year Cuba stood sixth in rank in the export trade of this country.

This remarkable economic advance has revolved around sugar. Cuba has been called the sugar bowl of the world. Although the island is no larger than the state of Mississippi, it produces every year a million more tons than India, the second largest sugar-producing country. Cuba produces 28 per cent of the world's sugar cane and over 85 per cent of Cuba's yearly sugar crop is sold to the United States; over half of the sugar consumed in the United States comes from Cuba.[4]

Sugar is to Cuba what oil is to Mexico, but in even greater measure. However, American economic interests in the little island extend beyond the sugar plantations. Of the 1,250,000,-000 American dollars invested in Cuban resources, sugar has

---

[1] Cuba; Camara de Comercio, "Boletin Oficial," v. 4, p. 53.
[2] Pan American Union, "Bulletin," v. 58, p. 729.
[3] U. S. "Foreign Commerce and Navigation," 1901-02, p. 103; 1923, p. X.
[4] U. S. "Commerce Year Book," 1923, p. 121 ff.

absorbed $750,000,000. The rest is invested in railroads, public utilities, urban real estate, tobacco, factories, mining, merchandising, agriculture, and ports and terminals.

2. The Platt Amendment

American economic predominance in Cuba has been paralleled by a political control which has caused one historian to declare that "Cuba is no more independent than Long Island." The history of early American political interest in Cuba will be found elsewhere in this book. The virtual, if not official, annexation of Cuba begins with the defeat of Spain in the Spanish-American War, and the temporary military occupation of Cuba by the United States in 1899. At the beginning of the war the attitude of the United States as expressed in official public documents was interpreted the world over as a magnanimous offer of complete independence to Cuba. The war resolution of April, 1898, contained a section declaring that "the United States hereby disclaims any disposition or intention to exercise sovereignty, jurisdiction, or control over said island except for the pacification thereof, and asserts its determination, when that is accomplished, to leave the government and control of the island to its people." [1]

The Spanish troops evacuated Cuba on January 1, 1899, and the government of the island was turned over to General Leonard Wood, who acted as military governor representing the United States. On November 5, 1900, General Wood called a convention at Havana to write a constitution for the Republic of Cuba, and draw up a treaty with the United States. The constitution provided for a president, senate, house of representatives, and supreme court, but the convention was silent on Cuba's relations to the United States. [2] Under instructions from Washington, General Wood requested the convention to incorporate into the new constitution a series of provisions drafted by the American Secretary of War, Elihu Root. These provisions bound Cuba, among other things, never to make any

[1] Latané, "America as a World Power," p. 27.
[2] U. S. War Dept., "Annual Report," 1902, v. 1, pt. 1, p. 84.

treaty impairing the independence of the island, and never to contract any public debt in excess of its ordinary revenues. At the same time the United States was to have the right to intervene to protect the independence of Cuba, the acts of its military occupation were to be recognized as legal, and Cuba was to grant the United States naval stations.[1]

Washington's request that these provisions be made an integral part of the Cuban constitution roused great indignation in the island. However, since Cuba was anxious to have its new constitution approved and the American troops withdrawn, the convention offered to append Secretary Root's provisions to the document they had drawn up with a few perfunctory statements indicating that the American addition in no way compromised Cuba's independence. But Secretary Root rejected the Cuban compromise, insisting that his articles be incorporated as an integral part of the Cuban constitution without comment of any kind.

Secretary Root's articles, with a few additions suggested by General Wood, came to be known as the Platt Amendment after Senator Platt of Connecticut who introduced them as a rider to the army appropriation bill March 2, 1901. The Platt Amendment was passed before any notice was served on the Cuban convention. The Amendment as adopted by Congress directed the President of the United States to leave the control of Cuba to the people of the island as soon as a government should be established under a constitution which defined the future relations with the United States as follows:

"1. That the Government of Cuba shall never enter into any any treaty or other compact with any foreign power or powers which will impair or tend to impair the independence of Cuba, nor in any manner authorize or permit any foreign power or powers to obtain, by colonization or for military or naval purposes or otherwise, lodgement in or control over any portion of said island.

"2. That said Government shall not assume or contract any public debt to pay the interest upon which, and to make reasonable sinking fund provision for the ultimate discharge of which,

[1] Root, "Military and Colonial Policy of U. S.," p. 211.

the ordinary revenues of the island, after defraying the current expenses of government, shall be inadequate.

"3. That the government of Cuba consents that the United States may exercise the right to intervene for the preservation of Cuban independence, the maintenance of a government adequate for the protection of life, property, and individual liberty, and for discharging the obligations with respect to Cuba imposed by the Treaty of Paris on the United States, now to be assumed and undertaken by the Government of Cuba.

"4. That all acts of the United States in Cuba during its military occupancy thereof are ratified and validated, and all lawful rights acquired thereunder shall be maintained and protected."

* * *

"7. That to enable the United States to maintain the independence of Cuba, and to protect the people thereof, as well as for its own defense, the Government of Cuba will sell or lease to the United States lands necessary for coaling or naval stations at certain specified points, to be agreed upon with the President of the United States.

"8. That by way of further assurance the Government of Cuba will embody the foregoing provisions in a permanent treaty with the United States." [1]

The Cuban constitutional convention was willing to accept the first and fourth proposals, but not the others. The third article was especially feared as a standing menace to Cuban sovereignty. A protest from Cuba declared that it was the duty of the United States to make Cuba "independent of every other nation, the great and noble American nation included." [2] But Secretary Root insisted on having the Platt Amendment incorporated in the Cuban constitution, and the convention was forced to yield after General Wood, under instructions from Secretary Root, stated that the third clause of the Platt Amendment did not mean "intermeddling or interference with the affairs of the Cuban Government, but the formal action of the Government of the United States, based upon just and substantial grounds." [3] The Platt Amendment was incorpo-

---

[1] U. S. "Foreign Relations," 1902, p. 321.   Ibid., 1904, p. 244.
[2] Ibid., 1902, p. 362.
[3] Root, "Military and Colonial Policy of U. S.," p. 214.

rated in the Cuban Constitution on June 1, 1901, after becoming a United States statute on March 2, 1901.[1]   Finally it was made the subject of a special treaty between Cuba and the United States on May 22, 1903.[2]

The general dissatisfaction of the Cuban people at this legal assertion of American control was somewhat assuaged by repeated and emphatic assurances by American public officials that the United States had no ulterior motives in forcing the Platt Amendment.   Nevertheless, presumptions on the basis of the Platt Amendment began almost immediately after the withdrawal of the American occupation and the establishment of a Cuban government under President Tomas Estrada Palma. Protests were sent by Cuba against direct and unofficial dealing with the Cuban Government by certain American consular officials, against the landing of marines on the south coast for making a magnetic survey without Cuban permission, against the American consul at Santiago who attempted to force local officials to improve sanitary conditions.   At least two of these cases were presumed on the basis of the Platt Amendment.   In every case, however, the United States admitted Cuba's right and sustained her protests, going so far as to remove the American minister, Herbert Squires, after his undiplomatic actions with regard to the Isle of Pines bloodless rebellion.

At the same time the United States almost at once took advantage of Article VII of the Platt Amendment to obtain two naval stations, one at Guantanamo on the south-east coast, the other at Bahia Honda on the north-west coast.[3]   The Bahia Honda station has not been occupied since 1912, when a new treaty, never ratified, gave it up in return for greater rights at Guantanamo, now more important because of the Panama Canal.   The strategic importance of these naval stations for the control of the Caribbean can be seen by a glance at Cuba's geographical position.   The island lies close to the United States, about one hundred miles from Key West.   The narrow strait

[1] U. S. "Statutes at Large," v. 31, pp. 897-8.
[2] Ibid., v. 33, p. 2248.
[3] U. S. "Foreign Relations," 1903, p. 350.

between Havana and Key West is the only entrance into the
Gulf of Mexico available to Northern shipping.

3. Second Military Occupation

In 1906 the United States under cover of the Platt Amendment intervened in Cuban affairs by force of arms. In August
of that year, following the re-election of President Palma, a
general insurrection took place in Cuba. Dr. Alfredo Zayas,
one of the leaders of this insurrection, described it as an "armed
protest against the frauds perpetrated at the last elecion." [1] The
American chargé d'affaires at Havana, Jacob Sleeper, urged
the Palma government to take energetic action against the
insurgents,[2] but the American most active in opposing the rebellion was Frank Steinhart, the American Consul General at
Havana. Steinhart came to Cuba as a sergeant in the first
American army of occupation; he became Official in Charge
of Archives under General Wood, and American Consul General
when the American troops were withdrawn. Today he figures
in the popular imagination as the Cuban Rockefeller, being head
of the Havana Electric Railway, Light and Power Company,
capitalized at $36,000,000, and interested in a number of other
important enterprises.

Steinhart, as Consul General at Havana, appealed to the
State Department for immediate American intervention. On
September 5, Assistant Secretary of State Robert Bacon informed him that President Roosevelt, "for your private information, believes actual, immediate intervention, to be out
of the question." [3]

On September 8, Steinhart cabled to Washington that President Palma requested two United States warships, one to
Havana and one to Cienfuegos.

"They must come at once," he wired. "The government
forces are unable to quell the rebellion. The Government is
unable to protect life and property. President Palma will

[1] U. S. "Foreign Relations," 1906, p. 469.
[2] Ibid., pp. 456–7.
[3] Ibid., p. 475.

convene Congress next Friday, and Congress will ask for our forcible intervention. It must be kept secret and confidential that Palma asked for vessels. No one here except President, secretary of state, and myself knows about it." [1]

Two days later Steinhart again cabled for the warships, saying that President Palma was worried because no reply had been received. To this Assistant Secretary Bacon replied on September 10: "Two ships have been sent, due to arrive Wednesday. The President (Roosevelt) directs me to state that perhaps you do not yourself appreciate the reluctance with which this country would intervene. President Palma should be informed that in the public opinion here it would have a most damaging effect for intervention to be undertaken until the Cuban Government has exhausted every effort in a serious attempt to put down the insurrection." [2]

In response to repeated appeals for action from Steinhart and Chargé d'Affaires Jacob Sleeper, President Roosevelt sent Secretary of War William Howard Taft and Assistant Secretary of State Robert Bacon to Havana. On their arrival, September 28, President Palma obtained the resignation of his entire cabinet, then resigned himself, preventing Congress from electing a provisional president by dissolving it, and appealing to the United States to take over the government of Cuba. A provisional government was established by Messrs. Taft and Bacon, exercising Cuban sovereignty under the authority of the President of the United States, [3] and sustained by American troops under the command of General Franklin Bell. On October 13, Secretary Taft turned the provisional government of Cuba over to General Charles E. Magoon and returned to Washington. [4]

The second military occupation of Cuba lasted from 1906 to 1909. It was undertaken under the Platt Amendment. From avowing reluctance to intervene in September, President

[1] U. S. "Foreign Relations," 1906, p. 473.
[2] Ibid., p. 474.
[3] Ibid., pp. 489–90.
[4] Ibid., p. 494.

Roosevelt reached the point where he could say in his congressional message of May 3 that while the United States did not wish to annex Cuba it was "absolutely out of the question that the island should continue independent" if the "insurrectionary habit" should become "confirmed." [1]

The three years of General Magoon's occupation have been described by Cubans as "the most disastrous in the island's history." [2] At the beginning of the second occupation Cuba had over $13,000,000 in the national treasury. When General Magoon left the island in 1909 there was a national deficit of over $12,000,000.

Much of this money was spent on extravagant and irregular contracts for public improvements. Many of the concessions granted by General Magoon were successfully disclaimed by the Cuban Government when he left, but most of them it was forced to sustain, since the United States declared itself "morally responsible" for their fulfillment. One of the most important concessions let by the American military governor to an American company was the concession for paving and sewage in Havana to the McGivney and Rokeby Construction Company. Others were let to H. J. Reilly.

The richest concession was granted to Consul General Frank Steinhart, who had worked hard for intervention. The American authorities found Steinhart invaluable during the military occupation. They officially acknowledged their debt to him in their reports.[3] The concession which he received from General Magoon was for the extension of the lines of the Havana Electric Railway, Light and Power Company referred to above. It is the most important public utility corporation in Cuba today, with a capitalization of $36,000,000, and Frank Steinhart is its president. It maintains a complete street railway system extending into every section of Havana and its suburbs, running through every street of business importance.

[1] U. S. "Foreign Relations," 1906, p. xlv.
[2] Sociedad Cubana de Derecho Internacional, "Anuario," 1922, p. 407.
[3] U. S. War Dept., "Annual Report," 1905–06, p. 450.

The company also supplies the entire city of Havana and the surrounding area with electric light and power.   It has two large wharves on Havana harbour.   In 1921, when the sugar crisis forced banks to suspend and when imports fell to one-fourth of their normal amount, the company reported a material gain in business, and the statement for that year announced net earnings of over $5,000,000.[1]

Among his other activities, Consul General Steinhart was also financial representative in Cuba of Speyer and Company.   In this capacity he put through for Speyer and Company the $16,500,-000 loan of 1909 to finance the sewerage concession mentioned above.

This was the second loan in Cuba's history.   The first loan ($35,000,000, 1904), also from Speyer, was used to pay war claims, many of which had been bought up at a discount by Americans.

4. *The Third Landing of Troops*

The second American military occupation ended in 1909 with the inauguration of President Gomez, but American intervention in Cuban affairs continued.   For three years the State Department under Secretary Knox repeatedly interfered in Cuban affairs.   In 1912, following the outbreak of race riots, the Platt Amendment was once more invoked and American troops were landed for a third time on Cuban soil.

The race riots were precipitated by the conflict between the Partido Independiente de Color and President Gomez.   The Negro party claimed it was deprived by President Gomez of political standing which it had been accorded by the provisional government under General Magoon.   Declaring that the Gomez administration was bound to carry out the acts of the American occupation, the Negro party raised the standard of revolt, to gain its political rights.[2]

Fears for American property in Cuba are repeatedly expressed in the official dispatches from the American minister at Havana.

[1] Havana Electric Railway Company, "Annual Report," 1921.
[2] U. S. "Foreign Relations," 1912, p. 240 ff.

On May 3, 1912, the Havana stevedores went on strike, and American warships and marines were at once sent to Guantanamo and Santiago. On May 25 the battleship *Nebraska* was sent to Cuba, and additional forces to Key West. A gunboat was also sent to Nipe Bay, where the United Fruit Company has large sugar plantations,[1] and the Spanish-American Iron Co., a subsidiary of Bethlehem Steel, has mines and mills.[2] These acts were accompanied by a note from Secretary Knox to the American minister to Havana ordering him to "inform the Cuban Government that in the event of its inability or failure to protect the lives or property of American citizens in Cuba the Government of the United States, pursuant to its uniform custom in such cases, will land forces to accord necessary protection." The note added: "This is not intervention." [3]

By June 5, however, Secretary Knox went so far as to threaten formal intervention: "Four large war vessels," he cabled to the American minister at Havana, "will forthwith be sent from Key West to Guantanamo. It is hoped these measures will at once awaken the Cuban Government to prompt and adequate discharge of its responsibilities, and you will vigorously impress upon the President of Cuba that a continued failure on the part of his Government adequately to protect life and property will inevitably compel this Government to intervene in Cuba under and in response to its treaty rights and obligations." [4]

The sending of American battleships and the landing of troops was accomplished over the continued protests of the Cuban Government that it was doing its best to meet the uprising and in a few days had succeeded in cornering it. The rebellion collapsed when its leader was killed. The American forces were then withdrawn.

The following year, 1913, saw the inauguration of Mario

[1] Moody's "Analyses of Investments: Industrials," 1916, p. 1145.
[2] Ibid., 1919, p. 916.
[3] U. S. "Foreign Relations," 1912, p. 248.
[4] Ibid., p. 254.

Garcia Menocal as President of Cuba. He was a wealthy sugar planter, a conservative, and as such acceptable to Washington; but his Secretary of Foreign Affairs, Dr. Cosme de la Torriente, resisted the encroachments of the American State Department in various minor cases. Pressure was brought to bear on Menocal to remove him, but Torriente resigned instead.[1]

5. *The Fourth Landing of Troops*

The military occupation of 1906 and the landing of American troops in 1912 were both occasioned by political quarrels in Cuba. Another political quarrel led the Wilson administration to follow the policy of its predecessors and to land troops on Cuban territory as the most effective means of enforcing American views. The occasion was the Cuban election of 1917. President Menocal was running for re-election on the Conservative ticket. Early election returns indicated that the Liberals would win. Delays followed. Finally Menocal was declared elected. The Liberals appealed to the Cuban Supreme Court and the court sustained [2] the claims of the Liberals that election boxes were opened, returns falsified, polls established in inaccessible places, and Liberals barred from voting by force of arms in remote provinces. On the basis of the Supreme Court decision new elections were held in two out of the six provinces. As these provinces usually went Liberal it seemed certain that the Liberals would win.

Meantime the Liberals appealed to the American Secretary of State, Robert Lansing, to request the Cuban Government to guarantee impartial elections. Secretary Lansing formally acknowledged the appeal but took no action. Failing in this, the Liberals attempted to confine Menocal at his country estate and to have the elections held under the Vice President, who was respected for his honesty. Several Liberals were at once jailed and the Conservative Party raised the cry of revolution. The State Department at Washington took notice of the strug-

[1] Sociedad Cubana de Derecho Internacional, "Anuario," 1922, p. 427.
[2] Ibid., p. 430.

gle by sending official warning that no government not duly elected would be recognized by the United States and that revolution would not be tolerated.[1]

Despite this warning, the Liberals occupied several towns including Santiago. The American minister at Havana, William E. Gonzalez, thereupon issued a proclamation to the revolutionists in the name of the United States threatening severe punishment if they did not lay down their arms. He warned them that they would be held responsible for all damage to property, and stated the doctrine evolved by President Wilson that no government founded on revolution would be recognized by the United States.[2] Significantly enough, this threat against the rebels came from a United States official rather than from the Cuban Government.

During this controversy, the Cuban Government, following the example of the United States, declared war on Germany. In the formal note of congratulations sent by the State Department to Cuba it was stated that the Liberal revolutionists would be regarded as the common foe of both the United States and Cuba.[3]

After several other notes of a similar nature, two hundred American marines landed at Santiago, taking the town from the Liberal revolutionists. This armed invasion was coincident with the holding of the appealed elections. As no precautions were taken to remove the conditions against which the Liberals had risen in arms, Menocal was elected by a narrow margin. Among the Liberals who took part in the revolution crushed by American arms were ex-President Gomez and Dr. Alfredo Zayas, one of the leaders of the 1906 revolt and subsequently president of Cuba.

The Menocal Government, secure in power with the assistance of American bayonets, now agreed to the presence of over 2,000 American marines, which Washington had sent to protect the sugar interests threatened during the revolution.

---

[1] Cuba; Estado, "Boletin," v. 14, pp. 74-5.
[2] Ibid., pp. 75-6.
[3] Cuba; Hacienda, "Boletin," v. 16, p. 469.

The explanation for their presence was that they were being trained for service in Europe! Despite this official explanation the troops remained until the end of January, 1912, when the last 350 sailed.

In February, 1919, the American Minister Gonzalez, in a proclamation [1] addressed "to the Cuban people," announced the coming of General Enoch H. Crowder, who had formerly served under General Magoon during the second American military occupation. General Crowder arrived on March 10 with a battleship for moral effect which remained in Cuba during his entire stay, or was relieved by another vessel. He undertook a study of the Cuban electoral law with a view to preventing disturbances. Finding it necessary to revise the census law for this purpose, he sent for another American, Harold E. Stephenson. The administration of Cuban affairs by Americans was carried on at Cuba's expense.[2]

6. The Civil Occupation of Cuba

The arrival of General Crowder marked the beginning of a new American policy in Cuba. Daily regulation was now substituted for occasional armed intervention. General Crowder continually sent notes and suggestions to the Cuban Government. Other American administrators continued to arrive in Cuba. In 1920, an American commission of steamship magnates arrived to clear up the congestion in Havana harbour. The Cuban Government received its report, enacted legislation, and the congestion continued.[3] The following year there came B. S. Wells and Oscar Wells, one to keep General Crowder in touch with Washington, the other to reorganize Cuban banking.

Meanwhile, in December, 1920, Albert Rathbone arrived to act as financial adviser to the Cuban Government. He was sent, it was stated, at the request of Cuba, but the Cuban Secretary of the Treasury, Leopoldo Cancio, who was supposed to

[1] Sociedad Cubana de Derecho Internacional, "Anuario," 1922, p. 451.
[2] Cuba, "Censo," 1919, pp. 2, 18.
[3] "La Prensa," July 15, 1920.

make the request, knew nothing about it. This official there-fore resigned and Mr. Rathbone took his place during the remainder of his stay.

The American financial adviser investigated the financial crisis of 1920–1921 brought about by the tremendous sugar deflation. Shortly after the war the United States Sugar Con-trol Board abruptly ceased to function. This precipitated a financial crisis in Cuba which was complicated by two other cir-cumstances: first, Cuba owed money to American contractors and investors who appealed to Washington; second, it fell into arrears to the extent of one interest payment on government loans held in the United States.

One of these loans was a credit for $30 million made by the United States Treasury when Cuba declared war on Germany. The credit was unrequested. Part of it was immediately dis-counted for four submarine chasers thrust upon Cuba, again unrequested. When interest on this loan fell in arrears one month the United States demanded that Cuba immediately re-organize its finances, threatening intervention as an alternative.

The National City Bank, which is behind practically all American sugar interests in Cuba and controls the Cuba Rail-road, took advantage of the Republic's financial difficulties to foreclose its mortgages on a number of native sugar planta-tions. These plantations were then taken over by the General Sugar Company, a National City Bank subsidiary. By this action, nearly ten per cent of the total Cuban crop was added to the part controlled by Americans.

To stabilize Cuban finances the American financial adviser, Albert Rathbone, made fourteen recommendations which Gen-eral Crowder, on the second visit, proceeded to enforce in the face of great opposition.[1]

1. To restore confidence by removing the moratorium.

2. To relieve dock congestion, which affected American ship-pers.

3. To make American paper money the only paper legal ten-der, prohibiting the issue of Cuban paper money.

[1] "Heraldo de Cuba," Jan. 8, 1921.

4. To secure a loan of from fifty to one hundred million dollars.

5. The bonds of this loan must be held in the United States.

6. To form a debt commission to take care of matters pertaining to this loan as long as it exists.

7. To continue the moratorium for thirty days to prepare for its removal.

8. Immediately sell the hoarded sugar crop, an enormous surplus, to Americans at the market price.

9. To ask the United States to sanction the loan officially.

10. To stop Cuban governmental control of sugar prices and not to approve the loan if this is disregarded.

11. To permit American gold to leave the country, repealing the decree forbidding it.

12. To establish a clearing house.

13. To insure the losses of bank depositors.

14. To seek American co-operation in formulating banking laws.

The loan referred to in these fourteen points was issued by J. P. Morgan & Co. in 1923 for the sum of $50,000,000 and was issued, as specified by Albert Rathbone, "with the acquiescence of the United States Government under the provisions of the Treaty dated May 22, 1903," which ratified the Platt Amendment. The conditions of the loans as set forth in the sales letter issued by J. P. Morgan & Co., on January 15, 1923, indicated the implications of the Platt Amendment and the connection between political control and financial concessions. "The principal and interest of these bonds," the letter states, "are to be forever exempt from any Cuban taxes now existing or which may hereafter exist. . . . By an act of the United States dated March 2, 1901, certain provisions were formulated which have been incorporated by amendment in the Cuban constitution and have also been embodied in a Treaty, dated May 22, 1903, between the United States and Cuba. Under these provisions, commonly referred to as the 'Platt Amendment,' the Republic of Cuba agrees not to contract any public debt the service of which, including reasonable sinking fund provisions, cannot be provided for by the ordinary revenues. In addition to this financial safeguard, the Republic also agrees not to enter into any foreign treaty or compact which may impair its independence, and furthermore grants to the United States the right to intervene for the purpose of preserving Cuban independence and maintaining a government adequate for the protection of life and property. . . . These bonds are to be the direct obligations of the Republic of Cuba, which pledges its good faith and credit for the prompt payment of principal and interest. In addition they are to be secured:

"(a) By a charge on certain revenues of the Republic, including the customs revenue, subject to existing charges, but prior to any future charges.

"(b) By a first charge on 10 per cent of the amount by which the revenues of the Government in each fiscal year exceed $60,000,000."

The sales letter quotes pertinent sections of the Platt Amendment, and adds that "Major General Enoch H. Crowder has been in Cuba during the past two years as the representative of the United States Government for the purpose of assisting the Cuban Government. As the result of his report and recommendations with respect to this loan, the Government of the United States has acquiesced in its issuance." J. P. Morgan & Co. were also able to state, as a result of the third of Albert Rathbone's recommendations, that "except for her subsidiary coinage, Cuba uses United States currency. The Cuban Nation, therefore, in a period of readjustment since the ending of the World War, has been entirely free from currency inflation."

In the process of coercing the Cuban Government to carry out these proposals, as well as other accessory ones of his own contriving, General Crowder for two years was engaged in an intimate intervention in all of the government's affairs, the infinite details of which can hardly be given in so limited an account. By means of a series of secret "memoranda" directed to the President of the Republic, legislative and administrative reforms desired by the State Department or the prospective bankers, were forced upon both the Cuban Congress and the President by thinly veiled threats of financial and military interventions, and legislative conferences at which General Crowder was present were completely overridden by him.

7. The Economic Occupation of Cuba

From the first military occupation of Cuba by the United States at the beginning of this century, through subsequent military and civil control, American economic interests have steadily developed their hold upon the island. One of President Roosevelt's earliest special acts was to urge Congress to reduce the tariff on Cuban imports, chiefly sugar.[1] A bill providing for reciprocity with Cuba and for a 20 per cent reduction on sugar, was introduced, but the American beet sugar interests, which had opposed the annexation of Hawaii, fought this bill which menaced the development of the beet sugar industry in the United States. The chief support for reciprocity came from the American Sugar Refining Co., generally known as the "Sugar Trust." The opposition was so strong that President Roosevelt sent a special message to Congress on June 13, 1902, urging the passage of the bill.[2]

In the course of the controversy the beet sugar interests showed that an active propagandist for the bill, F. B. Thurber, president of the United States Export Association, who had been distributing reciprocity leaflets, was in the pay of the American Sugar Refining Company and of General Leonard Wood, military governor of Cuba. General Wood submitted an explanation to the War Department on July 1, 1902, in which he admitted spending over $15,000 for reciprocity propaganda.[3] This exposure killed the bill in Congress, but by a treaty signed with Cuba, December 11, 1902, the Roosevelt administration established reciprocity. Cuban products were to be admitted at a 20 per cent reduction; American products

---

[1] U. S. "Foreign Relations," 1901, p. xxxi.
[2] U. S. Congress, 57:1; "Sen. Doc." 405, p. 1.
[3] U. S. Congress, 57:1; "House Doc." 679, p. 2.

were to enter Cuba at 25, 30, and 40 per cent reductions. The treaty also provided that so long as it was in force no sugar was to be admitted into the United States at a lower rate of duty than that provided by the Dingley tariff.[1] Following the signing of this treaty American exports to Cuba rose from $25 million in 1902 to $48 million in 1906, while imports from Cuba rose from $34 million to $86 million.[2]

This preferential tariff works chiefly to the advantage of the American sugar refiners, who import 85 per cent of Cuba's total sugar output. The workings of the tariff are described by H. C. Prinsen Geerligs.[3]

"Through the active cooperation of the American buyers this preference does not altogether go to the Cuban producers, but chiefly falls to the organized American refiners, as in most years the Cubans have no option but to go to the American market. The refiners make the most of it by bidding less for Cuban sugar than for Java or other foreign sugar of the same quality, which, being unprotected, corresponds in price with free sugar and can fetch the world's price. They can easily do this as they take care to bid so much below the world's price as will keep it within 20 per cent of the import duty, in which case their price will still be a little higher than the net world's price. Only when their margin exceeds the 20 per cent will it become profitable for the Cuban planters to offer their sugar in the open market; but the buyers take good care to prevent this until their wants are provided for."

Next to sugar, the railroads and ports represent the most important American investments in Cuba. These depend for their income chiefly on the handling of the Cuban sugar crop. Cuban railways can be grouped under two systems. In the eastern and central provinces are the lines of the Cuba Railroad, which is controlled by the Cuba Company, an American concern owning large sugar lands and mills. This road bears the brunt of the sugar traffic as it passes through the heaviest sugar producing sections of the island,

[1] U. S. "Foreign Relations," 1903, p. 375.
[2] U. S. "Foreign Commerce and Navigation," 1901–02, p. 103; 1905–06, p. 51.
[3] Prinsen Geerligs, "World's Cane Sugar Industry," p. 184.

and is, besides, the only railroad at the eastern end of the island. The Cuba Railroad also owns the Camaguey and Nuevitas Railroad, which has given it a deep-water terminal on Nuevitas, which is considered to be potentially the greatest sugar-port in the world. It also owns the Compania Industrial y Naviera Cubana, a company running tugs, lighters, and dredges.[1] This first great railway system is run by the Consolidated Railways of Cuba, which controls the Cuba Northern along the north coast, built and owned by Colonel José Tarafa. This line is the only public service railway in the section through which it runs, and has transported on an average of 6,500,000 bags of sugar yearly during the past three years. Its eastern terminal is at Puerto Tarafa.[2] Nearby are twelve warehouses owned by the railroad. A summary of the ports served by these two railroad systems would include practically all the sugar ports in Cuba.

The second great Cuban railway system is run by the United Railways of the Havana and Reglas Warehouses. It was incorporated in England and most of its directors are English. It controls, however, the Havana Central Railway, a company with a perpetual concession, incorporated in New Jersey in 1905, the majority of whose directors are Americans living in New York. The majority of lines carrying the sugar crops are American controlled.

In 1923 Colonel Tarafa, owner of the Cuba Northern Railways, a veteran of the Cuban wars of independence, was responsible for the introduction of a bill authorizing the consolidation of his road with the Cuba Railroad and the Camaguey and Nuevitas and giving this combined system a legal monopoly of the sugar crop transportation and all future railroad development on the island. In this action, Tarafa actually represented the Cuba Railroad, but it was said that the bill was the result of a controversy between Tarafa and sugar planters using his

[1] Moody's "Analyses of Investments: Steam Railroads," 1924, pp. 2003-7.
[2] Ibid., pp. 2008-9.

lines who violated their contracts and sent their sugar through private ports of their own.[1] The bill provided for the following:

(1) The formation of the Consolidated Railways of Cuba, which it was claimed would result in an immediate reduction of 20 per cent in the rates for hauling sugar over 100 miles.

(2) The association of all other railway companies with the Consolidated system, since only one such system was to be permitted.

(3) The establishment of about twenty authorized ports and the closing of all other private ports by revoking concessions.

(4) The taxation on all sugar exported through unauthorized ports in cases where railway facilities failed to connect them with an authorized port.

American sugar interests at once protested to the State Department against this bill. They were joined by other American enterprises in Cuba, such as the American Metal Company, which benefited by private ports. The protests objected that the bill was confiscatory in character and would entail loss of property; also that hauling sugar hundreds of miles instead of shipping direct was economically insane. The Rotary Club of Cuba also protested that the sugar industry and consequently the economic life of the country would suffer.[2]

Martin W. Littleton, counsel for the Cuba Railroad, replied to these objections that the fight was between two sets of American interests, and Washington must not seek to coerce Cuba either way. Owners of private ports, he declared, enjoyed special privileges for which they should be taxed. He added that Colonel Tarafa had consulted American interests before introducing the bills,—notably C. E. Mitchell of the National City Bank, with 24 branches in Cuba, and whose directors own the Cuba Railroad!

The State Department protested against what it called the confiscatory features of the bill, although it looked favourably on the consolidation as promoting efficiency and "correcting

[1] "New York Times," Aug. 12, 1923, p. 1, 4.
[2] Idem.

customs abuses." The Cuban Congress had to wait for the State Department's assent before passing the bill, after Washington had obtained easier terms for American mill owners who would suffer from the proposed taxation.[1] On the other hand, Cuban public opinion was inflamed against creating a railway monopoly favourable to American interests. The Cuban minister to London was recalled because he spoke against the bill and joined in the accusations. The Veterans of the Wars of Independence, and the economic organizations protested with great violence, and carried public opinion behind them. Organized bribery secured its passage in the Cuban Congress.

On September 1, 1924, Colonel Tarafa's Cuba Northern Railways and all its property became part of the Cuba Railroad system, and Colonel Tarafa became a director of both companies. The directors of the Cuba Railroad are the same as those of the Cuba Company and are almost all Americans. The transfer agent is the National City Bank, and three of the Cuba Company directors, including Percy A. Rockefeller, are also National City Bank Directors.[2]

One of the most striking facts brought out during the controversy over the Tarafa Bill was stated as follows by Colonel Tarafa: "Fully 85 per cent . . . of the sugar interests involved in opposition to the Tarafa bill is held in the United States. . . . And also an equal amount of the capital interested in the railways also is in American hands." [3]

Theoretically, Cuba is a sovereign state. Practically, the economic and political life of the island is dominated from New York and Washington. This method of control avoids the costs of colonization while it leaves a free field to the American interests. The ownership of Cuba lies almost completely in the hand of the National City Bank. The bank controls directly the General Sugar Company. Its directors control the

[1] Ibid., Aug. 23, 1923, p. 8.
[2] Moody's "Analyses of Investments: Steam Railroads," 1924, p. 2003.
[3] "New York Times," Aug. 23, 1923, p. 8.

Consolidated Railways and the immense sugar holdings of the
Cuba Company, as well as many other Cuban corporations.
In addition; the twenty-four branches of the National City
Bank in Cuba lend money to native planters on sugar security
—at 10 per cent interest. The Consolidated Railways under
the Tarafa Bill make money on what sugar it does not directly
or indirectly control. Cuban political life is directed by the
State Department's representative. American domination of
the island is thorough.

VII

CONQUEST AND PURCHASE

1. *From Economic Expansion to Political Sovereignty*

The process of acquiring interests outside of the United States begins with the setting up of trading ventures and other enterprises which imply no control over the political life of the country in which they are established. The process ends with complete political domination over the outlying territory.

There are two principal ways in which the sovereignty of the United States is extended over new territories; the first is by conquest and the second by purchase. It may be true, as the Declaration of Independence states, that all just governments derive their powers from the consent of the governed, but the fact remains that history—and particularly modern history—tells the story of hundreds of millions, in Asia and Africa, who have been brought under the control of some powerful European state without being consulted as to their wishes in the matter. With the exception of the Mexican War, certain of the Indian wars and the Spanish War of 1898, the United States has done little in the direction of acquiring control over foreign territory. There are instances, however, particularly in recent years, in which the sovereignty of the United States has been extended over populations that had expressed no desire for its presence.

The story is simple. It has been told repeatedly and is well known. There is no serious difference of opinion as to the facts. The matter is treated with sufficient fulness in any of the current histories.

The annexation of Porto Rico, the conquest of the Philippines and the purchase of the Virgin Islands are three type cases of the extension of United States sovereignty. Porto

195

Rico was occupied during the war with Spain (1898) without opposition from the inhabitants. The Philippines were conquered during a war that lasted from 1899 to 1901. The Virgin Islands were purchased from Denmark in 1917.

Porto Rico may be dismissed in a few sentences. The island was occupied by the United States army beginning July 25, 1898; ceded to the United States under the Treaty of April 11, 1899 (note: President McKinley, on July 30, 1898, in his negotiations with Ambassador Cambon demanded the cession of Porto Rico by way of indemnity),[1] and after a long controversy the Porto Ricans were given their American citizenship by the Act of March 2, 1917. There has never been, in Porto Rico, any organized opposition to the presence of the United States. The island was a war prize whose inhabitants were for the most part satisfied to make the change of sovereignty which the fortunes of war brought about.

2. *The Philippine Republic*

The conquest of the Philippines is a different story. These islands, which had been in open rebellion against Spain before the outbreak of the Spanish-American War, refused to accept the American occupation as the Porto Ricans had done, preferring to fight a war of independence, even against overwhelming odds.

The Philippine Rebellion of 1896, led by Aguinaldo, had wrung from Spain an agreement (the treaty of Briac-na-bato) under which the Governor-General agreed to introduce certain reforms, and the leaders of the revolution agreed to withdraw from the islands on payment of a million dollars. Pursuant to this agreement, Aguinaldo was living in Singapore in May, 1898.

While Admiral Dewey was at Hong Kong, preparing to leave for Manila, he was advised by the American Consul at Singapore that Aguinaldo was willing to co-operate with the Americans. Dewey cabled back: "Tell Aguinaldo come soon as possible." After the battle of Manila Bay, Aguinaldo was

[1] U. S. "Foreign Relations," 1898, p. 820.

brought to Manila with thirteen members of his staff, in the United States gunboat *McCullock*. He was allowed to land at Cavite, was encouraged to organize the revolutionists, and was given guns from the Spanish arsenal.[1]

The Filipinos assumed from the outset that the Philippines were to be treated substantially as Cuba was treated. Aguinaldo hailed the Americans as the liberators of his people. In a proclamation of May 24, 1898, he wrote: "Now that the great and powerful North American nation have come to offer disinterested protection for an effort to secure the liberation of this country."[2]

Plans were drawn up for the organization of a Philippine Republic. On June 18, Aguinaldo proclaimed a temporary "Dictatorial Government."[3]

Aguinaldo and his followers then proceeded to clear the Philippines of Spanish garrisons to such good purpose that, by the end of the year, they held practically the entire archipelago. On January 21, 1899, Aguinaldo, in the name of the Revolutionary Government, proclaimed the "Constitution of the Philippine Republic."[4]

3. *"Co-operating with Aguinaldo"*

On July 4, 1898, General Anderson, in command of the United States army in the Philippines, wrote to Aguinaldo: "I desire to have the most amicable relations with you, and to have you and your people co-operate with us in military operations against the Spanish forces."[5]

The negotiations between the American authorities and Aguinaldo, and the extent to which the two co-operated in the days following Aguinaldo's arrival, is well illustrated in the testimony given by Admiral Dewey before the Senate Committee in 1902.[6] Aguinaldo and his forces participated with the United

---

[1] U. S. Philippine Commission, "Report," 1900, v. I, p. 171 ff.
[2] U. S. Congress, 57:1; "Sen. Doc." 331, p. 2955.
[3] Ibid., 55:3; "Sen. Doc." 62, pp. 432–7.
[4] Elliott, "Philippines," Appendix G.
[5] U. S. Congress, 56:1; "Sen. Doc." 208, p. 4.
[6] Ibid., 57:1; "Sen. Doc." 331, p. 2934 ff.

States forces in the capture of Manila. Indeed, the Filipinos had completely invested the city, and withdrew from a part of the lines in favour of the American troops under General Merritt. The city was assaulted on August 13, 1898, by the joint forces of the Filipinos and the Americans. When the city capitulated, under the terms of the agreement the Americans occupied the walled city, and the Filipinos remained in the outer town.

General Merritt had come to the Philippines with specific instructions not to recognize the Philippine Republic, but to establish a provisional government. General Otis, who succeeded General Merritt, refused to continue the joint occupation of Manila with Aguinaldo, and on September 8, 1898, directed Aguinaldo to withdraw his troops, in these words: "Unless your troops are withdrawn beyond the line of the city's defenses before Thursday, the fifteenth instant, I shall be obliged to resort to forcible action." [1] Aguinaldo withdrew as directed.

On December 21, President McKinley ordered General Otis to extend the military government to the entire Philippine archipelago. His instructions ended with this paragraph:

"It should be the earnest and paramount aim of the military administration to win the confidence, respect, and affection of the inhabitants of the Philippines by assuring them in every possible way that full measure of individual rights and liberties which is the heritage of free peoples, and by proving to them that the mission of the United States is one of benevolent assimilation, substituting the mild sway of justice and right for arbitrary rule. In the fulfillment of this high mission, supporting the temperate administration of affairs for the greatest good of the governed, there must be sedulously maintained the strong arm of authority, to repress disturbance and to overcome all obstacles to the bestowal of the blessings of good and stable government upon the people of the Philippine Islands under the free flag of the United States" [2]

[1] U. S. War Dept., "Annual Report," 1899, v. 1, pt. IV, p. 9.
[2] U. S. Congress, 57:1; "Sen. Doc." 331, p. 777.

The Presidential proclamation sealed the fate of the Philippine Republic. Henceforth the outbreak of hostilities was only a question of time and occasion. The publication of the proclamation greatly strengthened the hands of the war faction among the Filipinos, and while Aguinaldo succeeded in preventing a declaration of war, a fight, starting between a handful of Filipinos and an American sentry, on February 4, 1899, began an "insurrection" which ended officially on July 4, 1902. During the Philippine War 4,067 United States officers and 122,401 enlisted men served in the Philippines, with losses of 140 officers and 4,234 men, killed or died of wounds, disease, etc., and 204 officers and 2,818 men wounded.[1]

4. Disposing of the Philippines

The war between the Revolutionary Government of the Philippines and the Government of the United States ended with the annihilation of the Philippine Republic. There remained the question of the political disposition of the islands.

While the victory of Dewey at Manila had put the capital of the Philippines under titular American control, there was at first no intention on the part of the American authorities to demand the islands from Spain. The protocol, signed August 12, 1898, provided only for the occupation by the United States of "the city, bay, and harbor of Manila pending the conclusion of a treaty of peace which shall determine the control, disposition, and government of the Philippines."[2]

A month later (September 16, 1898) in his letter of instructions to the Peace Commissioners, President McKinley wrote:

"Without any original thought of complete or even partial acquisition, the presence and success of our aims at Manila imposes upon us obligations which we cannot disregard. The march of events rules and overrules human action. Avowing unreservedly the purpose which has animated all our effort, and still solicitous to adhere to it, we cannot be unmindful that, without

[1] Heitman, "Historical Register," v. 2, p. 293.
[2] U. S. "Foreign Relations," 1898, p. 824.

any desire or design on our part, the war has brought us new duties and responsibilities which we must meet and discharge as becomes a great nation on whose growth and career from the beginning the Ruler of Nations has plainly written the high command and pledges of civilization.

"Incidental to our tenure in the Philippines is the commercial opportunity to which American statesmanship cannot be indifferent. It is just to use every legitimate means for the enlargement of American trade; but we seek no advantages in the orient which are not common to all. Asking only the open door for ourselves, we are ready to accord the open door to others." . . . "The United States cannot accept less than the cession in full right and sovereignty of the island of Luzon." [1]

The Philippine discussion occupied the Peace Commission at Paris for a month. Late in October, the American Commission cabled for further instruction. Secretary Hay replied:

"The information which has come to the President since your departure convinces him that the acceptance of the cession of Luzon alone, leaving the rest of the islands subject to Spanish rule, or to be the subject of future contention, cannot be justified on political, commercial, or humanitarian grounds. The cession must be of the whole archipelago or none. The latter is wholly inadmissable, and the former must therefore be required." [2]

The Spanish Commission opposed this demand on the ground that it violated the protocol. Finally, the United States agreed to pay $20,000,000 and Spain ceded the islands.

José S. Reyes has made a very careful study of President McKinley's change of mind with regard to the retention of the Philippines. [3]

At the time of the cession, the Spaniards had been practically driven from the islands. Manila was held by the armed forces of the United States and the remainder of the territory was being administered by a provisional government of the Philippine Republic.

[1] U. S. "Foreign Relations," 1898, p. 907.
[2] Ibid., p. 935.
[3] Reyes, "Legislative History of America's Economic Policy Toward the Philippines."

5. *Pacification and the Civil Government*

The change in American opinion regarding the desirability of keeping the Philippines, had been brought about, as President McKinley repeatedly suggested, by the commercial fields which the islands presented. An immediate effort was therefore made to re-establish law and order under the direction of a civil governor—William H. Taft—who was inaugurated July 4, 1901.

The work of the civil government centred about the establishment of public order, education, road building, and sanitation. In all of these directions immense strides were made.[1] While the Filipinos themselves had not abandoned their hope of independence, it was generally assumed in the United States that the islands were not yet capable of self-government.

Between 1902, when the civil government bill was before Congress, and 1916, when the Jones Act was passed, the Democratic Party championed a system of "qualified independence." The election of Woodrow Wilson in 1912, on a platform which stated: "We reaffirm the position thrice announced by the democracy in national convention assembled against a policy of imperialism and colonial exploitation in the Philippines, or elsewhere. . . . We favour an immediate declaration of the nation's purpose to recognize the independence of the Philippine Islands as soon as a stable government can be established," [2] had been hailed as a harbinger of immediate independence. These hopes were strengthened when Francis B. Harrison, the new Governor General, was sent to the Phillippines in August, 1913, with this message from the President:

"We regard ourselves as trustees acting not for the advantage of the United States, but for the benefit of the people of the Philippine Islands.

"Every step we take will be taken with a view to the ultimate independence of the Islands and as a preparation for that independence. And we hope to move towards that end as rapidly as the

[1] Elliott, "Philippines," chs. VIII–X, XIII.
[2] "Democratic Text Book," 1912, p. 30.

safety and the permanent interests of the Islands will permit.
After each step taken experience will guide us to the next.

"The administration will take one step at once and will give
to the native citizens of the Islands a majority in the Appointive
Commission, and thus in the Upper as well as in the Lower
House of the Legislature a majority representation will be secured
to them.

"We do this in the confident hope and expectation that immediate
proof will be given in the action of the Commission under the
new arrangement of the political capacity of those native citizens
who have already come forward to represent and to lead their
people in affairs." [1]

Following out this policy, Governor Harrison replaced American officials by Filipinos, with the assurance that as soon as
the necessary aptitude for self-government was demonstrated,
the islands would be granted their independence. Congress,
in March, 1916, gave its approval to this policy by passing the
Jones Law, with the following preamble:

"Whereas it was never the intention of the people of the United
States in the incipiency of the War with Spain to make it a war
of conquest or for territorial aggrandizement; and

"Whereas it is, as it has always been, the purpose of the people
of the United States to withdraw their sovereignty over the Philippine Islands and to recognize their independence *as soon as a
stable government can be established therein;* and

"Whereas, for the speedy accomplishment of such purpose, it
is desirable to place in the hands of the people of the Philippines
as large a control of their domestic affairs as can be given them
without in the meantime impairing the exercise of the rights of
sovereignty by the people of the United States in order that by
the use and exercise of popular franchise and governmental
powers they may be the better prepared to fully assume the responsibilities and enjoy all the privileges of complete independence." [2]

Education, civil government, commerce and industry made
great strides during the years between 1913 and 1920.[3]   At

[1] Harrison, "Corner-Stone of Philippine Independence," p. 50.
[2] U. S. Congress, 67:4; "House Doc." 511, p. 14.
[3] Ibid., p. 8 ff.

the same time there arose a very emphatic desire among the Philippine leaders to have the Philippines for the Filipino. The great areas of uncultivated land (the Filipinos report 6,356,927 hectares of public land "available for home seekers"[1]), the 65,000 square miles of timber, but above all the situation of the islands "at the cross-roads to the greatest trade routes of the future" make them rich prizes.[2]

Filipino leaders have had another reason for insisting that the Philippines must do their own developing. They fear that the investment of large sums of American capital will "become an excuse or a pretext for postponing or even putting off indefinitely the day of their national independence."[3] By way of further safeguard, the Philippine National Bank, much to the displeasure of competitive institutions already in the field, was organized in 1915. In addition, the government bought the Manila Railroad, organized a National Coal Company and a National Development Company, "for the purpose of financing isolated enterprises that the government may desire to establish for the general welfare of the country."[4]

6. Growing American Interests

Meanwhile American economic interests in the islands had grown apace. By 1920, 135 United States corporations, with a total capital stock of $433 million, were registered in the islands. Among these organizations, 87 were engaged in commerce, 16 in mining and agriculture, and 25 in manufacturing.[5]

The available and unexploited resources of the Philippines, the considerable investments of United States citizens in the islands, the effort of the Philippine leaders to governmentalize business in order to increase the control of the Philippine people over their own economic affairs, combined to favour the conflict between the United States investors and the movement for Philippine independence.

[1] U. S. Congress, 67:4; "House Doc." 511, p. 68.
[2] "Annalist," v. 23, p. 159.
[3] "Current History Magazine," v. 19, p. 283.
[4] U. S. Congress, 67:4; "House Doc." 511, pp. 73-4.
[5] Philippine Islands, "Statistical Bulletin," No. 3, p. 255.

7. *The Wood-Forbes Report*

The issue was brought to a head by the appointment (March 20, 1921) of a special mission, headed by Major-General Leonard Wood, which made a study at first hand of the position of the Philippines and which submitted a report reviewing these conditions, and concluding that:

1. "The great bulk of the Christian Filipinos have a very natural desire for independence; most of them desire independence under the protection of the United States; a very small percentage desire immediate independence with separation from the United States; a very substantial element is oppòsed to independence, especially at this time.

2. "The Moros are a unit against independence and are united for continuance of American control and, in case of separation of the Philippines from the United States desire their portion of the islands to be retained as American territory under American control.

3. "The Americans in the islands are practically a unit for the continuance of American control." [1]

Public order is well maintained by the constabulary: "The progressive development of the school system has been phenomenal." [2] Economic development has been "very gratifying" particularly since 1913. The national debt is unusually small (only $1.81 per capita, as compared with $25 in Cuba and $237 in the United States). The Philippine National Bank has fared badly, partly because of mismanagement and partly because of the severe business depression of 1920–1921.

"The Government has entered into certain lines of business usually left to private initiative. . . . In our judgment the government should as far as possible get out of and keep out of business." [3]

Among the general conclusions of the mission are the following:

[1] U. S. Philippine Islands, Special Mission to, "Report," 1921, p. 21.
[2] Ibid., p. 28.
[3] Ibid., p. 42.

"We find the people happy, peaceful, and in the main prosperous, and keenly appreciative of the benefits of American rule.

"We find everywhere among the Christian Filipinos the desire for independence, generally under the protection of the United States. The non-Christians and Americans are for continuance of American control.

"We find a general failure to appreciate the fact that independence under the protection of another nation is not true independence. . . .

"We feel that with all their many excellent qualities, the experience of the past eight years, during which they have had practical autonomy, has not been such as to justify the people of the United States in relinquishing supervision of the government of the Philippine Islands, withdrawing their army and navy, and leaving the island a prey to any powerful nation coveting their rich soil and potential commercial advantages." [1]

Recommendation number one, as presented by the mission, is that "the present general status of the Philippine Islands continue until the people have had time to absorb and thoroughly master the powers already in their hands." And number three reads: "In case of a deadlock between the Governor General and the Philippine Senate in the confirmation of appointments that the President of the United States be authorized to make and render the final decision." [2]

Following the report, General Wood was made Governor of the Philippines. A struggle ensued between the Filipino legislature and the Governor General, in the course of which the Filipino leaders sought by political pressure to force President Coolidge to fulfil the promise of the Jones Act, and to make good the statement of President Wilson in his message of December 7, 1920:

"The people of the Philippine Islands have succeeded in maintaining a stable government since the last action of the Congress in their behalf, and have thus fulfilled the condition set by the Congress as precedent to a consideration of granting independence to the Islands. I respectfully submit that this condition precedent having been fulfilled, it is now our liberty and our duty to keep our prom-

[1] U. S. Philippine Islands, Special Mission to, "Report," 1921, p. 42.
[2] Ibid., p. 46.

ise to the people of those Islands by granting them the independence which they so honorably covet." [1]

President Coolidge's letter of February 21, 1924, to Manuel Roxas strikes a far different note:

The White House,
Washington,
Feb. 21, 1924.

MY DEAR MR. ROXAS:

The resolutions adopted by the Senate and House of Representatives of the Philippines, touching upon the relations between the Filipino people and the Government of the United States, have been received. I have noted carefully all that you have said regarding the history of these relations. I have sought to inform myself so thoroughly as might be, as to the occasions of current irritation between the Legislature of the Philippines and the executive authority of the islands.

In your presentment you have set forth more or less definitely a series of grievances, the gravamen of which is that the present executive authority of the islands, designated by the United States Government, is in your opinion out of sympathy with the reasonable national aspirations of the Filipino people.

If I do not misinterpret your protest, you are disposed to doubt whether your people may reasonably expect, if the present executive policy shall continue, that the Government of the United States will in reasonable time justify the hopes which your people entertain of ultimate independence.

. . . .

The world is in a state of high tension. . . . The possibility of either economic or political disorders calculated to bring misfortune, if not disaster, to the Filipino people unless they are strongly supported, is not to be ignored.

It should not be overlooked that within the past two years, as a result of international arrangements negotiated by the Washington Conference on Limitation of Armament and problems of the Far East, the position of the Filipino people has been greatly improved and assured. For the stabilizing advantages which accrue to them in virtue of the assurance of peace in the Pacific, they are directly indebted to the initiative and efforts of the American Government.

[1] U. S. "Congressional Record," v. 60, p. 26.

They can ill afford in a time of so much uncertainty in the world to underrate the value of these contributions to their security.

. . . .

Although they have made wonderful advances in the last quarter century, the Filipino people are by no means equipped, either in wealth or experience, to undertake the heavy burden which would be imposed upon them with political independence. Their position in the world is such that without American protection there would be the unrestricted temptation to maintain an extensive and costly diplomatic service and an ineffective but costly military and naval service.

It is to be doubted whether, with the utmost exertion, the most complete solidarity among themselves, the most unqualified and devoted patriotism, it would be possible for the people of the islands to maintain an independent place in the world for an indefinite future.

. . . .

A fair appraisal of all these considerations and others which suggest themselves which do not require enumeration will, I am sure, justify the frank statement that the Government of the United States would not feel that it had performed its full duty by the Filipino people, or discharged all of its obligations to civilization, if it should yield at this time to your aspirations for national independence.

. . . .

I should be less than candid with you, however, if I did not say that in my judgment the strongest argument that has been used in the United States in support of immediate independence of the Philippines is not the argument that it would benefit the Filipinos, but that it would be of advantage to the United States.

Feeling as I do, and as I am convinced the great majority of Americans do regarding our obligations to the Filipino people, I have to say that I regard such arguments as unworthy. The American people will not evade or repudiate the responsibility they have assumed in this matter.

The American Government is convinced that it has the overwhelming support of the American nation in its conviction that present independence would be a misfortune and might easily become a disaster to the Filipino people. Upon that conviction, the policy of this Government is based.

Thus far I have suggested only some of the reasons related to international concerns, which seem to me to urge strongly against independence at this time. I wish now to review for a moment some domestic concerns of the Philippine Islands which seem also to urge against present independence. The American Government has been most liberal in opening to the Filipino people the opportunities of the largest practicable participation in, and control of, their own Administration.

. . . .

It has been charged that the present Governor General has in some matters exceeded his proper authorities, but an examination of the facts seems rather to support the charge that the legislative branch of the Insular Government has been the real offender, through seeking to extend its own authority into some areas of what should properly be the executive realm.

The Government of the United States has full confidence in the ability, good intentions, fairness and sincerity of the present Governor General. It is convinced that he has intended to act and has acted within the scope of his proper and constitutional authority. Thus convinced, it is determined to sustain him, and its purpose will be to encourage the broadest and most intelligent co-operation of the Filipino people in this policy.

Looking at the whole situation fairly and impartially, one cannot but feel that if the Filipino people cannot co-operate in the support and encouragement of as good administration as has been afforded under Governor General Wood, their failure will be rather a testimony of unpreparedness for the full obligations of citizenship than an evidence of patriotic eagerness to advance their country.

. . . .

If the time comes when it is apparent that independence would be better for the people of the Philippines, from the point of view of both their domestic concerns and their status in the world, and if when that time comes the Filipino people desire complete independence, it is not possible to doubt that the American Government and people will gladly accord it.

. . . .

Yours very truly,
CALVIN COOLIDGE.[1]

Evidently the Filipinos will be compelled, despite their vigorous and repeated protests, to live for some time to come "under the free flag of the United States" as President McKinley phrased it on December 21, 1898.

[1] "New York Times," March 6, 1924, p. 1:1.

8. *The Virgin Islands—A Strategic Key*

The Virgin Islands are neither a sphere of influence nor a protectorate; they were not conquered in war nor were revolutions fomented to obtain them. They were bought as a valuable piece of property, and with the purchase came complete domination over 26,000 people.

The value of the Virgin Islands to the United States is almost entirely military. They are located in the Caribbean Sea, of which one naval strategist has said: "One thing is sure. In the Caribbean Sea is the strategic key to the two great oceans, the Atlantic and the Pacific, our own chief maritime frontiers." [1]

The Virgin Islands are divided into three groups. One group includes the islands of Culebra, Vieques and adjacent smaller islands. These formerly belonged to Spain but were acquired by the United States following the Spanish American War. The second group, including the islands of Tortola, Anegada and Virgin Gorda belong to Great Britain. The third group, known until 1917 as the Danish West Indies, include the islands of St. Thomas, St. John and St. Croix and about fifty smaller islands, comprising a total area of about one hundred and fifty square miles. This group is located east of Porto Rico—St. Thomas about forty miles to the east, and St. Croix about a hundred miles.

The islands were discovered by Columbus on his second voyage in 1493. They were first settled by Danes who came to St. Thomas in 1666. Eight years later negro slaves were imported and by 1680 there were about fifty flourishing plantations cultivating chiefly tobacco. The islands of St. Thomas, St. John and St. Croix remained the property of Denmark for 250 years, except for a brief period during the Napoleonic Wars when they were seized by Great Britain for strategic purposes. The population of the islands has remained to this day predominantly negro. [2]

[1] Mahan, "Naval Strategy," p. 382.
[2] U. S. Congress, 66:2; "House Doc." 734, pp. 5-6.

The first attempts of the United States to acquire the Danish West Indies were made during President Lincoln's second administration in 1865. Secretary of State Seward was impressed by their strategic value, chiefly because during the Civil War St. Thomas afforded refuge to Southern privateers and blockade runners. In 1866 Seward visited the islands, and the following year offered Denmark $5,000,000 for the group. Negotiations were carried on in great secrecy.[1] They were for a time delayed by the assassination of Lincoln and the wounding of Seward, but finally the State Department and Denmark compromised on $7,500,000 for the two islands of St. Thomas and St. John. A plebiscite in the islands—insisted upon by Denmark—resulted in a large vote for cession to the United States. A treaty was drawn up for the transfer of the islands. It was immediately ratified by the Danish Rigsdag and signed by King Christian IX. The United States Senate, however, failed to ratify it, mainly because of the political feud between President Andrew Johnson and Congress.[2]

Plans to purchase the Danish West Indies were revived during the Harrison and Cleveland administrations; but nothing of a definite nature was done until, in 1898, when the United States was entering the arena of world imperialism, the Senate Foreign Relations Committee, headed by Senator Lodge, urged the acquisition of the islands as a naval and coaling station. The Lodge report emphasized the strategic importance of the islands as follows:

"From a military point of view the value of these islands to the United States can hardly be overestimated. We have always been anxious to have a good naval and coaling station in the West Indies. Important in time of peace, such a station would be essential to our safety in time of war. . . . The fine harbor of St. Thomas fulfils all the required naval and military conditions."[3]

[1] U. S. Congress, 57:1; "Sen. Doc." 284, p. 10, 17.
[2] Ibid., pp. 18–19.
[3] Ibid., p. 19.

The Lodge report referred to the opinions of Captain A. T. Mahan, regarded as an authority on naval strategy. Of the island of St. Thomas Captain Mahan said: "It remains still a desirable position for the United States to obtain. If it had come into her possession . . . there would have been matter for serious consideration whether it or Culebra were the more advantageous as an advance base, secondary or subservient to Guantanamo. My study of the two, though not exhaustive, inclines me decidedly in favor of St. Thomas both for situation and for defensive strength based upon topographical conditions. To these is to be added the offensive value that results from greater ease of handling a battle fleet, and greater security of egress owing to hydrographic conditions." [1]

On the basis of the Lodge report, Congress authorized President McKinley to buy the Virgin Islands from Denmark. Secretary Hay negotiated a treaty for their purchase at $5,000,000. This time the Senate ratified the treaty but the Danish Rigsdag failed to ratify it.[2]

In 1902 the Senate Foreign Relations Committee again reported in favour of buying the islands. The report emphasized the strategic value of the islands, pointing out that St. Thomas is "an important coaling station and depot of trade with the West Indies," and that its harbour is excellent. "These islands," the report added, "together with Porto Rico, are of great importance in a strategic way, whether the strategy be military or commercial." The Committee quoted a military report by Major Glassford of the United States Signal Corps in which he said:

"The island of St. Thomas offers conditions suitable for developing a first class military outpost. This island possesses all the natural advantages, enabling it to be converted into a second Gibraltar." [3] On the strength of these recommendations President Roosevelt submitted to the Senate on January

---

[1] Mahan, "Naval Strategy," p. 322.
[2] U. S. Congress, 66:2; "House Doc." 734, p. 7.
[3] U. S. Congress, 57:1; "Sen. Doc." 284, pp. 11-12.

27, 1902, a treaty with Denmark for the purchase of St. Thomas, St. John and St. Croix for $5,000,000. Again the scheme fell through.[1]

9. Purchasing the Islands

The completion of the Panama Canal and the growing power of the United States in the Caribbean made possession of the Virgin Islands a cardinal point in the State Department's policy. In 1915 Maurice Francis Egan, the American Minister to Denmark, was instructed to open negotiations. Mr. Egan has told the story of these negotiations in his book "Ten Years Near the German Frontier."

Briefly, the story is as follows: The Wilson administration, like its predecessors, was impressed by the strategic importance of the islands. "Puerto Rico was of little value in a strategic way without the Danish Antilles. A cursory examination of the map will show that Puerto Rico, with no harbors for large vessels and its long coast line, would offer no defences against alien forces."[2] America's anxiety to have the islands was heightened by the European war. There was fear that Germany might seize Denmark and Danish possessions in the Caribbean. By the middle of 1915 "it was plain to all who read the signs of the times, that we could not long keep out of the war."[3]

Minister Egan was authorized to approach the Danish Foreign Minister on the subject of selling the islands. When the conversation opened the American Minister thought: "He will ask $50,000,000. . . . He knows better than anybody that we shall be at war with Germany in less than a year." The American Minister "felt dizzy at the thought of losing the Gibraltar of the Caribbean."[4] However, instead of asking for $50,000,000 the Danish Foreign Minister asked for only $30,000,000, adding apologetically: "The price is dazzling, I know."

---

[1] U. S. Congress, 57:1; "Sen. Doc." 284, pp. 1-6.
[2] Egan, "Ten Years Near the German Frontier," p. 239.
[3] Ibid., p. 259.
[4] Ibid., p. 265.

Minister Egan replied: "My country is more generous even than she is rich. The translation must be completed before . . ." The Danish Foreign Minister understood the pause, according to Mr. Egan, who explains significantly that the United States "was neutral *then*." This was in 1915. The purchase of the Virgin Islands the following year appears to have been part of a war program prepared by the Wilson administration.[1]

Many Danes opposed the sale of the islands to the United States, and Minister Egan decided to overcome this opposition. When liberal Danish women objected that the United States was not democratic enough to give its women the vote, the American Minister staged a public lecture in Copenhagen in which he advocated woman suffrage. Another widespread objection, one which the Queen of Denmark shared, was that the United States would treat the Negroes in the Virgin Islands as it treated them in the South. The Danish Government insisted that a plebiscite be held in Denmark on the question of the sale. Shortly before the balloting a news dispatch from the United States brought the story of the brutal lynching of a Negro. Minister Egan prevented publication of the story.[2] The plebiscite in Denmark and another in the Virgin Islands both favoured cession to the United States. A treaty was signed in New York on August 4, 1916. It was ratified by the Senate and President Wilson and by the Danish Rigsdag, and proclaimed in January, 1917.[3]

By this treaty Denmark ceded to the United States for $25,-000,000 the islands of St. Thomas, St. John and St. Croix, together with the adjacent islands and rocks. The United States bound itself to maintain the concessions granted by the Danish Government in the islands, covering chiefly harbour improvement, telephone, telegraph and electric lighting.

The treaty also provided that Danish citizens residing in the islands might remain there or leave at will, retaining in either

[1] Egan, supra, p. 266.
[2] Ibid., pp. 268–88.
[3] U. S. "Treaty Series," no. 629.

event their property rights.   In case they remained, they were
entitled to all their rights under the local laws then in force.
Those who remained in the islands were permitted to preserve
their Danish citizenship by making a declaration to that effect
before a court of record.   However, unless they did so, within
a year after exchange of treaty ratifications, they would be presumed to have renounced Danish citizenship and to have accepted citizenship in the United States.

10. *Naval Rule*

No such detailed provisions were made for over 20,000 native Negroes who were bought by the United States with the
islands.   Article Six of the treaty stipulated that "the civil
rights and political status of the inhabitants of the islands shall
be determined by the Congress."   Congress has not yet taken
permanent action under this clause.   Instead, a temporary
naval dictatorship was established by the Act of March 3, 1917,
replacing the civil government which the natives had under
Danish rule.   This Act provided that:

"All military, civil and judicial powers necessary to govern the
West Indian Islands acquired from Denmark shall be vested in a
Governor and such persons as the President may appoint, and shall
be exercised in such manner as the President shall direct until
Congress shall provide for the government of said islands:
"*Provided,* that the President may assign an officer of the army
or navy to serve as such Governor and perform the duties appertaining to said office, *and provided further,* that the Governor of
said islands shall be appointed by and with the advice and consent
of the Senate; *and provided further* that the compensation of all
persons appointed under this Act shall be fixed by the President."

Although naval rule was established as a temporary measure
it still exists, eight years after the islands were bought, and
seven years after the armistice.   The Colonial Councils existing under Danish rule have been continued, but they are under
the complete domination of the naval governor who can veto
their acts or dissolve them at any time.   The usual conditions
of a quasi-military dictatorship have followed.   Officers of the

army and navy have been appointed judges.[1] The naval governor of the Virgin Islands, Admiral Oman, deposed Judge Malmin during the latter's absence in the United States. The United States Circuit Court sent Malmin back, but President Harding intervened, and Judge Malmin was forced to give up his office and to return to the United States. In 1922 Admiral Kittelle, who succeeded Admiral Oman as governor of the Virgin Islands, tried to force the Colonial Council to give him the power to depose judges. When the Council refused he dissolved it.[2]

The early days of American occupation were marked by savage attacks on natives by American marines and sailors stationed in the islands. Though the situation has improved in that respect, there is great dissatisfaction among the natives because the Virgin Islands police, the rank and file of whom are native Negroes, cannot arrest marines and sailors, and the insular courts cannot try them. Under Danish rule the courts of the islands had authority over soldiers and sailors in public places. This is the case in the United States and almost everywhere else in the world.[3]

The fears expressed by the Danish queen and Danish Liberals in 1915 as to American treatment of Negroes have been justified by the introduction of race prejudice into the islands. Danish residents in the islands often married Negro women, and took them to Denmark when they returned. Negroes were invited to official and private social functions. Under American rule native Negroes have been subjected to a social ostracism which they had not known before.

The Naval Government has acted dictatorially in the Colonial Councils, the courts, and the press. In 1922, Rothschild Francis, editor of the *Emancipator* of St. Thomas, and local labour leader, was threatened with censorship because he had criticised editorially the action of the United States in Santo Domingo. The editor of the St. Thomas *Mail Notes* was fined and im-

[1] U. S. Attorney General, "Opinions," v. 31, p. 118.
[2] "Federal Reporter," v. 272, p. 785.
[3] "Nation," v. 116, pp. 650-2.

prisoned for editorial comment. D. Hamilton Jackson, editor
of the St. Croix *Labor Herald,* was sentenced for contempt
of court for the publication of an article. In January, 1923, a
native of the British West Indies was deported from St.
Thomas for criticising the police department in the *Emancipator.*[1]

One of the bitterest complaints of the natives has been regarding their political status. The State Department has ruled
that the Virgin Islands are not a territory but a possession like
the Philippines. Consequently the Constitution of the United
States and all laws which are not locally applicable have no
force in the islands.[2] In 1920 the State Department ruled that
the citizenship status of the islanders is like that of the Filipinos. They are not citizens of the United States, and have not
the civil and political status of citizens. Nevertheless they are
American nationals, owing allegiance to the United States Government and wholly within that government's power. Passports issued to natives of the islands describe them as
"inhabitants of the Virgin Islands entitled to the protection of
the United States." [3] Under this decision, each of the 10,000
Virgin Islanders now residing in New York City is literally "a
man without a country." He is not an American citizen; and
since he is not an alien either, he cannot become a citizen
through naturalization.

Natives may vote only for members of the Colonial Councils,
the local legislatures established under Danish rule and retained
by the Treaty of August 4, 1916. However, voting is restricted to men of twenty-five years or over owning real estate
producing $60 a year or having a personal income of at least
$300 a year. As wages in the islands are extremely low, this
ruling excludes nearly all the industrial workers.[4]

---

[1] "Nation," v. 116, p. 267.
[2] U. S. House For. Aff. Com., "Cession of Danish West Indian
Islands," 1917, pp. 3-4.
[3] U. S. Congress, 66:2; "House Doc." 734, pp. 31-2.
[4] Ibid., p. 8.

As early as 1919 some officials at Washington favoured a change in the status of the islands. A joint congressional committee headed by Senator Kenyon was appointed to investigate conditions in the Virgin Islands. To this committee Secretary of the Navy Daniels wrote: "The Department feels that the time has arrived when some more permanent provision should be made for their government." The joint committee visited the islands and submitted a report early in 1920. After summarizing conditions in the islands the report declared: "It is the judgment of the commission that it is inexpedient to change the existing system of government at present." [1] The commission recommended that a change of government be postponed until the local laws were revised. The revision was completed in 1921 and has been in force ever since.

On the other hand, a Federal Commission appointed in 1924 by the Secretary of Labour to investigate industrial and economic conditions in the islands, recommended that "a new organic act should be passed, so as to authorize the adoption of a new code of laws based upon American ideals and calculated to insure an administration and enforcement of the laws in keeping with American practices. Especially, the courts should be so reorganized that in this important connection the people will enjoy a feeling of confidence, and every man however humble, be assured of 'his day in court.'" The Commission recommended particularly that the Appellate Court for the islands, which is now situated in Philadelphia, out of reach of poverty-stricken islanders, "be made more accessible." [2]

The report adds, however, that "the most perfect political system will not avail to relieve this distress unless founded upon an industrial and economic readjustment of the Virgin Islands." The Commission on its visit to the islands found "unemployment, inadequate wages and even hunger on every hand." Natives engaged in the coaling of vessels, two-thirds of them women, earn about $1.20 a week, while living costs are

[1] U. S. Congress, 66:2; "House Doc." 734, p. 38.
[2] U. S. Virgin Islands, Commission to the, "Report," p. 26.

practically as high as in the United States. Sugar plantation workers receive about forty cents first class and twenty cents second class for a day of nine hours.[1]

When the United States took over the islands they were already running down hill economically. Since then the situation has grown progressively worse. St. Thomas is a port of call, not a port of entry. The Volstead Act and the Supreme Court ruling regarding the carrying of liquor under seal into United States ports has had the effect of diverting shipping from St. Thomas to competing foreign ports of the West Indies.[2] For lack of shipping, the bay rum industry, important to the islands, has declined. Economic distress has also been increased by the recent substitution of oil burning for coal burning ships; this has crippled St. Thomas as a coaling port.[3]

Attempts to obtain economic assistance and a permanent form of civil government have been made by natives. Active in this movement have been the two labour unions of the islands. One of these, at St. Thomas, is affiliated with the American Federation of Labor; the other at St. Croix is independent. A bill abolishing naval rule was drafted in 1924 by the Virgin Islands committee representing natives and American Liberals. It was introduced in the Senate on March 10 by request. The bill (1) provides for a permanent form of civil government for the Virgin Islands; (2) guarantees Bill of Rights similar to the one in effect in Porto Rico; (3) grants citizenship to natives residing in the Virgin Islands or in the United States; and (4) establishes a simplified form of local government.[4]

Meantime abuses under naval rule continue. In the summer of 1924 the natives protested to Governor Philip Williams and to President Coolidge against the appointment of District Attorney George Washington Williams to the post of District Judge in the islands. It was charged that Williams was a white

[1] Ibid., pp. 22–3.
[2] Ibid., p. 4.
[3] U. S. Congress, 66:2; "House Doc." 734, p. 6.
[4] U. S. Congress, 68:1; "Senate Bill," 2786.

Marylander who had brought his racial prejudice to the islands; that in 1923 he had attempted to block the passage of Senate Bill 2786 granting the islands a civil government, and that the bitter feeling existing between him and the natives unfitted him for a judicial post. Despite these protests, Williams was appointed as District Judge.

Chief among the political critics of Williams has been Rothschild Francis, editor of the *Emancipator*, leader of the A. F. of L. labour union at St. Thomas, and a member of the Colonial Council, the local legislature. Francis and Williams have attacked each other in print. On January 6, 1925, Francis was arrested on a charge of criminal libel for publishing an editorial criticising the St. Thomas police department. He was brought for trial before Judge Williams, whose appointment he had actively opposed. It was urged that the political enmity between the judge and the defendant would prevent Williams from rendering a fair decision. Nevertheless, Judge Williams tried his critic without a jury and sentenced him to thirty days in jail for an editorial opinion. Francis appealed the case and criticised his conviction in the *Emancipator*, on the grounds that it was impossible for him to obtain a fair trial under the circumstances. For this editorial he was convicted of contempt of court by Judge Williams on April 25, 1925. In addition to these judicial abuses, the Colonial Council has been dissolved by the Governor for refusing to obey his orders. This is the second time under American naval rule that the local legislature has been dissolved. (For documents in the Francis case and dissolution of Colonial Council, see files of American Civil Liberties Union, 100 Fifth Avenue.)

11. *Summarizing Imperial Policy*

Across Mexico and Central America, through the countries surrounding the Caribbean, as far west as the Philippines, in China and Turkey, the pioneers of the American Empire have been active during the past generation, laying economic and political foundations. There is one principle that dominates the imperial policy on which these fore-runners have been acting. Senator Kenyon's Joint Committee crystallized it in a paragraph dealing with the Virgin Islands:

"It is, of course, generally understood that the United States did not purchase the Virgin Islands as an investment. They were purchased primarily for strategic purposes. St. Thomas and its harbor is the strongest and most easily fortified spot in the West Indies. It can be made for us both an impregnable fortress and a valuable commercial and shipping station." [1]

"An impregnable fortress and a valuable commercial and shipping station,"—military power and economic advantage: it is in these terms that practically the entire imperial program of any of the great modern industrial empires may be summarized. The pattern is simple. Its details and ramifications are endless. For its completion there are required, not months and years, but decades and generations. It is a structure based on deep-lying economic and social forces.

The Philippines lay in the path of these forces. They were conquered by the United States Army and added to the territory of the American Empire. The Virgin Islands were a part of the frame-work. They were bought and paid for, and are now ruled by the United States Navy. Nicaragua and Honduras, Haiti and Cuba, Santo Domingo and Porto Rico, Panama and Colombia are also within the area that falls logically to the share of the United States. They, too, have heard the tramp of United States marines or felt the diplomatic and economic pressure of which the marines are but the symbol.

[1] U. S. Congress, 66:2; "House Doc." 734, p. 7.

VIII

WAR DEBTS AND SETTLEMENTS

1. *War Debts and Financial Imperialism*

Since the opening of the war, in 1917, the United States has established official financial relations with sixteen European countries. These relations have taken the form of loans and credits from the United States Treasury for the purchase of war supplies and for relief and reconstruction. The Treaty obligations imposed on the defeated countries have also played a leading rôle in official post-war imperialism.

Loans are frequently made by one government to another. The war indemnities imposed as a result of the Versailles Treaty are merely the extension and the application of an accepted practice in the struggle for national supremacy. But the loans and indemnities resulting from the War of 1914 are so vast as to give them quite a new significance in international relations.

Strong, rich countries have frequently subjugated poor and weak countries. Originally this was done crudely, by military victory and by slavery. The devices employed subsequent to the recent war, built upon modern business experience, accomplish the result by substituting dictated treaties for vassalage, and guaranteed bonds for slavery.

The really novel feature of the present situation is that the debts between the Allied Nations, resulting from the war, seem to be as onerous, in some cases, as the penalties imposed by the victors upon the vanquished. During the war the Government of the United States loaned to its European Allies about $9,600 million. Under the Treaty and the provisions for reparations payments the United States is a beneficiary in a very minor degree. Germany owes the United States Government nothing beyond some minor claims for war damages and for the costs of the army of occupation, while Great Britain owes about $4.6 billion; France about $4 billion; Italy about $2 billion, and Belgium about half a billion.[1]

2. *War Mortgages*

Similar creditor-debtor relations developed very widely as a result of the War of 1914. The United States was by no means the only lender. From the outset, Great Britain, France and Germany carried a part of the burdens which their weaker allies were unable to shoulder. These inter-ally loans grew, during the war years, to an unprecedented volume. Great Britain, for example, while borrowing heavily from the United States, loaned to Belgium, Czecho-Slovakia, Esthonia, France, Greece, Italy, Latvia, Lithuania, Poland, Russia, and other countries about $11.2 billion. France borrowed largely from both Britain and the United States, while at the same time lending to Belgium, Jugo-Slavia, Roumania, Poland, Russia, Greece, and other nations a total of about $3.5 billion.[2] In fact, practically all of the Baltic and Balkan states have drawn heavily on France during the past eight years.[3]

With the termination of the war and the resumption of normal business relations, each of these debts became, for the lender, a potential source of revenue, both as to interest and principle. The obligations were so large that Britain, had she been able to collect four per cent interest and one per cent sinking fund on her war loans would have been in receipt of about half a billion dollars per year, or the equivalent of one-half of the return on her entire pre-war foreign investment of approximately $20 billion. To be sure, no such payments were made, but the existence of the loans involved potential assets of immense proportions on the one side and potential liabilities of a formidable character on the other.

[1] Fisk, "Inter-Ally Debts," pp. 348-9.
[2] Idem.
[3] "Annuaire Général de la France," 1923, p. 279.

3. *United States Claims Against European Governments*

The United States was the largest lender of the war and the post-war periods, although the loans made by Great Britain were only a little less than those made by the United States. The loans to European Governments under the Liberty Loan Acts were:[1]

		Amounts in Millions
Belgium		$ 349.2
Czecho-Slovakia		67.3
France		2,997.5
Great Britain		4,277.0
Greece		48.2
Italy		1,648.0
Roumania		25.0
Russia		187.7
Serbia		26.8
	Total	$9,626.7

These loans placed nine European governments in the debt of the United States to the extent of more than nine billion. Later they were supplemented by the sale, to these and other European countries, of surplus war material in a total amount of $574.8 million.[2]

The net result is an economic advantage in favour of the United States of such magnitude that if all of these nations should pay four per cent interest and one per cent toward the amortization of the debt, the Treasury of the United States would be in receipt of more than half a billion dollars per year or enough to carry one-fifth of the total federal budget.

4. *The British Debt Settlement* [3]

The situation is well illustrated by the British debt settlement which is evidently regarded both by the British and American Treasury officials as a fair adjustment of these inter-allied financial relations.

[1] U. S. "Statistical Abstract," 1922, p. 555.
[2] Ibid., p. 556.
[3] U. S. World War Foreign Debt Commission, "Great Britain, Proposal, etc."

By mutual agreement, the principal of the British debt to the United States Government was fixed at $4.6 billion, for which the British Government issues 3–3½ per cent bonds at par. Beside paying interest on the bonds the British Government agrees to pay the principal in annual instalments on a fixed schedule, according to which the payments for the first ten years average about $160 million per year and for the following fifty-two years about $180 million per year. Under this arrangement the British Government will pay back $4.6 billion of principal and $6.5 billion of interest, making a total of $11.1 billion. The last payment is due in 1984.

The total net income of the British state for 1923 was 910.8 million pounds Sterling. On the basis of the debt settlement, the demands of the United States for the year 1923 will equal about 3.6 per cent of the total British revenue. Should the revenue remain approximately the same during the next sixty-two years, it will require the equivalent of the total British revenue for two and a quarter years to meet its obligations under the debt settlement plan.

Should the British debt settlement be accepted as a precedent, and a similar arrangement be made with France, Italy and Belgium, the United States would receive, from the treasuries of these four countries alone, about $425 million annually, the last payments being made somewhere about 1985 or 1990. The total volume of these payments, interest and principal, if made in full, would exceed $25 billion.

Britain, France, Italy, and Belgium were the four principal allies of the United States in the War of 1917. The United States fought with them and rendered them economic assistance. The cost to these nations of the economic assistance rendered by the United States will exceed four hundred millions per year for the next half century.

Historically, it is no uncommon thing for the victor to impose onerous burdens upon the vanquished. But there is no modern instance where it has cost four nations $25 billion to call in a sympathetic ally.

There is, of course, no certainty that the debts will be paid, either as to principal or interest. Yet, as the United States Secretary of the Treasury (Mr. Mellon) has repeatedly pointed out, these debts represent business obligations, and should they be scrapped, a serious blow would be struck at the whole creditor-debtor relation upon which modern business rests. If this point of view is finally accepted, and if the British Debt Settlement is followed in principle, sixteen European nations will remain official debtors to the United States until nearly the end of the present century, and capitalist empires, in their future dealings with one another, will be able to point to this very important instance as a precedent for future exactions along similar lines.

5. *Stripping Economic Rivals*

So much for the relation which recent imperial practice establishes among allies who lend and borrow. As a result of the late war the great nations of Europe are actual or potential tribute payers to the United States for at least two generations. The same principle of creditor and debtor, worked out in far more elaborate detail, appears in the treatment accorded to the defeated enemy nations by the victorious Allies. This is particularly true of Germany, which was the strongest, economically, of the defeated nations.

Austria-Hungary was dismembered as a result of the war. Turkey was stripped and humiliated. Germany alone remained to carry the economic burdens which the Allies chose to impose. While the populations of the Allied countries were assured that the war was being waged against militarism and as a means of preserving world peace, the secret treaties, signed in 1915, 1916 and 1917 between the representatives of the various Allied Governments made it very clear that the Allies were seeking important economic advantages.

The Treaty which brought Italy into the War on the side of the Allies (April 26, 1915) contained specific provisions for a loan of $250 million and for the cession of certain territory lying along the Adriatic to Italy. The sixteen articles of this treaty are very precise as to the exact nature of the economic gains which Italy is to receive.[1]

A note from the Minister of Foreign Affairs to the French Ambassador at Petrograd notes that the Government of the Republic intends to demand, among other peace terms, Alsace and Lorraine. "At the same time strong economic demands must be taken into consideration so as to include within French territory the whole of the industrial iron basin of Lorraine and the whole of the industrial coal basin of the valley of the Saar." Later, in a secret telegram to the Russian Ambassador in Paris the aspirations of France are described as including Alsace and Lorraine, the Saar and the establishment of an independent state in the German trans-Rhenish territory.[2]

The same Russian publication gives the essence of the treaty by which it was proposed to divide Turkey, and in addition, the economic offers that were made to Italy and to Greece as a price for joining the cause of the Allies.[3]

Had there remained any doubt as to the economic plans and ambitions of the Allied powers, it was dispelled by the provisions of the Treaty of Versailles. This point has been sufficiently elaborated in a number of books, among which "The Economic Consequences of the Peace"[4] and "Germany's Capacity to Pay"[5] are as well-reasoned and as clear as any others

Keynes points out[4] that the German economic system before the war depended on three main factors:

1. Overseas commerce, represented by the merchant marine, the colonies, foreign investments and overseas business connections;

2. The exploitation of German coal and iron resources, with the interests built on them.

---

[1] Russia, "Secret Diplomatic Documents," p. 13 ff.
[2] Ibid., pp. 19–20.
[3] Ibid., p. 11 ff., 21 ff.
[4] Keynes, "Economic Consequences of the Peace."
[5] Moulton & McGuire, "Germany's Capacity to Pay."

3. The transport and traffic systems inside of Germany. Moulton and McGuire [1] carry this argument one step farther, and show that, through transport, banking, commerce and investment Germany was a heavy buyer and seller in Britain, France, Belgium, Italy, Russia, the Balkans and so on, so that German business was an essential link in the chain of European business.

Two forces contended at the Treaty Table—one that desired to render Germany economically impotent, and the other that desired to make Germany pay for the war. While neither side won a complete victory, the Treaty contained all of the provisions that were considered necessary to destroy the efficiency of German economic life:

1. Germany ceded to the Allies all of her merchant vessels, built and building, of more than 1600 gross tons; half of those between 1000 and 1600 tons, and a quarter of those under 1000 tons; all of the over-seas possessions, thus practically destroying the elaborate commercial system which Germany had erected, and upon which she depended for the purchase of her raw materials and imported food.

2. The iron of Lorraine, the coal of the Saar for a long period, the coal of Upper Silesia, were lost to Germany under the Treaty. In addition, heavy mortgages were laid on the coal of the Ruhr. In 1913, three-quarters of the iron produced in Germany came from Lorraine, while Upper Silesia, the Saar and the Ruhr provided four-fifths of Germany's coal. The Treaty therefore dealt a severe blow to German heavy industry.

3. Under the Dawes Plan the railroads of Germany, which were formerly state owned, pass under the control of a private company.

6. *A Technique of Exploitation*

Ostensibly the Treaty was sufficiently rigorous to destroy Germany's capacity to compete, particularly in the heavy industries. Actually, German heavy industry came back with astonishing rapidity, threatening to take from the French iron masters

[1] Moulton & McGuire, supra.

the markets of Central Europe. The story of this conflict between German and French heavy industry is brilliantly told from the German side by Phillips Price,[1] and on the French side by Francis Delaisi.[2]

There were other critical elements in the situation. The currencies of Germany, Austria, Poland, and certain Baltic and Balkan states passed through a period of disastrous liquidation. The currencies of France, Belgium and Italy threatened to follow the same lead. Such a general dislocation of financial affairs would have added to the chaos in which European economic life found itself in 1923.[3]

Added to this economic dislocation was the political tension incident to the occupation of the Ruhr. When the British Labour Ministry took office, early in 1923, the Ruhr situation seemed likely to involve Britain and France as well as France and Germany in serious controversies. Throughout the year the situation became more aggravated, until finally, on November 30, 1923, the Allied Governments agreed to the appointment by the Reparations Commission of two expert committees to consider the balancing of the German budget, the stabilization of the currency, and to investigate the amount of German capital exported. Two weeks later the Reparations Commission decided to invite Charles G. Dawes and Owen D. Young to serve as American experts in connection with the inquiry into Germany's financial situation. Four months later, on April 9, 1924, the two committees submitted their reports.[4]

Part I of the Dawes Report begins with the words: "We have approached our task as business men anxious to obtain effective results." It is in these terms that the Report must be read and accepted—as an effort of the most advanced business elements of the Allied countries to stabilize the business life of Europe.

There are four particularly significant provisions in the

[1] Price, "Germany in Transition."
[2] "Manchester Guardian Commercial: European Reconstruction," pp. 846-9, 879-82. "Manchester Guardian Commercial," v. 7, pp. 197-8.
[3] "Year Book of the Exchange Rates of the World."
[4] "World Peace Foundation," v. 6, pp. 329-444.

Dawes Plan. The first involves the organization of a bank "entirely free from Government control or interference" which has "the exclusive right to issue paper money in Germany for the period of its charter, fifty years." The bank is under the control of a General Board, consisting of .seven Germans and seven foreigners, one each of the following nationalities: British, French, Italian, Dutch, Belgian, American and Swiss. The Commissioner, or head of this General Board, is to be a foreigner, and while it is true that under the plan ten of the fourteen members of the Board must approve of each proposition involving an issue between the Germans and the Allies, the fact remains that the Bank is under foreign (non-German) control. Thus the ultimate financial policy of Germany is directed by foreigners, and the central financial system of the German Empire is a private and alien institution.

The second important provision involves the assignment, to the Reparations Commission, of the following German Government revenues: receipts from customs, alcohol, tobacco, beer and sugar. All of these revenues, in excess of 1,250 millions of gold marks per year will be turned back to the German Government. This billion and a quarter will be allotted, from the budget, to reparations payments.

The third provision calls for the payment of about 960 million gold marks per year through the bonding of German industry. The railroads, the largest single economic unit in Germany, were Government owned before the Dawes Plan took effect. Under the plan a private company is organized under the direction of a board of eighteen members, nine to be nominated by the German Government and the remaining nine to be named by the trustee of the railway bonds. The railroads have been assessed at 26 billion gold marks. Against this property the new company will issue eleven billions of bonds, two billions of preferred stock and thirteen billions of common stock. The bonds go to a representative of the Reparations Commission; three-fourths of the preferred stock is to be sold by the railroad to provide working capital and to eliminate certain debts; the balance of the preferred stock and all of the common stock goes to the German Government. The bonds carry a five per cent rate of interest, and a payment of one per cent for sinking fund. According to this schedule, the eleven billions of bonds, held by the Reparations Commission, will yield 660 million gold marks per year.

Similar provisions are made in the case of German industry. A bond issue of five billion gold marks is to be issued against German industries. These bonds are also to be held by the Reparations Commission and are to yield the same gross six per cent, or a total of 300 millions.

The fourth provision of the plan is unique. The budget, the railway and industrial bonds, and a transport tax of 290 million gold marks will yield a total of 2,500 gold marks after 1928. Up to that year the amounts are graduated. This is a minimum payment. The Report adds to this minimum an indefinite amount in the form of a Prosperity Index. Trade; budget receipts and expenditures; railroad traffic; value of sugar, tobacco, beer and alcohol consumed; total population, and the consumption of coal are all to be tabulated for the years 1927, 1928 and 1929. The result will be a base on which the Prosperity Index is to be computed. Should these items, for 1930, exceed the base by ten per cent, then in addition to paying 2,500 million gold marks for that year, Germany would pay 2,500 million plus ten per cent, or 2,750 millions in all. In this way, with the years 1927–9 as a base, the prosperity of Germany will be computed, and the payments will be graduated from a minimum of 2,500 millions to a maximum of 5,000 millions, which would mark a hundred per cent increase in prosperity.

At the outset of the Treaty negotiations, an attempt was made to fix an amount which the Germans could pay over a series of years. With the acceptance of the Dawes Report, this effort is abandoned. In its place there is set up a bank, under Allied control, which is the virtual master of German economic life; bonds are issued against the railroads and certain of the industries, from which the Reparations Commission will draw a stated income, supplemented by a budgetary, secured

charge and a transport tax.   In order to insure the Allies
against any considerable increase in the efficiency of German
economic life, there is established a device enabling the Allies
to collect payments in proportion to the economic progress of
Germany.

The payments per year are stated. The Dawes Report
does not specify the number of years during which these payments are to be made.   Virtually, Germany will pay until the
Reparations Commission decides that she has paid enough.

This is the most complete modern system of exploitation
ever devised and applied in the relations between great powers.
Financial empires, dealing with weak and bankrupt countries,
have frequently imposed terms that are equally harsh.   The
Nicaraguan loans, for example, involved more control of the
economic life of that country than does the Dawes Plan in the
case of Germany.   Financial imperialism has meant the adoption
of methods that would insure weak borrowing nations paying
their debts to strong lending nations.   The details of such
transactions have already been given at length.   These methods
have not ordinarily been applied, however, in the dealings
between strong nations.

Ordinarily, in transactions involving a weak and a strong
nation, a simple assignment of revenue is all that is necessary.
The Dawes Report provides additional safeguards in the form
of rail industrial bonds.   Thus the revenues of industry as
well as the revenues of the state are pledged to the payment
of the obligation.

The Dawes Report has won the approval of all of the
principal nations of the world.   It may be accepted, therefore,
as the model which will serve for the guidance of relations
between great empires in the future.

7. The Principles of World Subjugation

The Dawes Plan is a new venture.   The relations between
the nations, resulting from the War of 1914, are as yet so
recent that they will not permit of more than a tentative general-
ization; nevertheless they represent the current results of the

competitive nationalism that has grown up in the world during the present epoch. Western civilization, in its experimenting with new things, has hit upon these methods of international exploitation. Whatever may be said as to their permanence, their reality at the present moment can scarcely be doubted.

Briefly that reality may be formulated into a number of quite obvious axioms or principles upon which the Versailles Treaty, the Treaty of Sèvres and the Dawes Plan were founded:

1. In the case of an enemy defeated in war, some combination of the following practices will be resorted to:
   a. Political dismemberment, as in the case of Austria-Hungary and Turkey.
   b. Or economic dismemberment, as in the case of Germany.
   c. This dismemberment will be carried to the point of economic ruin unless that ruin will also involve the victor nation. In that case,
   d. Indemnities and penalties will be imposed which must be paid over a long series of years, and which will be designed to transfer the surplus of the vanquished nation to the rulers of the victor state.
   e. The collection of this tribute will be made possible by attaching the income of the defeated nation and mortgaging its industrial properties.

2. Automatically, under these rules, the nation with the greatest economic reserves, and which is not defeated in war, will speedily have the whole world, ally as well as enemy, paying tribute into its coffers.

It must be perfectly obvious that the methods heretofore applied by capitalist empires to the exploitation of weaker nations will hereafter be applied to the exploitation of defeated rivals. The principles that have governed the internal affairs of capitalist empires in the past are now being introduced into the world struggle. As to the soundness of these principles, we are not here passing judgment. Their import is to place large sections of the world's populations in a position where they must pay regular tribute to the world's conquering and dominant nationalist groups.

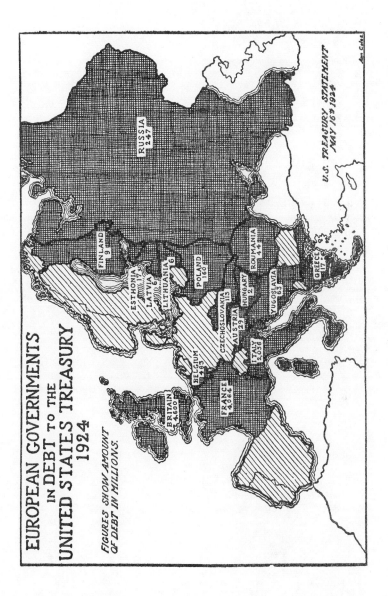

EUROPEAN GOVERNMENTS
IN DEBT TO THE
UNITED STATES TREASURY
1924

FIGURES SHOW AMOUNT
OF DEBT IN MILLIONS.

RUSSIA
247

FINLAND
9

ESTHONIA
17
LATVIA
6
LITHUANIA
6

POLAND
160

ROUMANIA
44

GREECE
17

CZECHOSLOVAKIA
115

AUSTRIA
29

HUNGARY
2

YUGOSLAVIA
63

ITALY
2,056

BELGIUM
483

FRANCE
4,064

BRITAIN
4,600

U.S. TREASURY STATEMENT
MAY 16TH 1924

IX

THE EVOLUTION OF AMERICAN IMPERIAL DIPLOMACY

1. *Imperial Purposes and Requirements*

From the day on which the republic of the United States was established, its foreign policy has paralleled its economic expansion. "Foreign policies," according to Secretary of State Charles E. Hughes, "are not built upon abstractions. They are the result of practical conceptions of national interest arising from some immediate exigency or standing out vividly in historical perspective. . . . Statesmen who carry the burdens of empire do not for a moment lose sight of imperial purposes and requirements."[1] The imperial purposes and requirements of the United States at the foundation of the republic were those involved in conquering the continent which stretched westward toward the Pacific, and in developing the commerce and the manufacture springing up along the Atlantic. The history of the United States during the first half of the nineteenth century is thus an almost unbroken record of territorial acquisition.

Even before the opening of the nineteenth century there were people like Alexander Hamilton who saw visions of an American empire uniting the United States, Central America and South America into a "great American system, superior to the control of all trans-Atlantic force of influence, and able to dictate the terms of connection between the Old and the New World."[2] The natural wealth of the Western Hemisphere led

[1] "Annals," v. 111, "Supplement," p. 7.
[2] "Federalist," no. 11, p. 58.

Washington as early as 1788 to hope that "the United States of America will be able to keep disengaged from the labyrinth of European politics and wars." [1]   In his Farewell Address he laid the cornerstone of the foreign policy which the United States followed for over half a century: "The great rule of conduct for us, in regard to foreign nations, is, in extending our commercial relations, to have with them as little political connection as possible. . . . It is true policy to steer clear of permanent alliances with any portion of the foreign world; so far, I mean, as we are now at liberty to do it." [2]   In the same way Jefferson laid down the policy of "peace, commerce and honest friendship with all nations, entangling alliances with none." [3]

The first corrollary to this policy of isolation was established in connection with the acquisition of new territory in 1803, when Jefferson, a life-long anti-expansionist on principle, was forced by the growing economic demands of the new nation to purchase the Louisiana tract from the French.   This met the demand for new land temporarily.   In 1810 Spanish subjects seized Baton Rouge and declared it independent.   President Madison believed that Spain was about to sell West Florida. The United States thereupon occupied that section over the protests of Great Britain, and Congress passed, on January 15, 1811, a resolution declaring that "the United States, under the peculiar circumstances of the existing crisis, cannot, without serious inquietude, see any part of the said territory pass into the hands of any foreign power; and that a due regard to their own safety compels them to provide, under certain contingencies, for the temporary occupation of the said territory." [4] Thus, under the necessity of territorial expansion, American foreign policy laid down the two rules that there was to be (1) no American interference in European affairs and (2) no European interference in American affairs.

---

[1] Washington, "Writings," v. 9, pp. 398–402.
[2] Ibid., v. 12, pp. 231–2.
[3] Jefferson, "Writings," v. 8, p. 4.
[4] U. S. "Statutes at Large," v. 3, p. 471.

2. The Monroe Doctrine

At this period, taking advantage of the turmoil following the Napoleonic wars, the Spanish colonies of South America revolted and declared themselves republics. In May, 1822, at the request of President Monroe that the United States recognize the South American colonies as independent states, Congress voted an appropriation to make the recognition effectual. On November 22, 1822, the Holy Alliance of Austria, Russia, Prussia and Great Britain met in Congress at Verona and signed a secret treaty "to put an end to the system of representative governments, in whatever country it may exist in Europe, and to prevent its being introduced in those countries where it is not yet known." [1]

Cotton had been enthroned in the South since the invention of the cotton gin in 1792; new cotton lands were in continuous demand; the slave states of the South, already exercising an enormous influence over the Federal Government, were searching for slave states to offset the free states growing up in the north-west, and were already pushing toward Florida and Texas, and thought of acquiring Cuba. The progress of the Holy Alliance would have made this impossible.

Great Britain opposed the plot of the Holy Alliance to restore the Latin-American colonies to Spain, and the British prime minister, Canning, proposed to join the United States in a declaration favouring the independence of the South American republics. Britain's reason for giving up her principle of "legitimacy" in this case was her rapidly increasing trade with Latin America which restoration to Spain would damage. The joint declaration which Canning proposed contained the following pledges: "We aim not at the possession of any portion of them ourselves. . . . We could not see any portion of them transferred to any other power with indifference." [2]

The chief opponent in President Monroe's cabinet of Canning's proposal was John Quincy Adams, at that time Secretary of State.

[1] Elliot, "American Diplomatic Code," v. 2, p. 179.
[2] Mahony, "Monroe Doctrine," p. 35.

"The object of Canning," he argued, "appears to have been . . . really or especially against the acquisition to the United States themselves of any part of the Spanish American possessions. . . . By joining with her (Britain), therefore, . . we give her a substantial and perhaps inconvenient pledge against ourselves, and really obtain nothing in return. . . . Without entering now into the enquiry of the expediency of our annexing Texas or Cuba to our Union, we should at least keep ourselves free to act as emergencies may arise, and not tie ourselves down to any principle which might immediately afterwards be brought to bear against ourselves." [1]   Instead of a joint declaration with Great Britain, Adams urged a separate and distinct declaration by the United States.

The situation was further complicated by Russia's claims to the Northwest Territory down to the fifty-first parallel, and the plans of Russian traders to establish a post in what is now California. In July, 1823, Adams informed the Russian ambassador "specially that we should contest the right of Russia to *any* territorial establishment on this continent, and that we should assume distinctly the principle that the American continents are no longer subjects for *any* new European colonial establishments." [2]

This idea was embodied in President Monroe's message of December 2, 1823, which laid down the principles of what has since been known as the Monroe Doctrine. Monroe's message reaffirmed the policy of "no entangling alliance" by declaring that Europe and America were different and incompatible; it emphasized the fact that Europe's political systems were not to be extended to the Western Hemisphere; and finally it declared that the period of colonization was at an end.

"Our policy, in regard to Europe, which was adopted at an early stage of the wars which have so long agitated that quarter of the globe, nevertheless remains the same, which is, not to interfere in the internal concerns of any of its powers; to consider the government *de facto* as the legitimate government for us. . . .

[1] Adams, "Memoirs," v. 6, pp. 177–8.
[2] Ibid., p. 163.

But, in regard to these (the American) continents, circumstances are eminently and conspicuously different. It is impossible that the allied powers should extend their political system to any portion of either continent, without endangering our peace and happiness; nor can anyone believe that our Southern Brethren, if left to themselves, would adopt it. . . . The occasion has been judged proper for asserting, as a principle in which the rights and interests of the United States are involved, that the American continents, by the free and independent condition which they have assumed and maintain, are henceforth not to be considered as subjects for future colonization by any European powers." [1]

This doctrine left the way open for Americans themselves to colonize the unoccupied sections of the continent, without European rivalry. Madison had already broached the idea that the whole Gulf Stream was American water; Monroe's declaration was aimed at Russian manœuvres in the north-west. Its immediate effect was that in 1824 Russia concluded a treaty with the United States fixing the parallel of 54–40′ as the southern limit of Russia's possessions in America. This added a link to the claim of the United States to the Oregon territory contested by Great Britain. The Monroe Doctrine fitted the needs of American territorial expansion.

3. Early Applications of the Monroe Doctrine

Among the foreign powers which saw in the Monroe Doctrine a threat to European empire and an indication of American territorial and commercial expansion was France, whose foreign minister, Chateaubriand, declared that the Doctrine "ought to be resisted by all the Powers possessing either territorial or commercial interest in that Hemisphere." [2] That the United States seriously intended to apply the Monroe Doctrine was made clear two years later. In 1825 it was rumoured that Spain intended to sell Cuba to France. When a French fleet arrived in Cuba the State Department at once declared that the United States would under no circumstances

---

[1] U. S. "Foreign Relations," 1823, pp. 14–15, 5.
[2] Hart, "Monroe Doctrine," p. 84.

permit any power other than Spain to hold Cuba or Porto Rico. The French fleet was withdrawn.[1]

In the same year the newly emancipated Spanish-American republics called a congress at Panama to which they invited the United States. Henry Clay advocated accepting the invitation, but a storm of opposition was raised by the slaveholding South, which was opposed to the emancipation of Negroes in Cuba and would not tolerate sitting at Panama with the delegates from Haiti and Santo Domingo, whom they considered Negroes. In fact, with the South becoming dominant in national politics, the official policy of the United States was becoming opposed to the policy of the new Spanish-American republics. Whereas these wanted to free Cuba and Porto Rico, which were still Spanish colonies, the United States wanted them to remain in the possession of Spain; for so long as the islands belonged to Spain they could be bought or conquered by the United States, but if they became free their sovereignty would stand in the way of America's expansion.[2] Eventually President Adams appointed delegates to the all-American conference at Panama, but the opposition of the South served to delay their arrival, and they came too late to a gathering which in the end miscarried.

In 1843, Cuba was again the touchstone of the Monroe Doctrine. The State Department, then under the direction of Daniel Webster, had occasion to reaffirm its determination not to allow the status of Cuba to be changed until such time as the United States should see fit to annex it. When a British fleet was reported on its way to Cuba, Webster stated that "the Spanish Government has long been in possession of the policy and wishes of this Government in regard to Cuba, which have never changed, and has repeatedly been told that the United States would never permit the occupation of that island by British agents or forces upon any pretext whatever; and that in the event of any attempt to wrest it from her, she might securely rely upon the whole naval and military re-

[1] U. S. "Foreign Relations," 1825, p. 855.
[2] Fish, "American Diplomacy," p. 217.

sources of this country to aid her in preserving or recovering it." [1]

A direct application of the Monroe Doctrine by name to American territorial expansion was made by President Polk in 1845. Polk had been elected on a platform pledged to the annexation of Texas, which had been wrested from Mexico by American slave-holders who had colonized the territory, and to the annexation of Oregon, which was demanded by the settlers in the north-west. In his message to Congress on December 2, Polk, referring to British claims to Oregon, declared: "It is well known to the American people and to all nations, that this government has never interfered with the relations subsisting between other governments. . . . We may claim on this continent a like exemption from European interference. . . . The present is deemed a proper occasion to reiterate and reaffirm the principle avowed by Mr. Monroe, and to state my cordial concurrence in its wisdom and sound policy." [2] The annexation of Texas which followed and the Mexican war which it provoked added immense territory to the domain of the slave-holding oligarchy. Polk's interpretation of the Monroe Doctrine, backed up by the force of American arms, rounded out the republic by the addition of Texas, New Mexico and upper California. Later, through negotiation, the Oregon territory was added.

Having pushed their power as far as the Gulf and the Rio Grande, the slave states proceeded to take up the old plan of annexing Cuba. On January 17, 1848, President Polk, in a secret dispatch, authorized R. M. Saunders, the United States Minister to Madrid, to offer Spain $100,000,000 for Cuba. Spain turned the offer down. [3] From that time until the Civil War the annexation of Cuba was one of the burning political issues. Between 1840 and 1852, American filibusters devoted to the slave system, aided Cuban uprisings against Spain. President Fillmore issued a proclamation forbidding the organiza-

---

[1] Crichfield, "American Supremacy," p. 442.
[2] U. S. "Foreign Relations," 1846, p. 14.
[3] Polk, "Diary," v. 3, p. 493.

tion of filibustering expeditions on American soil and ordered the civil, naval, and military authorities at the ports of New York and New Orleans to prevent such expeditions from sailing.[1]

The South, however, continued to support filibusterers in Cuba, and when some of them were captured and executed by the Spanish authorities in Cuba, riots broke out against the Spaniards in New Orleans and the Spanish consulate was mobbed. Passion ran so high in the slave-holding states that France and Great Britain ordered their fleets in West Indian waters to repel by force "any adventurers of any nation from landing with hostile intent upon the island of Cuba." [2]

Though President Fillmore had himself forbidden filibustering, he now (1852) invoked the spirit of the Monroe Doctrine and declared that the United States regarded this naval demonstration as ill-advised.[3] In reply, the French minister proposed that if at some future time Spain should part with Cuba, "the possession of that island, or the protectorship of the same, ought not to fall upon any of the great maritime powers of the world." The United States turned this proposal down.[4]

The question of Cuban annexation continued to agitate the country. It was an issue in the presidential campaign of 1852. While the South was agitating for annexation and attempting to create revolts in Cuba, American vessels landing on the island were now and again seized and searched by the Spanish authorities. Claims were filed but the Spanish Government refused reparation. Partly as a threat to bring about a settlement and partly to announce a sharp foreign policy President Pierce in 1854 requested the United States ministers to Spain, Great Britain and France "to compare opinions and to adopt measures for perfect concert of action in aid of the negotiations at Madrid." [5] These three ministers all came from below the Mason and Dixon line and were intimately connected with the

---

[1] U. S. Congress, 32:1; "Sen. Ex. Doc." 1, p. 27.
[2] Ibid., p. 74.
[3] Curtis, "Life of Webster," p. 551.
[4] U. S. Congress, 32:1; "Sen. Ex. Doc." 1, p. 81.
[5] "American History Leaflets," no. 2, p. 2.

Southérn slave-holding autocracy. They met at Ostend and drew up a manifesto which, instead of confining itself to the claims at Madrid, urged the annexation of Cuba.

The United States, they declared in the Ostend Manifesto, ought "to buy Cuba because of its nearness to our coast; because it belonged naturally to that great group of States of which the Union was the providential nursery; because it commanded the mouth of the Mississippi whose immense and annually growing trade must seek that way to the ocean, and because the Union could never enjoy repose, could never be secure, till Cuba was within its boundaries." [1] They also urged that if Spain refused to sell Cuba the United States should wrest it by force of arms.[2] The Ostend Manifesto was promptly repudiated by the State Department, but the question of Cuban annexation continued to stir the country. It was a feature in the Lincoln-Douglas debates of 1858 and was fought over in Congress the following year.

The outbreak of the Civil War postponed action on the Cuban issue; but in another direction European interference in the Western Hemisphere gave the Lincoln administration an opportunity to assert the Monroe Doctrine once more. Mexico, which had gained its independence from Spain in 1821, was disturbed by a series of revolutionary outbreaks from 1851 to 1859, during which the Mexican Government went into bankruptcy. In 1861 the Mexican Congress voted to defer payment on foreign bonds. France, Great Britain and Spain signed an agreement to collect their debts, and on October 31 their ships seized the customs houses at Vera Cruz and proceeded to collect duties. Eventually Spain and Great Britain withdrew, but Napoleon III, taking advantage of America's preoccupation with the Civil War, decided to set up a Mexican empire which would resist the expansion of the United States toward the south. The Austrian Prince Maximilian was named emperor, and all Seward could do was to protest mildly.[3]

[1] McMaster, "History of the People of U. S.," v. 8, pp. 185-6.
[2] Rhodes, "History of U. S.," v. 2, p. 41.
[3] Mahony, "Monroe Doctrine," pp. 48-9.

When the Civil War was over, however, Washington was in a position to take more vigorous measures. On April 4, 1864, the House of Representatives passed a resolution that "it does not accord with the policy of the United States to acknowledge any monarchical government erected on the ruins of any republican government in America under the auspices of any European power." [1] The following year more than 100,000 federal troops, released from the war, were massed on the Mexican border, and Secretary of State Seward notified France that ".the presence and operations of a French army in Mexico, and its maintenance of an authority there, resting upon force and not the free will of the people of Mexico, is a cause of serious concern to the United States." [2] On February 12, 1866, the French army was withdrawn; with its support gone, Maximilian was executed, and his empire wiped out.

4. Commercial Diplomacy

Until the Civil War the foreign policy of the United States was fundamentally in the service of territorial expansion, and was particularly influenced by the need of the South for more slave territory. The triumph of the North in the Civil War meant the end of the slave power and the rise of a new industrial civilization. The new order did not for the time being need additional territory. There were three thousand miles from coast to coast of vast forest tracts, mineral deposits, and fertile land; there were railroads to be built, factories to be established, and banks to be opened. Manufacturing plants increased at a tremendous rate supplying a growing national market. Toward the last two decades of the nineteenth century American manufacturers had reached the stage where a surplus had been created which could not be disposed of in the home market. By 1880 the foreign commerce of the United States had reached a value of 93 million dollars; by 1898 it had risen to 223 million dollars. The great change of

[1] Moore, "Digest of International Law," v. 6, p. 496.
[2] U. S. Congress, 39:1; "Sen. Ex. Doc." 6, p. 71.

this period has been well described in a recent circular issued by the Bankers Trust Company of New York:

"In the first century of our national existence, our producers were primarily concerned with meeting the local demand which steadily increased with our enormous growth in population, and were content to leave the foreign markets to the producers of the older countries excepting only those raw materials of which we have always had a surplus. The tremendous development of our manufactures in recent years, however, totally changes the aspect of our trade. We can no longer maintain our conservative attitude of doing business in our own way and on our own terms. The exigencies of foreign trade force us not only to meet the requirements as we find them, but to seek the best methods of stimulating the demand for American products in the markets of South America, Russia and the Orient, if we would more successfully meet the competition of the European producers.

"Our prosperity will be permanent only when a market can be found for all the goods we can produce. . . . In order to keep invested capital employed at the point of most economical production, by finding a market for all it can produce, our manufacturers are compelled to seek constantly greater outlets in foreign trade. . . ." [1]

In its need for markets, the United States turned to South America. James G. Blaine, leader of the Republican Party, and political spokesman for the manufacturing classes, described the new commercial policy of the American government as follows: "We seek the conquests of peace. We desire to extend our commerce, and in an especial degree with our friends and neighbors on this continent. . . . While the great powers of Europe are steadily enlarging their colonial domination in Asia and Africa, it is the especial province of this country to improve and expand its trade with the nations of America. No field promises so much. No field has been cultivated so little. Our foreign policy should be an American policy in its broadest and most comprehensive sense,—a policy of peace, of friendship, of commercial enlargement." [2] As a result of Blaine's efforts— known as the "Big Sister" policy—Congress passed a bill in

[1] Bankers Trust Company, "Our United States," pp. 24-5.
[2] Blaine, "Letter Accepting Nomination for President," pp. 15-6.

1888 convoking a Pan-American congress. This conference of American states met at Washington in 1889. Blaine, in his capacity as Secretary of State, presided. He did his utmost to secure the commercial supremacy of the United States in Latin America through the formation of a customs union in which "the United States, supplanting Europe, should become the industrial provider of the agricultural nations in Latin America."[1] Blaine and the State Department also sought to open markets for American goods in Spanish America by reciprocity treaties with Brazil, Honduras, Nicaragua, and with Spain for Cuba and Porto Rico.

The results of the first Pan-American congress were slight. The United States was not yet in an economic position to export large enough quantities of goods to capture the South American markets. European countries, particularly Great Britain, had large investments in South America and extensive commercial relations; the United States, being herself dependent on Europe for the capital necessary for the exploitation of its own vast resources, was not yet ready to invest in Latin America. Another obstacle to increasing commerce was the lack of direct communications by land or by sea between the two continents of the western hemisphere. The only permanent result of the conference of 1889 has been the Pan-American conference which meets to this day.

5. The Dawn of Modern Imperial Diplomacy

The year 1878 marked a turning point in the history of the world. "From that date the relations between European nations were less affected by questions arising in Europe itself than by the struggle carried on outside of Europe for the possession of colonies and markets."[2] In that year the Congress of Berlin marked the entrance of Europe on the path of modern economic imperialism; in that same year the United States signed a treaty which passed unnoticed at the time, but which silently foreshadowed America's first step as a modern

[1] Viallate, "Economic Imperialism," p. 29.
[2] Ibid., p. 19.

imperialistic power. The treaty was with the kingdom of Samoa, below the equator in the southern part of the Pacific. It gave the United States the right to use the harbour of Pagopago in the island of Tutuila as a naval station. In return the United States promised that "if, unhappily, any differences shall have arisen, or shall hereafter arise, between the Samoan Government and any other Government in amity with the United States, the Government of the latter will employ its good offices for the purpose of adjusting those differences upon a satisfactory and solid foundation."[1] The treaty was used by the State Department to maintain the independence of Samoa and to prevent its control by Germany or Great Britain. This became evident in 1885 when the German consul at Samoa, under pretext of an agreement with King Malietoa, raised the German flag over the royal hut, and the United States protested. The following year the American consul proclaimed a formal American protectorate over Samoa. His act was at once repudiated by the State Department, and under the treaty of 1888 Washington sent a committee to investigate the conflict and to reach an agreement with the German and British consuls.[2] The situation became so tense by 1889 that American, German, and British warships arrived in Samoan waters and there was talk of war; a clash was avoided only by a hurricane which drove the ships to shelter and the officials to reconsider the issues.[3] By the General Act of Berlin, Samoa was made a protectorate of Great Britain, Germany and the United States. Thus, in taking up again its expansion westward, the United States left its own shores, crossed half an ocean and entered into an international agreement which, according to Secretary of State Gresham, was a departure from our "traditional and well-established policy of avoiding entangling alliances with foreign powers in relation to objects remote from this hemisphere."[4]

[1] U. S. Congress, 50:1; "House Ex. Doc." 238, pp. 124-5.
[2] Ibid., p. 19
[3] Fish, "American Diplomacy," p. 401.
[4] Beard, "Contemporary American History," p. 203.

The Samoan episode was a minor event in a tremendous imperialist movement which was beginning to take shape in the United States. While the bulk of American industries were still absorbed in exploiting the domestic field, others, such as the sugar interests, were beginning to spread out to Cuba, Porto Rico, and Hawaii. It was this fact which produced a change in American diplomacy. Just as American foreign policy in the first half of the nineteenth century had been accommodated to the need of territorial expansion, and later had become essentially commercial to meet the needs of the rising manufacturing class, it now assumed, in addition, the rôle of assisting American investments in foreign, and particularly tropical, countries. The United States was beginning to reach the point which had driven European countries into the Far East and into Africa. The search for markets and for trade was now supplemented by the search for opportunities to invest capital abroad. Since 1844, when Caleb Cushing was sent to open the doors of trade with China, the Far East had become an important American market. Furthermore, the United States had the largest Pacific coastline in the world. The importance of Hawaii as a source for raw material, in this case sugar, as an uncultivated tropical country where American capital could find investment, and as a stepping stone to a rapidly expanding trade with Asia, was frankly stated by Secretary of State Hamilton Fish as early as 1873.

"There seems to be a strong desire on the part of many persons in the islands, representing large interests and great wealth, to become annexed to the United States. And while there are . . . many and influential persons in this country who question the policy of any insular acquisitions, perhaps even any extension of territorial limits, there are also those of influence and of wise foresight who see a future that must extend the jurisdiction and the limits of this nation, and that will require a resting spot in the mid-ocean, between the Pacific coast and the vast domains of Asia, which are now opening to commerce and Christian civilization." [1]

[1] Fish, supra, p. 404.

As the American sugar planters in Hawaiian islands became more and more insistent that the United States take over the islands, the State Department adjusted itself to the tactics required by modern economic imperialism. "Throughout the continent, north and south," Secretary of State Blaine wrote in 1881 in a confidential dispatch to the American minister of Hawaii, "wherever a foothold is found for American enterprise, it is quickly occupied, and this spirit of adventure, which seeks its outlet in the mines of South America and the railroads of Mexico, would not be slow to avail itself of openings of assured and profitable enterprise even in ·mid-ocean." Having marked Hawaii for its own, the United States at first fell back on the policy of watchful waiting that it had followed in the early part of the nineteenth century toward Cuba and South America. Because of the alleged "priority of our interests" it refused in 1888 to join with France and England in a joint guarantee of the independence of the Hawaiian Government.[1]

The revolution engineered by American investors in Hawaii, the assistance rendered by the American minister, and the final annexation of the islands in 1898, has been dealt with in another chapter. As the annexation of Hawaii marked a profound change in American economic development, so the conduct of the American minister marked a corresponding change in foreign policy. It was the beginning of a diplomacy which was to serve the requirements of American investments in foreign countries, as the old diplomacy served the requirements of territorial expansion and of commerce. In the last decade of the nineteenth century American capital was still sunk in the development of domestic industries and in organizing gigantic trusts. Prior to the Spanish-American War, however, an occasion arose for the United States once more to assert the Monroe Doctrine with its implication of the supremacy of the United States in the western hemisphere. Great Britain and Venezuela disputed the boundary line of British Guiana. The

[1] Fish, supra, pp. 403–4.

issue involved some 30,000 square miles of territory. Venezuela had offered to submit the question to arbitration, but
Great Britain refused. During Cleveland's second administration the State Department urged Great Britain to arbitrate.
Finally President Cleveland decided to intervene in the dispute.
In 1895 Secretary of State Richard Olney notified Great
Britain that . . . "Today the United States is practically
sovereign on this continent, and its fiat is law upon the subjects
to which it confines its interposition. Why? It is not because
of the pure friendship or good will felt for it. It is not simply
by reason of its high character as a civilized state, nor because
wisdom and justice and equity are the invariable characteristics
of the dealings of the United States. It is because in addition
to all other grounds, its infinite resources combined with its
isolated position render it master of the situation and practically
invulnerable against any or all other powers." [1] This militant
extension of the Monroe Doctrine was supported in President
Cleveland's message to Congress of that year, which declared
that the acquisition of territory in the western hemisphere
through the arbitrary advance of a boundary line was a violation
of the Monroe Doctrine, and asked Congress for an appropriation to finance a commission to decide on the boundary line. It
would be the duty of the United States to uphold the findings of
this commission, President Cleveland declared, and added: "In
making these recommendations I am fully alive to the responsibility incurred and keenly realize all the consequences that may
follow." [2] Congress voted the appropriation, and excitement
ran so high in this country and in England that the two nations
seemed to be on the point of war. However, before the
American boundary commission concluded its investigation,
Great Britain agreed to arbitrate the matter.

6. *The Far-Flung Battle Line*

America's emergence as a modern imperialist power became a
generally recognized fact with the outbreak of the Spanish-

[1] U. S. "Foreign Relations," 1895, p. 558.
[2] U. S. "Congressional Record," v. 28, p. 191.

American War, the avowed object of which was the liberation of Cuba from Spanish domination. The interest of the United States in annexing Cuba, it has been pointed out, was as old as the United States. Following the Civil War the chief aim of the State Department in regard to Cuba was the extension of commercial relations with the island and the protection of American interests there. During the Ten Years War from 1868–1878, in which Cuba sought to break away from Spain, the United States threatened to intervene, with the implication of annexing the island.[1] In 1895 Cuba began its final insurrection against Spain, and a bitter struggle followed in which the insurrectionists carried on a guerilla war while the Spaniards herded the population into concentration camps.

In addition to the unbroken interest which the United States had shown toward Cuban annexation for almost a century, American investments in Cuba by 1893 amounted to over $50,000,000; the trade of the United States with the island had reached a value of $100,000,000; while American claims amounted to over $16,000,000.[2] Consequently the McKinley administration, which took office in 1897, began to negotiate with Spain for a cessation of hostilities.

Spain offered to grant Cuba autonomy, but the insurrectionists insisted on complete independence. On January 13, 1898, a riot took place in Havana as a deliberate demonstration against the plan for autonomy; and the American consul-general advised Washington that a warship might be necessary to protect Americans in Havana. The *Maine* was promptly dispatched and anchored in Havana harbour on January 25. Meantime the Hearst press, which had been carrying on a sensational campaign for war, published a private letter written by the Spanish ambassador at Washington, in which President McKinley was criticised for "keeping on good terms with the jingoes of his party." [3] This letter, according to Secretary of State Day, was "surreptitiously if not criminally obtained." [4]

[1] Latané, "U. S. and Latin America," p. 124.
[2] U. S. "Congressional Record," v. 31, p. 3776.
[3] Latané, supra, p. 129.
[4] U. S. "Foreign Relations," 1898, p. 680.

However, it served its purpose; the popular clamour for war increased. On the evening of February 15 the *Maine* blew up in the harbour of Havana, and two officers and 258 men were killed. Although "there was no evidence whatever that any one connected with the exercise of Spanish authority in Cuba had had so much as guilty knowledge of the plans made to destroy the *Maine*"[1] it was assumed that the ship had been blown up by the Spanish, and the demand for war became louder.

Meantime the American Minister at Madrid was discussing the purchase of Cuba by the United States. On March 17, 1898, he wrote to the Secretary of State that "if we have war we must finally occupy and ultimately own the island. If today we could purchase at reasonable price we should avoid the horrors and expense of war."[2] Spain refused to sell; but in response to an offer by President McKinley for an armistice with the Cuban revolutionists and adjustment through the assistance of the United States, the Spanish government offered to submit the question involved in the explosion of the *Maine* to arbitration, and to leave the pacification of the island to a Cuban parliament.[3] Representatives of Germany, Austria-Hungary, France, Great Britain, Italy, and Russia made a formal appeal to President McKinley for peace, and the Pope prevailed upon Spain to suspend hostilities. By this time most of the disputed points between the United States and Spain had been settled; there were no Americans in Cuban prisons; the reconcetrado policy had been stopped; American relief had been admitted on the island; arbitration of the *Maine* incident had been offered; and amnesty had been granted.[4] Nevertheless, President McKinley submitted the question to Congress on April 11 in a message which practically made no mention of Spain's offer of peace.

The president's message and the debates on it in Congress

[1] Wilson, "History of the American People," v. 5, p. 270.
[2] U. S. "Foreign Relations," 1898, p. 688.
[3] Latané, supra, p. 131.
[4] Fish, "American Diplomacy," p. 415.

showed that the interest of the United States in the fate of Cuba was not entirely humanitarian. Senators pointed out that "for three-fourths of a century this Government has persistently asserted its right to control the ultimate destiny of Cuba." [1] The message advocated "the forcible intervention of the United States as a neutral to stop the war" on the following grounds:

"First. In the cause of humanity and to put an end to the barbarities, bloodshed, starvation, and horrible miseries now existing there. . . . Second. We owe it to our citizens in Cuba to afford them that protection and indemnity for life and property which no government there can or will afford. . . . Third. The right to intervene may be justified by the very serious injury to the commerce, trade, and business of our people and by the wanton destruction of property and devastation of the island. Fourth, and which is of the utmost importance. The present condition of affairs in Cuba is a constant menace to our peace, and entails upon this Government an enormous expense.[2]

American "trade has suffered," the message said; "the capital invested by our citizens in Cuba has been largely lost." [3] What McKinley's real intentions toward "Cuba libre" were, he indicated in the following words:

"Nor from the standpoint of expediency do I think it would be wise or prudent for this Government to recognize at the present time the independence of the so-called Cuban Republic. Such recognition is not necessary in order to enable the United States to intervene and pacify the island. To commit this country now to the recognition of any particular government in Cuba might subject us to embarrassing conditions of international obligation toward the organization so recognized. In case of intervention our conduct would be subject to the approval or disapproval of such government. We would be required to submit to its direction and to assume to it the mere relation of a friendly ally." [4]

On April 19 Congress passed a joint resolution declaring that "the people of the Island of Cuba are, and of right ought to be, free and independent, and that the Government of the

---

[1] U. S. "Congressional Record," v. 31, p. 3789.
[2] Ibid., p. 3701.
[3] Idem.
[4] Idem.

United States hereby recognizes the Republic of Cuba as the true and lawful government of that island," and empowered the President to use the army and navy to carry out the provisions of the resolution. That there were elements in the United States opposed to the annexation of Cuba was indicated by the addition of the Taller amendment which declared that "the United States hereby disclaims any disposition or intention to exercise sovereignty, jurisdiction, or control over said island, except for the pacification thereof, and asserts its determination when that is accomplished to leave the government and control of the island to its people."[1] Two days later President McKinley ordered a blockade of Cuban ports and the war was on. At the same time Commodore George Dewey, in command of the Asiatic squadron at Hongkong, was ordered to proceed to Manila Bay in the Philippine Islands, which belonged to Spain, and to capture or destroy the Spanish fleet there.[2]

7. America: An Oriental Power

War having been declared to liberate Cuba, what was an American fleet doing in the Philippines? During the autumn of 1897, while humanitarian appeals were being made on Cuba's behalf, Commodore Dewey had approached Assistant Secretary of the Navy Theodore Roosevelt and asked for the command of the Asiatic squadron in expectation of a war with Spain. He obtained the command; on February 25, 1898, almost two months before war was declared, Roosevelt wired Dewey: "Order the squadron to Hongkong. Keep full of coal. In the event of declaration of war Spain, your duty will be to see that the Spanish squadron does not leave the Asiatic coast, and then offensive operations in Philippine Islands."[3] The meaning of this secret order and of America's interest in the Philippine Islands did not become clear until, after a brief conflict of four months, in which the United States easily defeated Spain on land and water, a peace treaty was signed at Paris on Decem-

[1] U. S. "Foreign Relations," 1898, p. 761.
[2] Latané, supra, p. 134.
[3] Rhodes, "McKinley and Roosevelt Administrations," p. 70.

ber 10, 1898, and ratified by Congress on February 6, 1899.

The Treaty provided for the independence of Cuba, the cession of Porto Rico, Guam, and the Philippines to the United States, and the payment of 20 million dollars by the United States to Spain for the Philippines.[1] The instructions which the American peace commissioners received and the subsequent discussion of the peace treaty revealed that the Philippines were acquired to meet the demands of expanding industry and commerce. Admiral Dewey received at Hongkong on August 13, 1898, the following message from the Navy Department: "The President desires to receive from you any important information you may have of the Philippines; the desirability of the several islands; the character of their population; coal and other mineral deposits; their harbor and commercial advantages, and in a naval and commercial sense which would be most advantageous." Admiral Dewey replied that "Luzon is in all respects the most desirable to retain. Contains most important commercial ports. Manila is farthest north. Produces all of the good tobacco. . . . Possible rich minerals. . . . Subig Bay best harbor for coaling purposes and military. Water deep; land-locked; easily defended. ' Strategically, command of bay and city of Manila, with arsenal at Cavite, most valuable." [2] The chief reason for taking the Philippines was not only their own value as sources of raw material, but what is more important, their strategic position for trade with China. The Philippines were to be for the United States what Kiauchow was for Germany and Hongkong for Great Britain: a base for developing America's growing sphere of influence in Manchuria.[3] "The ruling motive for accepting the responsibility (of taking over the Philippines) was commercial; given those islands, it was said, our trade with Asia must be large." [4]

---

[1] MacDonald, "Documentary Source Book of American History," pp. 602–8.

[2] U. S. Navy Dept., "Annual Report," 1898, v. 2, pp. 122–3. Pettigrew, "Triumphant Plutocracy," p. 320.

[3] See Chapter III.

[4] Viallate, "Economic Imperialism," p. 34. "Annals," v. 13; "Supplement," p. 109.

From 1889 to 1898 the value of American exports to China was $62,289,980, of which 87 per cent was made up of cotton cloth and refined mineral oil.[1] From 1890 until the outbreak of the Spanish-American War, American exports to China had increased threefold, so that by 1898 our entire volume of trade with that country equalled "that of the whole of continental Europe, outside of Russia."[2] The value of the Philippines as a base for Chinese trade was thus described by the Secretary of the American Asiatic Association in 1899: "Had we no interests in China, the possession of the Philippines would be meaningless. . . . In December, 1897, it became evident that a situation had been created under which the trade and treaty rights secured by the United States in China might be seriously imperilled. These had already been adversely affected by an agreement made in regard to the Russo-Manchurian Railway, in which it was provided that" Russia pay one-third less duty than other nations. "The existing status had been further threatened by the virtual supremacy of Russia in Manchuria and the Liaotung Peninsula and the consequent danger that the treaty port of Newchwang—more than half of whose imports of cotton textiles come from the United States—might at any time be declared a part of the Russian Empire, and therefore subject to its tariff. In short, the beginnings were only too obvious of a process of alienation of sovereignty under which the whole of the North China might pass under the dominion of the Czar. As it happens that over 80 per cent of all the cotton drills, and over 90 per cent of all the sheetings which the United States exports to China, find their way to the three northern treaty ports of Tientsin, Chefoo, and Newchwang, this was a process to which the manufacturing interests of our country could hardly be indifferent. The first body to take action in regard to the threatening situation in China was the New York Chamber of Commerce," which in February, 1898, "addressed a memorial to the President of the United States in which it was set forth that the trade of the United States with

[1] "Annals," v. 13; "Supplement," p. III.
[2] Hill, "Greater America," p. 8.

China is rapidly increasing, and is destined with the further opening of that country to assume large proportions, unless arbi- trarily debarred by the action of foreign governments." [1]

The New York Chamber of Commerce requested President McKinley to take steps "for the preservation and protection of their important interests in that empire." This demand of American business for better facilities for trading with China, including an Open Door policy, led McKinley to include in his instructions to the peace delegation at Paris the following:

"Incidental to our tenure in the Philippines is the commercial opportunity to which American statesmanship cannot be indif- ferent."

The peace commissioners at Paris wired back to the State Department details about the economic value of the Philippines, especially as a source for sugar, hemp, and tobacco. They urged buying all of the Philippine Islands "to keep out Germany, the great trade rival of . . . United States in next genera- tion." [2]

8. *Manifest Destiny*

The acquisition of the Philippines, Porto Rico and Guam by the Treaty of Paris and the formal annexation of Hawaii dur- ing the war and Samoa in 1900, made the United States a world power. For the first time since its inception as a union of thirteen colonies, it had to face the problem of colonial ad- ministration. Before the signing of the treaty, one of the peace commissioners in Paris urged Washington that there is "no place for colonial administration or government of subject people in American system." [3] A resolution was introduced into the Senate "that under the Constitution of the United States, no power is given to the Federal Government to acquire

[1] "Annals," v. 13; "Supplement," pp. 148-9.
[2] U. S. "Foreign Relations," 1898, pp. 925-7.
[3] Ibid., p. 935.

territory to be held and governed permanently as colonies." [1] The resolution failed, the islands were annexed and officially the American government was committed to a policy of imperialism. The profound change which this acquisition heralded raised a great deal of opposition, and was reflected in the arguments of the imperialists and anti-imperialists.

Defenders of the new departure declared expansion was the "manifest destiny" of the United States. "Every expansion of our territory has been in accordance with the irresistible law of growth," Senator O. H. Platt of Connecticut said in the Senate. "The history of territorial expansion is the history of our nation's progress and glory. It is a matter to be proud of, not to lament. We should rejoice that Providence has given us the opportunity to extend our influence, our institutions, and our civilization into regions hitherto closed to us, rather than contrive how we can thwart its designs." [2] The great popular opposition to imperialism made it necessary for Whitelaw Reid, one of the Paris Peace commissioners and editor of the *New York Tribune,* to tour the country during 1899 in defense of the new acquisitions. He emphasized the importance of the Philippines in the Far East where "lies now the best hope of American commerce. . . . The Pacific Ocean," Reid stated, "is in our hands now. Practically we own more than half the coast on this side, dominate the rest, and have midway stations in the Sandwich and Aleutian Islands. To extend now the authority of the United States over the great Philippine Archipelago is to fence in the China Sea and secure an almost equally commanding position on the other side of the Pacific—doubling our control of it and of the fabulous trade the Twentieth Century will see it bear. Rightly used, it enables the United States to convert the Pacific Ocean almost into an American lake. . . . Nobody doubts the advantage our dealers have derived in the promotion of trade from controlling political relations and frequent intercourse. There are those who deny that 'trade follows the flag,' but

[1] Beard, "Contemporary American History," p. 216.
[2] Idem.

even 'they admit that it leaves if the flag does. . . . The trade in the Philippines will be but a drop in the bucket compared to that of China, for which they give us an unapproachable foothold." [1]

Reid described the statesmanship which guided him and his fellow commissioners in Paris as follows: "The statesmanship of the past has been to develop our vast internal resources by the protective policy. The statesmanship of the present and future is to extend our commercial relations and secure markets for our marvellous surplus productions. We are today the most wealthy nation on the face of the globe. The amount of our commerce exceeds that of any of the great powers of the world, being well on to two billion dollars. . . . New York, not London, is to be the money centre of the world."

The dawn of modern American imperialism was described by Robert Hutcheson as follows: "Wish it, vote for it, pray for it as we may, isolation is no longer possible for the United States. We are not as free as in the time of Washington to avoid European complications. Steam and electricity have annihilated space and brought the great nations of the world to elbow and jostle one another' like pedestrians on a crowded street. The old eastern question no longer centres at Constantinople, but by the completion of the Trans-Siberian railway has been transferred to Port Arthur. The Muscovite has found the sea just off our western coast and henceforth we must reckon with him. The eagle and the bear are face to face. . . . The feeble governments and low civilization of Central America must in time disappear. With the completion of an isthmian waterway we will be brought in more immediate contact with those people, . . . and ought to have more to say about their future destiny than any other power." [2] John Hay, then Secretary of State, also saw the dawn of a new age. "The 'debtor nation,'" he declared, "has become the chief creditor nation. The financial centre of the world, which required thou-

---

[1] Reid, "Problems of Expansion," pp. 41-2, 191-2.
[2] Hutcheson, "Expansion, the Traditional Policy of the U. S.," p. 19.

sands of years to journey from the Euphrates to the Thames and the Seine, seems passing to the Hudson between daybreak and dark." [1]

9. *The Open Door Doctrine*

The Philippines, Porto Rico and Guam were outright possessions obtained by conquest, a mode of imperialist acquisition which began to go out of existence at the end of the nineteenth century. Hawaii had been obtained by fomenting a revolution. Having embarked on a policy of imperial expansion the United States developed a series of policies in the Far East and in Latin America, where the chief interests of its ever-growing foreign trade and investment lay, which in essence was the European policy of "spheres of influence" and protectorates.

It was America's sphere of influence in Manchuria which gave rise to the Open Door doctrine.[2] In his instructions to the Peace Commissioners at Paris drawing up a treaty with Spain, President McKinley had already stated that "we seek no advantages in the Orient not common to all. Asking the open door for ourselves we are ready to accord the open door to others." The division of China into spheres of influence provoked the note which John Hay sent in September, 1899, calling for an open door to Chinese markets. The origin and application of the Open Door doctrine has been described by Secretary of State Knox thus: "Following the lease in 1898 and 1899 of various portions of Chinese territory to Germany, Russia, France, and Great Britain, with exchanges of notes in which these Powers, together with Japan, were recognized each as having special interests within certain provinces of the Chinese Empire, the United States secured from each of these Powers a declaration giving assurance of equality of treatment within these so-called 'spheres of interest' for nationals of all the Powers; and, preliminary to the settlement of the Boxer trou-

[1] U. S. "Congressional Record," v. 35, p. 2201.
[2] See Chapter III.

bles, the United States again addressed the interested Powers, securing their assent to the principle of the preservation of Chinese territorial and administrative entity and equality of commercial opportunity. It was especially to safeguard these principles that the United States Government interested itself so actively in the question of municipal government at Harbin in Manchuria, in that of the working of mines along the Mukden-Antung Railway, in the proposed constructions of the Chinchou-Aigun Railway, and made the proposal to neutralize the railways of Manchuria, and sought for American capital a participation in the loan for the Hukuang Railways." [1] On the basis of this policy, the State Department has actively co-operated with American bankers to obtain concessions both in the Near East and the Far East.[2]

The Philippines continue to play a rôle as the American base of operations for extending commercial and financial interests in the Orient. "The business background of the independence question becomes of far-reaching importance in any decision," a financial journal recently stated. "In dollars-and-cents terms it is a question of foreign investment. East or West, trade follows not the flag but the dollar—and the pound sterling, and the yen. . . . In the last analysis, the American business man and the Filipino politician have split upon the rock of foreign investment. . . . Within this 1700 mile radius . . . lies the key to Pacific commercial supremacy. To the north are the great Japanese business centres of Yokohama, Kobe, and Osaka; then the North China ports of Dairen and Tientsin; the China coast from Shanghai to Canton and Hongkong; Saigon, Bangkok, and Singapore, the British-held gateway to the wealth of the Indies; Batavia and Sourabaya in the Netherlands East Indies, and southward to Australia—all within that five day steaming radius. With Manila the centre of a 2,500 miles radius, the imagination merchandises almost half the world's population; for 761,205,000 people live and toil in this circle engir-

[1] Knox, "Spirit and Purpose of American Diplomacy," pp. 27-9.
[2] See Chapter III.

dling Vladivostok, the Pacific door to Siberia, India to the Arabian Sea, and Oceanica to Perth and Brisbane in Australia." [1]

10. *Protectorates*

While the State Department has been assisting American investors in the Orient and the Near East on the basis of the Open Door policy, an intensification of the Monroe Doctrine has served as the diplomatic façade of the economic conquest of Latin America, particularly of the Caribbean. "Steadily, quietly, almost unconsciously, the extension of international responsibilities southward has become practically a fixed policy with the State Department." [2] There was a great rush of American capital to Cuba immediately after the Spanish-American War, and the United States did not allow its promise not to exercise "sovereignty, jurisdiction, or control" over Cuba to stand in the way. By the Platt Amendment, "proposed by General Leonard Wood, carefully drafted by Elihu Root, at that time Secretary of War, discussed at length by President McKinley's cabinet, and entrusted to Senator Platt of Connecticut," and passed by Congress on March 2, 1901, Cuba was practically made a protectorate of the United States. [3] The technical legal status of Cuba is that of a "protected independent state," according to a document issued by the State Department on January 10, 1919, [4] marked "Confidential: For Official Use Only." This official document, now on file at the New York Public Library, declares that:

"It would appear that 'independence' as a technical term employed in treaties relating to such protected States does not mean full freedom of action as a positive attribute, but rather the absence of any such restrictions upon the protected State as would amount to an infringement of its international personality and take from it a certain theoretical legal competence to be the arbiter of its

[1] "Annalist," v. 23, p. 159.
[2] Jones, "Caribbean Interests of the U. S.," p. 125.
[3] Latané, "U. S. and Latin America," pp. 138–9. See above, Chapter VI.
[4] Willoughby, "Types of Restricted Sovereignty," p. 7.

own destiny. . . . Cuba represents perhaps the best example of an independent State under the protection of a single power." [1]

Shortly after the Platt Amendment practically turned Cuba into an American protectorate, the United States began to interpret the Monroe Doctrine in connection with business opportunities. These interpretations eventually led to the establishment of protectorates over Santo Domingo and Haiti.[2] An important interpretation of the Doctrine was made in 1902, when Great Britain, Germany, and Italy blockaded Venezuela to collect debts due to the investors; the United States minister to Venezuela, acting under State Department orders, prevailed upon Venezuela to submit the question to arbitration. Great Britain and Italy withdrew, but Germany continued the blockade. At this point President Roosevelt informed the German ambassador that unless Germany withdrew her fleet and submitted to arbitration, American warships would be ordered to Venezuela in ten days.[3] Germany agreed to arbitrate.

11. *The Big Stick*

Although this incident strengthened the Monroe Doctrine in so far as it applied to European influence, President Roosevelt had declared in his annual message of December 3, 1901, that the United States would not guarantee any Latin-American state "against punishment if it misconducts itself, provided that punishment does not take the form of the acquisition of territory." [4] In 1904, when Santo Domingo was in financial difficulties, he established a protectorate, first by executive agreement, later by treaty. In his annual message of 1904 Roosevelt formulates the policy of intervention by declaring that "Chronic wrongdoing, or an impotence which results in a general loosening of the ties of civilized society, may in America, as elsewhere, ultimately require intervention by some civilized nation, and

---

[1] Willoughby, "Types of Restricted Sovereignty," pp. 6–7.
[2] See Chapter V.
[3] Latané. "U. S. and Latin America," pp. 252–3. Mahony, "Monroe Doctrine," pp. 51–2.
[4] U. S. "Foreign Relations," 1901, pp. xxxvi–vii.

in the Western Hemisphere the adherence of the United States to the Monroe Doctrine may force the United States, however reluctantly, in flagrant cases of such wrongdoing or impotence, to the exercise of an international police power." [1] This "big stick" policy was applied to Santo Domingo by a later administration in the shape of armed intervention. Following the establishment of the Dominican protectorate the largest sugar plantations of the island republic fell into American hands. American investors bought up large tracts of land, and obtained a practical monopoly of the fruit trade.[2] That Santo Domingo and Cuba were not to be the only Caribbean protectorates of the United States was prophesied by Elihu Root in 1908, when he declared that the causes which led to American intervention in Cuba "would lead to similar action in Haiti or Nicaragua if American interests there were of equal magnitude," [3] and again in 1912, when he told the Chamber of Commerce in New York that "it is a question of time until Mexico, Central America and the islands, which we do not possess in the Caribbean, shall come under our banner." [4] The precedent set in Santo Domingo was followed in 1912, when on behalf of Brown Brothers & Co., and J. and W. Seligman & Co., New York bankers, the Taft administration intervened and established a protectorate over Nicaragua; and again in 1915 the Wilson administration established a protectorate in Haiti.[5] Santo Domingo also became a precedent for American diplomatic pressure in Honduras in 1911, on behalf of a banking syndicate headed by J. P. Morgan & Co.[6] At that time Secretary Knox, who had developed "dollar diplomacy" in China and Latin America, summed up the assistance given by the Government to American investors as follows: "During the course of a year it is many times necessary for the United States to send forces to the

[1] U. S. "Congressional Record," v. 39, p. 19.
[2] Jones, supra, p. 30.
[3] Coolidge, "U. S. as a World Power," p. 297.
[4] Inman, "Problems in Pan-Americanism," p. 339.
[5] For details see Chapter V.
[6] Stuart, "Latin America and the U. S.," p. 278. U. S. "Foreign Relations," 1911, p. 573 ff.

ports of some of the Central American republics in order to afford protection to foreign life and property. This is done at an enormous expense, an informal estimate from some of the naval officers showing that the annual cost to this Government amounts to over $1,000,000." [1]

12. *The American Gibraltar*

America's acquisitions in its first imperialistic war offered important military and naval as well as economic advantages. Through the occupation of Hawaii, Samoa and the Philippines, the United States had footholds from which with a powerful navy she could dominate the Pacific Ocean. Porto Rico was annexed and Cuba turned into a protectorate at a time when a canal across the Isthmus of Panama and an alternative or additional canal across Nicaragua were being planned to connect the two great oceans flanking America. Henceforth, American diplomacy, in addition to safeguarding investments through negotiation, loan conventions, treaties, and bayonets, was to extend and safeguard the American empire through the establishment of naval bases in the Caribbean. The Hay-Pauncefote Treaty of 1901, which gave the United States control over the proposed Panama Canal, and which aroused no protests, marked European recognition of America's hegemony over the Caribbean region. [2] The building of the canal was intended, in the words of President McKinley, immediately after the Spanish-American War, to afford "that intimate and ready intercommunication between our eastern and western seaboards demanded by the annexation of the Hawaiian Islands and the prospective expansion of our influence and commerce in the Pacific." [3] When the canal was completed, after the United States had fomented a revolution in Panama, [4] the map of the world was changed, and the Caribbean was transformed into a great commercial and investing centre. [5] In addition, by the

[1] U. S. "Foreign Relations," 1912, p. 586.
[2] Viallate, "Economic Imperialism," p. 37.
[3] U. S. "Foreign Relations," 1898, p. lxxii.
[4] See Chapter IV.
[5] Inman, supra, p. 15.

treaty forced upon Nicaragua in 1916 after armed intervention,[1] the United States obtained the right to build another canal across Nicaragua. A series of naval bases beginning with Key West, Florida, and including Guantanamo (obtained by the treaty with Cuba), Porto Rico, and the Virgin Islands (purchased in 1917), give the United States absolute control of the Caribbean region. The treaty of 1907 with Santo Domingo gives the United States the right to build a naval base at Samana Bay; the treaty of 1915 with Haiti gives her the same right to the Mole of St. Nicholas; and the Bryan-Chamorro treaty of 1916, permits her to build naval bases on Fonseca Bay and the Corn Islands off Nicaragua.

In connection with the extension of naval power the Monroe Doctrine was modified in 1912, when it was rumoured that a Japanese trading concern had bought land which would give Japan a naval base on Magdalena Bay in Lower California, which is Mexican territory. Although the report later proved to be groundless the Senate passed a resolution introduced by Senator Lodge which provided that "when any harbor or other place in the American continents is so situated that the occupation thereof for naval or military purposes might threaten the communications or the safety of the United States, the Government of the United States could not see without grave concern the possession of such harbor or other place by any corporation or association which has such a relation to another Government, not American, as to give that Government practical power of control for national purposes."[2]

13. Dollar Diplomacy

During the Taft administration the assistance which the State Department gave to American investors had developed into so definite and clear-cut a policy that it became generally known as "dollar diplomacy."

This assistance was extended in the Far East for the purpose of obtaining financial and railway concessions for an

[1] See Chapter V.
[2] U. S. "Congressional Record," v. 48, p. 10045.

American banking syndicate headed by J. P. Morgan & Co., in connection with the Hukuang Railway loan and the Manchurian bank scheme.[1] Dollar diplomacy in China was thus described by President Taft in his message on foreign relations communicated to Congress on December 3, 1912: "In China the policy of encouraging financial investment to enable that country to help itself has had the result of giving new life and practical application to the open-door policy. The consistent purpose of the present administration has been to encourage the use of American capital in the development of China by the promotion of those essential reforms to which China is pledged by treaties with the United States and other powers." [2] At the same time the State Department helped American financiers to entrench themselves in Nicaragua, Honduras, and elsewhere in Latin America.

The rôle of the Monroe Doctrine in the Caribbean region and its relation to the interests of American bankers has been described by President Taft as follows: "It is obvious that the Monroe doctrine is more vital in the neighborhood of the Panama Canal and the zone of the Caribbean than anywhere else. . . . It is therefore essential that the countries within that sphere shall be removed from the jeopardy involved by heavy foreign debt and chaotic national finances and from the ever-present danger of international complications due to disorder at home. Hence the United States has been glad to encourage and support American bankers who were willing to lend a helping hand to the financial rehabilitation of such countries. . . . The Republics of Central America and the Caribbean possess great natural wealth. They need only a measure of stability and the means of financial regeneration to enter upon an era of peace and prosperity, bringing profit and happiness to themselves and at the same time creating conditions sure to lead to a flourishing interchange of trade with this country." The in-

---

[1] See Chapter III.
[2] U. S. "Foreign Relations," 1912, p. xi. For details of the "Government's co-operation with the Morgan banking group in efforts to exploit China," see Chapter III.

terests of American investors were protected by the landing of
"over 2000 marines and blue-jackets in Nicaragua. Owing to
their presence the constituted Government of Nicaragua was
free to devote its attention wholly to its internal troubles, and
was thus enabled to stamp out the rebellion." [1]

The policy of protecting American investments led the Taft
administration to interfere in Ecuador "to the end that Amer-
can interests in Ecuador might be saved from complete extinc-
tion." [2] Similarly in the same year American marines were
landed in Cuba to protect American Investments. [3] The chief
tenet of dollar diplomacy with its corollary of intervention in
weak states was outlined by President Taft as follows: "While
our foreign policy should not be turned a hair's breadth from
the straight path of justice, it may well be made to include active
intervention to secure for our merchandise and our capitalists
opportunity for profitable investment which shall inure to the
benefit of both countries concerned." [4]

The policy of rendering active assistance to American investors was continued and amplified by the Wilson administration. Armed intervention, such as had taken place in Santo
Domingo on behalf of the Santo Domingo Improvement Company and in Nicaragua on behalf of Brown Brothers and J. and
W. Seligman & Co., was in 1915 undertaken in Haiti on behalf of the National City Bank. The Department of State also
continued American control in Nicaragua through the Bryan-
Chamorro treaty of 1916. Another example of interference on
behalf of American finance in the Caribbean region is disclosed
in the following instructions sent by the State Department to
the American legation in Cuba, 1913: "Information received
by Department forecasts an attempt to renew a project of
British capitalists to rush through Cuban Congress concession
for railroad from Nuevitas to Caibarien.

"You will earnestly urge upon the President the desirability

[1] U. S. "Foreign Relations," 1912, pp. xii–xiii. See above, Chapter V.
[2] Ibid., p. xxiii.
[3] Ibid., p. xxv. See above, Chapter VI.
[4] Viallate, "Economic Imperialism," p. 62.

of postponing final action on this bill sufficiently to allow the fullest investigation and consideration, emphasizing the burden it would impose on the Cuban Treasury in favor of capital which is neither American nor Cuban." [1]

This was a definite step in the direction of an economic Monroe Doctrine. In fact, before long government assistance to American oil interests resulted in an elaboration of the Monroe Doctrine by President Wilson which implied that the United States in the future would not only oppose European territorial acquisition in the Western Hemisphere, but would also oppose concessions to foreign investors. [2] In 1913 the United States Government prevented a British oil syndicate from obtaining a concession in Colombia. Shortly afterward President Wilson declared in a speech at Mobile, Alabama:

"You hear of 'concessions' to foreign capitalists in Latin America. You do not hear of concessions to foreign capitalists in the United States. They are not granted concessions. They are invited to make investments. . . . States that are obliged, because their territory does not lie within the main field of modern enterprise and action, to grant concessions are in this condition, that foreign interests are apt' to dominate their domestic affairs, a condition of affairs always dangerous and apt to become intolerable . . . I rejoice in nothing so much as the prospect that they will now be emancipated from these conditions, and we ought to be the first to take part in assisting in that emancipation." [3]

14. Oil and Intervention

American oil investments in Mexico led to political interference and armed intervention by the Wilson administration in 1914. The United States Government, which had supported or fomented revolutions in Hawaii, Panama, and Nicaragua, and had on the whole followed a policy of recognizing de facto governments, [4] now refused to recognize the Huerta government. The doctrine of recognition was distinctly American, having

[1] U. S. "Foreign Relations," 1913, p. 381.
[2] Viallate, supra, p. 69.
[3] Scott, "President Wilson's Foreign Policy," pp. 22-3.
[4] Latané, "From Isolation to Leadership," p. 160.

been laid down by Jefferson to off-set the European doctrine of Divine Right, and as a corollary to the principle expressed in the Declaration of Independence that governments derive their just powers from the consent of the governed. It was first disregarded by President Roosevelt in the case of Santo Domingo when he told the revolutionary leaders that he would not recognize them even if they succeeded.[1] President Wilson's refusal to recognize Huerta was followed by the landing of American troops at Vera Cruz and the capture of the customs house on April 20, 1914. This intervention alarmed all of Latin America; the A B C group—Argentina, Brazil, and Chile—hastened to offer mediation, and as a result of a conference held at Niagara on May 20, Huerta resigned. By August, General Carranza, head of one of the revolutionary factions, took control of the Mexican Government, but his power was contested by General Francisco Villa. After unsuccessful attempts to reconcile the warring factions, the United States recognized the Carranza government in October, 1915. In retaliation, Villa began a series of raids on American citizens, some of which brought him across the border. A punitive expedition under General Pershing was dispatched into Mexico in March, 1916, and later large bodies of troops were massed on the Mexican border. A loud demand for war was raised by American investors in oil, land, mines, and rubber in Mexico.[2] But President Wilson pursued a policy of "watchful waiting" which staved off war with Mexico until the United States was ready to enter the World War.

Behind these bare facts of Mexican intervention lies a story of attempts by American investors to exploit an undeveloped country with immense resources, and active aid by the United States Government to some of these investors. That policy has been increasingly followed wherever American money has been invested in appreciable quantities. It may be described as a policy of using diplomatic pressure to modify either the laws or the administration of the country in which Americans have

---

[1] Fish, "American Diplomacy," p. 484.
[2] Latané, supra, p. 163.

concessions. In his testimony before a Senate Committee, Henry Lane Wilson, United States ambassador to Mexico from 1909 to 1913, declared: "There were instances, of course, where I was called upon to represent some important interests before the Mexican Government, but that was almost without exception under instructions from the Department of State."[1] John Lind, special representative of President Wilson to Mexico, in 1913, stated that "Those who had oil interests . . . all wanted intervention. They wanted Uncle Sam, as they usually put it, to come down and clean up Mexico and protect them and their purchases or concessions that they had obtained."[2]

In 1917 the Carranza government adopted a new constitution, Article 27 of which provided: "(a) No foreign corporation or individual can legally acquire or hold any mines, oil wells, land or other real property in Mexico unless he renounces his citizenship.

"(b) No corporation, either domestic or foreign, can own agricultural, grazing, or other rural lands in Mexico, and if title to such property is already vested in a corporation provision is made for its acquisition by the respective State governments in exchange for state bonds.

"(c) No corporation owning a mine, oil well, factory, or other industrial enterprise can hold or acquire land in excess of its actual immediate requirements, the area to be determined by the Federal or State executive.

"(d) No foreign corporation or individual can, under any condition, hold or acquire ownership to lands or waters within 60 miles of its frontiers or 30 miles from the sea-coast.

"(e) The ownership of all minerals, solid, liquid, or gaseous, is declared to be vested in the nation, regardless of existing rights based upon the old constitution.

"(f) All contracts relating to the acquisition of natural resources made since the year 1876 are subject to revision by the present government, and the executive is authorized to declare them null and void." Article 27 furthermore provided that

[1] U. S. Congress, 66:2; "Sen. Doc." v. 10, p. 2252.
[2] Ibid., p. 2325.

"the nation shall have at all times the right to impose on private property such limitations as the public interest may demand, as well as the right to regulate the development of natural resources . . . in order to conserve them and equitably to distribute the public wealth. . . .

"In the nation is vested direct ownership of all minerals. . . .

"In the nation is likewise vested the ownership of the waters of territorial seas."[1]

This attempt by Mexico to nationalize its natural resources met with the most powerful opposition by American concessionaires, and consequently the United States Government took active measures to protect the investors. On January 19, 1916, Secretary of State Lansing wired to Consul John R. Silliman in Mexico: "Department reliably informed de facto authorities contemplate issuing a decree providing for the nationalization of petroleum, which, if we are correctly informed, would affect most seriously the interests of numerous American citizens and other foreigners who have heretofore engaged in the business of producing and selling petroleum in Mexico. Point out to General Carranza in unequivocal terms the dangerous situation which might result from the issuance of any decree of a confiscatory character. Request that definite action be delayed until department shall have had opportunity to examine proposed decree, and mail copy thereof to department."[2] On January 22, 1917, the State Department informed the Carranza government that "the American government cannot acquiesce in any direct confiscation of foreign-owned properties in Mexico or indirect confiscation."[3]

To give effect to the Constitutional provision nationalizing natural wealth, Carranza on February 18, 1918, issued a decree "for the imposition of certain taxes on the surface of oil lands, as well as on the rents, royalties, and production derived from the exploitation thereof."[4] Again the State Department pro-

[1] U. S. Congress, 66:2; "Sen. Doc." v. 9, p. 446.
[2] Ibid., v. 10, p. 3121.
[3] Ibid., v. 10, p. 3123.
[4] Ibid., v. 9, p. 266.

tested, declaring that "'the United States cannot acquiesce in any procedure ostensibly or nominally in the form of taxation or the exercise of eminent domain but really resulting in the confiscation of private property and arbitrary deprivation of vested rights."[1] The decree called for the filing of documents showing the basis of their titles by concessionaires. The American oil companies, according to Edward L. Doheny, a leading American oil investor in Mexico, refused to file these statements "with the consent and approval and at the suggestion of our own State Department."[2] On April 2 the State Department again made a "formal and solemn protest . . . against the violation or infringement of legitimately acquired American private property rights involved in the enforcement of said decree."[3] Passing from protests to threats the State Department added: "It becomes the function of the Government of the United States most earnestly and respectfully to call the attention of the Mexican Government to the necessity which may arise to impel it to protect the property of its citizens in Mexico divested or injuriously affected by the decree above cited."[4]

15. *The State Department as a Business Solicitor*

In addition to extending commerce through treaties, acquiring naval bases, establishing protectorates, intervening in elections, withholding recognition, and using the army and navy to coerce debtors, the United States Government has also acted as a business solicitor for American investors in China, the Near East, and Latin America. Naval intelligence missions sent to various countries of the world not only report on naval matters but supply the Department of Commerce with information about opportunities for investment.

Secretary of State Hughes has stated that "in order to accord adequate protection to American interests in the Near East during the period following the Great War, the Department of

---

[1] U. S. Congress, 66:2; "Sen. Doc." v. 9, p. 266.
[2] Ibid., p. 267.
[3] Ibid., v. 10, pp. 3157-8.
[4] Ibid., v. 9, p. 267.

State has maintained its representatives throughout this area, and a naval force has been stationed in Near Eastern waters since 1919. Until October, 1922, this force consisted of from three to nine destroyers with various other craft from time to time. . . . These vessels have been of inestimable service to the representatives of the Department of State and to all American interests in the Near East."[1]

This rôle of advance agent for American business, and particularly for American finance, was increasingly assumed by the government after the outbreak of the European war, when capital began to flow into this country, and the surplus accumulated at an enormous rate. The upheaval in the economic life of the world was reflected in American foreign policy as soon as it became evident that finance, as distinguished from industry and commerce, was about to become a leading activity of American capitalists. The foreign business of American bankers began in a small way at the beginning of the twentieth century; before the outbreak of the war financial investments had already received government aid in China and Latin America; with the outbreak of the World War, the United States began to play the dominant financial rôle in the world. A sign of the new times was the Pan-American Financial Conference called in Washington on May 24, 1915, attended by the finance ministers and leading bankers of the United States and twenty Latin-American countries. Just as the Pan-American conference inaugurated by Blaine represented the interests of American manufacture and commerce, so the new conferences represented the interests of those bankers who were ready to invest in foreign loans, the building of railways, canals, public utilities, and in developing mines and other natural resources.[2] The purpose of the new type of conference was thus described by Secretary of the Treasury William Gibbs McAdoo in greeting the delegates: "The time is ripe for the establishment of closer financial relations betwen the people of the United States and the nations of Central and South America. In order that

[1] "Foreign Affairs," v. 2; "Supplement," p. xviii.
[2] Academy of Political Science, "Proceedings," p. 598.

these conferences may be productive of important and permanent results, the Secretary, interpreting what he believes to be the wish of the members of the Conference, has arranged to have a group of eminent financiers and leading business men of the United States meet with each of the delegations from the sister republics. In a sense, therefore, the Conference will partake of the nature of a series of meetings between the official delegates of the Republics . . . and the representatives of the Secretary of the Treasury." [1] In reality, the bankers were not the representatives of the Secretary of the Treasury; it was the Secretary who was the representative of the bankers.

A year later the trend of the new times was formulated by President Wilson in these words: "These are days of incalculable change. . . . We must play a great part in the world whether we choose it or not. Do you know the significance of this single fact that within the last year or two we have . . . ceased to be a debtor nation and have become a creditor nation; that we have more of the surplus gold of the world than we ever had before, and that our business hereafter is to be to lend and to help and to promote the great peaceful enterprises of the world? We have got to finance the world in some important degree, and those who finance the world must understand it and rule it with their spirits and with their minds." [2]

During and following the war the State Department worked in the closest co-operation with American finance to obtain concessions in foreign countries. An outstanding example is the Chinese Consortium loan of 1920, in reference to which the United States Government pledged itself to aid in every way possible and "to make prompt and vigorous representations, and to take every possible step to ensure the execution of equitable contracts made in good faith by its citizens in foreign lands." [3] A feverish activity to obtain concessions for American oil interests has been carried on with equal ardour

[1] Pan American Financial Conference, "Proceedings," 1915, p. 73.
[2] Robinson and West, "Foreign Policy of Wilson," pp. 338–40.
[3] See Chapter III.

and persistence by the Wilson and Harding administrations. Oil had become one of the dominant factors in modern economic life, and the governments of the great powers are struggling for control of the world's oil supply. "The country which dominates by means of oil," one oil magnate has declared, "will command at the same time the commerce of the world. Armies, navies, money, even entire populations, will count as nothing against the lack of oil." A revolution has taken place in fuel, and petroleum has become one of the chief stakes of diplomacy. No sooner did it become known in 1920 that Great Britain was to receive the mandate over Mesopotamia than the State Department began to pound on the gates demanding that Standard Oil be admitted to the oil fields of that region. The policy of the open door, which had been disregarded in keeping British oil interests out of Colombia in 1913, was invoked on behalf of American oil interests in 1920. The first note addressed by Ambassador John W. Davis to the British Foreign Office referred to "unfortunate impression in the minds of the American public, that the authorities of His Majesty's Government in the occupied region had given advantage to British oil interests which were not accorded to American companies, and further that Great Britain had been preparing quietly for exclusive control of the oil resources in this region. . . . The United States Government believes that it is entitled to participate in any discussions relating to the status of such concessions, not only because of existing vested rights of American citizens, but also because the equitable treatment of such concessions is essential to the initiation and application of the general principles in which the United States Government is interested." [1] The vested interests of American citizens in the Near East referred to in Davis's note were the Chester concession, including the Mosul section, and Standard Oil claims in Palestine. On behalf of the latter Washington continued to demand participation in the exploitation of the petroleum fields in and around Mosul for which the Turkish petroleum com-

[1] Great Britain; Foreign Off., "Miscellaneous," no. 10, (1921), p. 2.

pany, a British-French-Dutch syndicate, claimed to have a concession.

"The fact cannot be ignored," Secretary of State Bainbridge Colby notified Great Britain, "that the reported resources of Mesopotamia have interested public opinion of the United States, Great Britain and other countries as a potential subject of economic strife. . . . Because of the shortage of petroleum, its constantly increasing commercial importance, and the continuing necessity of replenishing the world's supply by drawing upon the latent resources of undeveloped regions, it is of the highest importance to apply to the petroleum industry the most enlightened principles recognized by nations as appropriate for the peaceful ordering of their economic relations." [1]

Both the Wilson and Harding administrations repudiated the San Remo agreement which gave the Turkish Petroleum Company a monopoly in Mesopotamia. As a result of the activities of the State Department, the Standard Oil Company obtained the right to explore its claims in Palestine.[2] The "unofficial" American representative at the Lausanne conferences carried on the fight for the Open Door until the controversy was settled by allowing Standard Oil to enter the Turkish Petroleum combine.[3]

The rôle of a business solicitor was frankly played by the State Department again in its attempts to obtain concessions for the Standard Oil Company in the Djambi oil fields of the Dutch East Indies. On April 19, 1921, the American Minister at the Hague pointed out to the Dutch Government that "in the future ample supplies of petroleum have become indispensable to the life and property of my country as a whole, because of the fact that the United States is an industrial nation in which distance renders transportation difficult and agriculture depends largely on labor-saving devices using petroleum products. In these circumstances my Government finds no alternative than the adoption of the principle of equal opportunity, with the provision that no foreign capital may operate in American pub-

[1] Great Britain; Foreign Off., "Miscellaneous," no. 10, (1921), p. 9.
[2] U. S. Congress, 68:1; "Sen. Doc." 97, pp. 60-67.
[3] Chapter III.

lic lands unless its Government accords similar or like privileges to American citizens."

The American minister went on to threaten that "in the light of the future needs of the United States such very limited and purely defensive provisions . . . might become inadequate should the principle of equality of opportunity not be recognized in foreign countries." [1] The American Government, the note stated, was "very greatly concerned when it becomes apparent that a monopoly of such far-reaching importance in the development of oil is about to be bestowed upon a company in which foreign capital other than American is so largely interested." [2] However, the efforts of the State Department could not prevent the concession in the Djambi fields from going to a subsidiary of the Royal Dutch. [3]

In its co-operation with American oil interests the State Department has fulfilled the advice of Edward L. Doheny, who told a Senate Committee that "the United States ought to hold for its industries and for its people . . . the oil lands that are owned and have been acquired by Americans anywhere in the world, and they should not be allowed to be confiscated by any Government, whether it be British, Mexican or any other. They ought to be maintained." [4]

The intimate relations between the State Department and American investments in foreign countries led the Department on March 3, 1922, to urge investment bankers to consult it before floating loans, which might involve the United States in the affairs of another country. A statement issued by the Department declared:

"At a conference held last summer between the President (Harding), certain members of the Cabinet and a number of American investment bankers, the interest of the Government in the public flotation of issues of foreign bonds in the American market was informally discussed, and the desire of the Govern-

[1] U. S. Congress, 68:1; "Sen. Doc." 97, p. 70.
[2] Ibid., p. 70-1.
[3] Davenport and Cooke, "The Oil Trusts," p. 108.
[4] U. S. Congress, 66:2; "Sen. Doc." v. 9, p. 254.

ment to be duly and adequately informed regarding such transactions before their consummation, so that it might express itself regarding them if that should be requested, or seem desirable was fully explained. Subsequently the President was informed by the bankers that they and their associates were in harmony with the Government's wishes and would act accordingly. . . . The flotation of foreign bond issues in the American market is assuming an increasing importance and on account of the bearing of such operations upon the proper conduct of affairs, it is hoped that American concerns that contemplate making foreign loans will inform the Department in due time of the essential facts and subsequent developments of importance. Responsible American bankers will be competent to determine what information they should furnish and when it should be supplied. . . . The Department believes that in view of the possible national interests involved it should have the opportunity of saying to the underwriters concerned, should it appear advisable to do so, that there is or there is not objection to any particular issue." [1]

The United States has travelled a long distance since the days of isolation and no entangling alliances. In addition to the territory which this government controls is the steady penetration of American finance into the industrially undeveloped countries of Latin America and Asia, and even into the highly developed countries of Europe. The penetration proceeds through the export of capital. State Department support for these investments expresses itself through the Monroe Doctrine in Latin America, the Open Door in Asia, and various forms of the Dawes plan in Europe.

The Washington Arms Conference openly marked the emergence of the United States as a dominant Far Eastern Power. With Great Britain and Japan its biggest rivals in that section of the world, it was a great triumph for American finance and diplomacy to break up the Anglo-Japanese Alliance by the Four Power Treaty, and to substitute for the old race for spheres of influence an international financial trust in the form of the Chinese Consortium.[2]

[1] "New York Times," Mar. 4, 1922, p. 2:8.
[2] See Chapter III.

Granting or withholding recognition of revolutionary governments is another method by which American diplomacy seeks
to exert pressure on behalf of American investors. For over a
century it was the policy of the United States to recognize de
facto governments. The policy was abandoned first in the
Caribbean region when American interests became dominant.
It has now been evoked in the case of Russia, and has been
applied on several occasions as a form of pressure in Mexico.
Control in this direction has also been exercised through
hipping or withholding arms. Secretary Hughes frankly admitted that America refused to adhere to the St. Germain convention relating to arms traffic because it "would prevent this
government from selling arms to our neighboring republics . . .
however necessary that course might be to the maintenance of
stability and peace in this hemisphere." [1]   In the case of Huerta
the United States withheld arms from the de facto government
and shipped them to the revolutionists; in the case of Obregon
the process was reversed. At the Geneva traffic-in-arms conference of 1925, the United States reserved the right to ship
arms to any government, whether recognized or not.

The relations between Washington and American investors
were indicated by Secretary Hughes when he declared that the
United States Government has at times "agreed to a measure of
supervision in the maintenance of security for loans." The
measure of supervision has been exercised by State Department
agents, naval officers, and marines, who imposed treaties on the
Caribbean republics giving Americans control over customs collection and government personnel, and forcing loans. Marines
continue to rule Haiti, and in 1922 an American High Commissioner was appointed "charged with the duty of coordinating
and supervising the work of treaty officials" carrying out the
provisions of the 1915 treaty. American troops left Santo
Domingo in 1924 only after the native government had signed
a treaty approving all the acts of the military occupation, and
providing for the protection of loans made by American bankers
in 1918 and 1922.[2]   American marines were withdrawn from

[1] Hughes, "Foreign Relations," p. 57.
[2] Ibid., p. 64. See also Chapter V.

Nicaragua in 1925, but control was retained through an American-commanded constabulary. In all three republics customs are collected by Americans.

Since 1919 the State Department's activities as a business solicitor have included sending protests against the British protectorate over Persia, where the Sinclair oil interests are seeking a foothold; against a monopoly of European oil interests in Mesopotamia, where the Standard Oil Company finally obtained a share; against the decision of the San Remo conference to partition most of the Ottoman Empire into spheres of influence among France, Italy and Great Britain, which affected the claims both of Standard Oil and of the Chester group; against Dutch discrimination in the Dutch East Indies, where Standard Oil was affected; against the attempts of France and Japan in Siberia and Manchuria and of Great Britain in the Caucasus and Northern Persia to acquire the interests of Russia in sections where the Morgan banking group has financial and railway interests through the Chinese Consortium and Standard Oil and Sinclair have oil interests; against Great Britain and Australia for alleged violation of the mandate terms agreed upon for the island of Nauru, and against Japan for similar violations of Pacific islands like Yap; against cable and wireless monopolies in the Far East, on behalf of the Federal Telegraph Company; against France for attempting to set aside the Open Door doctrine in regard to Morocco; against the attempts of China and Soviet Russia to come to an agreement on the Chinese Eastern Railway, which American finance has sought to obtain since the days of E. H. Harriman, and against the attempts of Japan to monopolize the Manchurian "sphere of influence" in connection with the new Chinese Consortium in which the Morgan banks play the dominant rôle.

A similar summary of Government co-operation with American finance in Latin America would show variations of the Monroe Doctrine ranging from mere warnings to armed intervention and the establishment of protectorates. It would include the determination of boundaries; the prevention of filibustering inimical to American financial interests and the helping of filibustering advantageous to American financial interests; the administration of Americans of the customs house in Santo Domingo, Haiti, and Nicaragua; the annexation of Porto Rico and the purchase of the Virgin Islands; the financial annexation of Central America and Cuba, where protectorates of one sort or another have been established; armed intervention to protect debt claims or banking interests or oil interests; the destruction of independent government in three republics; the fomenting of revolution in Panama, Honduras, and perhaps Mexico; the building of the Panama Canal; the option on a canal route in Nicaragua, and attempts to obtain a third Canal route; interference with elections; the refusal to recognize governments not subject to the control of American interests and the active support of governments backed by American interests; the acquisition of naval bases at Guantanamo, Samana Bay, the Corn Islands, Fonseca Bay, and St. Thomas; the establishment of native constabularies under American officers, similar to the British colonial system; diplomatic interference by an economic interpretation of the Monroe Doctrine, for the purpose of blocking Latin-American concessions to European investors; the active soliciting of loan business for New York banking houses; and the carrying on of a ceaseless campaign on behalf of the oil interests against the attempts of Mexico to nationalize its natural resources.[1]

[1] Blakeslee, "Mexico and the Caribbean," pp. 186-7.

THE TERRITORY OF THE UNITED STATES

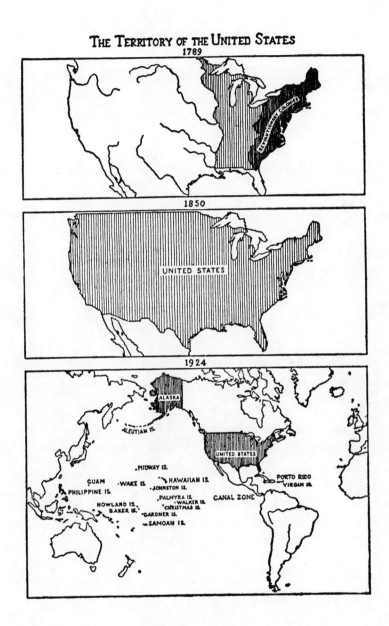

APPENDIX I

Name	Date	Relationship	Area in Square Miles	Population
Hawaii	1898	Annexed	6,450	250,000
Cuba	1898	Virtual protectorate	44,150	2,900,000
Porto Rico	1898	Annexed after war with Spain	3,600	1,250,000
Philippine Islands	1898	Annexed after war with Spain	115,025	8,500,000
Guam	1898	Annexed after war with Spain	210	14,500
Tutuila (Samoa)	1899	Annexed by treaty with Great Britain and Germany	77	7,250
Panama	1903	General supervision	32,400	450,000
Santo Domingo	1907 1916	Supervision of finances Military administration	18,500 11,000	955,000 2,500,000
Haiti	1915	Supervision of finances	49,500	746,000
Nicaragua	1913 1916	Virtual protectorate Grant of canal rights and naval base to U. S.		
Virgin Islands	1917	Ownership by purchase	132	26,000
		Totals	281,044	17,598,750 [1]

[1] Bowman, "The New World," p. 561.

APPENDIX II

Department of State.
Washington, February 1, 1902.

An agreement by which China cedes to any corporation or company the exclusive right and privilege of opening mines, establishing railroads, or in any other way industrially developing Manchuria, can but be viewed with the gravest concern by the Government of the United States. It constitutes a monopoly, which is a distinct breach of the stipulations of treaties concluded between China and foreign powers, and thereby seriously affects the rights of American citizens; it restricts their rightful trade and exposes it to being discriminated against, interfered with, or otherwise jeopardized, and strongly tends toward permanently impairing the sovereign rights of China in this part of the Empire, and seriously interferes with her ability to meet her international obligations. Furthermore, such concession on the part of China will undoubtedly be followed by demands from other powers for similar and equal exclusive advantages in other parts of the Chinese Empire, and the inevitable result must be the complete wreck of the policy of absolute equality of treatment of all nations in regard to trade, navigation, and commerce within the confines of the Empire.

On the other hand, the attainment by one power of such exclusive privileges for a commercial organization of its nationality conflicts with the assurances repeatedly conveyed to this Government by the Imperial Russian ministry of foreign affairs of the Imperial Government's intention to follow the policy of the open door in China, as advocated by the Government of the United States and accepted by all the treaty powers having commercial interests in that Empire.

It is for these reasons that the Government of the United States, animated now, as in the past, with the sincerest desire of insuring to the whole world the benefits of full and fair intercourse between China and the nations on a footing of equal rights and advantages to all, submits the above to the earnest consideration of the Imperial Governments of China and Russia, confident that they will give due weight to its importance and adopt such measures as will relieve the just and natural anxiety of the United States.[1]

[1] U. S. "Foreign Relations," 1902, pp. 275–6.

APPENDIX III

(Notes exchanged between the United States and Japan November 30, 1908, declaring their policy in the Far East.)

The Japanese Ambassador to the Secretary of State.

Imperial Japanese Embassy
Washington, November 30, 1908.

SIR: The exchange of views between us, which has taken place at the several interviews which I have recently had the honor of holding with you, has shown that Japan and the United States holding important outlying insular possessions in the region of the Pacific Ocean, the Governments of the two countries are animated by a common aim, policy, and intention in that region.

Believing that a frank avowal of that aim, policy, and intention would not only tend to strengthen the relations of friendship and good neighborhood, which have immemorially existed between Japan and the United States, but would materially contribute to the preservation of the general peace, the Imperial Government have authorized me to present to you an outline of their understanding of that common aim, policy and intention:

1. It is the wish of the two Governments to encourage the free and peaceful development of their commerce on the Pacific Ocean.

2. The policy of both Governments, uninfluenced by any aggressive tendencies, is directed to the maintenance of the existing status quo in the region above mentioned and to the defense of the principle of equal opportunity for commerce and industry in China.

3. They are accordingly firmly resolved reciprocally to respect the territorial possessions belonging to each other in said region.

4. They are also determined to preserve the common interest of all powers in China by supporting by all pacific means at their disposal the independence and integrity of China and the principle of equal opportunity for commerce and industry of all nations in that Empire.

5. Should any event occur threatening the status quo as above

described or the principle of equal opportunity as above defined, it remains for the two Governments to communicate with each other in order to arrive at an understanding as to what measures they may consider it useful to take.

If the foregoing outline accords with the view of the Government of the United States, I shall be gratified to receive your confirmation.

I take this opportunity to renew to your excellency the assurance of my highest consideration.

(Signed) K. TAKAHIRA.[1]

[1] U. S. "Foreign Relations," 1908, pp. 510-11.

APPENDIX IV

LANSING-ISHII AGREEMENT

Hearings before the Com. on For. Rel. U. S. Senate, on the Treaty of Peace with Germany, signed at Versailles on June 28, 1919, and submitted to the Senate on July 10, 1919, by the President of the United States.

Agreement effected by exchange of notes between the United States and Japan—mutual interest relating to the Republic of China—signed November 2, 1917.

(The Secretary of State to the Ambassador Extraordinary and Plenipotentiary of Japan on special mission.)

Department of State
Washington, November 2, 1917.

EXCELLENCY: I have the honor to communicate herein my understanding of the agreement reached by us in our recent conversations touching the questions of mutual interest to our Governments relating to the Republic of China.

In order to silence mischievous reports that have from time to time been circulated, it is believed by us that a public announcement once more of the desires and intentions shared by our two Governments with regard to China is advisable.

The Governments of the United States and Japan recognize that territorial propinquity creates special relations between countries, and consequently the Government of the United States recognizes that Japan has special interests in China, particularly in the part to which her possessions are contiguous.

The territorial sovereignty of China, nevertheless, remains unimpaired, and the Government of the United States has every confidence in the repeated assurances of the Imperial Japanese Government that while geographical position gives Japan such special interests they have no desire to discriminate against the trade of other nations or to disregard the commercial rights heretofore granted by China in treaties with other powers.

The Governments of the United States and Japan deny that they have any purpose to infringe in any way the independence or territorial integrity of China, and they declare, furthermore, that

287

they always adhere to the principle of the so-called "open door" or equal opportunity for commerce and industry in China.

Moreover, they mutually declare that they are opposed to the acquisition by any government of any special rights or privileges that would affect the independence or territorial integrity of China, or that would deny to the subjects or citizens of any country the full enjoyment of equal opportunity in the commerce and industry of China.

I shall be glad to have Your Excellency confirm this understanding of the agreement reached by us.

Accept, Excellency, the renewed assurance of my highest consideration.

(Signed) ROBERT LANSING.

His Excellency Viscount Kikujiro Ishii,
    Ambassador Extraordinary and Plenipotentiary
        of Japan, on Special Mission.[1]

[1] U. S. Congress, 66:1; "Sen. Doc." 106, p. 225.

APPENDIX V

An agreement made the fifteenth day of October, 1920, between
The Hongkong and Shanghai Banking Corporation, having its
offices at 9 Gracechurch Street in the City of London (hereinafter
called "the Hongkong Bank") of the first part
The Banque de L'Indo Chine having its office at 15bis Rue Laf-
fitte Paris (hereinafter called "the French Bank") of the second
part and
The Yokohama Specie Bank Limited having its office at Yoko-
hama in Japan (hereinafter called "the Japanese Bank") of the
third part and
Messrs. J. P. Morgan & Co., Messrs. Kuhn Loeb & Co., The
National City Bank of New York, Chase National Bank, New
York, The Guaranty Trust Company of New York, Messrs. Lee,
Higginson & Co. of Boston and the Continental and Commercial
Trust and Savings Bank of Chicago (hereinafter called "the
American Managers") acting as to the United Kingdom by Messrs.
Morgan, Grenfell & Co., of 22 Old Broad Street in the City of
London and as to France by Messrs. Morgan Harjes & Co. of
Paris of the fourth part
Whereas the Hongkong Bank the French Bank the Japanese Bank
and the American Managers are acting for the purposes of this
agreement as the representatives of the British, French, Japanese
and American Groups respectively
And Whereas the British, French, Japanese and American
Groups were formed with the object of negotiating and carrying
out Chinese loan business
And Whereas their respective Governments have undertaken to
give their complete support to their respective national groups the
parties hereto in all operations undertaken pursuant to the agreement hereinafter contained and have further undertaken that in
the event of competition in the obtaining of any specific loan contract the collective support of the diplomatic representatives in
Peking of the four Governments will be assured to the parties
hereto for the purpose of obtaining such contract.

And Whereas the said national groups are of the opinion that the interests of the Chinese people can in existing circumstances best be served by the cooperative action of the various banking groups representing the investment interests of their respective countries in procuring for the Chinese Government the capital necessary for a programme of economic reconstruction and improved communications

And Whereas with these objects in view the respective national groups are prepared to participate on equal terms in such undertakings as may be calculated to assist China in the establishment of her great public utilities and to these ends to welcome the co-operation of Chinese capital

Now It Is Hereby Agreed by and between the parties hereto as follows:

1. Each Group reserves to itself the right of increasing or reducing the number of its own members but so that any member of a group dropping out shall remain bound by the restrictive provisions hereof and any member of a group coming in shall become subject to the restrictive provisions hereof and so that no group shall (without the consent of the others) be entitled to admit into its group a new number who is not of its nationality and domiciled in its market. The admission of any new group shall be determined by the parties hereto subject to the approval of their respective Governments.

2. This Agreement relates to existing and future loan agreements which involve the issue for subscription by the public of loans to the Chinese Government or to Chinese Government Departments or to Provinces of China or to companies or corporations owned or controlled by or on behalf of the Chinese Government or any Chinese Provincial Government or to any party if the transaction in question is guaranteed by the Chinese Government or Chinese Provincial Government but does not relate to agreements for loans to be floated in China. Existing agreements relating to industrial undertakings upon which it can be shown that substantial progress has been made may be omitted from the scope of this Agreement.

3. The existing Agreements and any future loan agreements to which this Agreement relates and any business arising out of such agreements respectively shall be dealt with by the said groups in accordance with the provisions of this Agreement.

4. This Agreement is made on the principle of complete equality in every respect between the parties hereto and each of the parties hereto shall take an equal share in all operations and sign all

contracts and shall bear an equal share of all charges in connection with any business (except stamp duties and any charges of and in connection with the realization by the parties hereto in their respective markets of their shares in the operations) and the parties hereto shall conclude all contracts with equal rights and obligations as between themselves and each party shall have the same rights, privileges, prerogatives, advantages, responsibilities and obligations of every sort and kind. Accordingly preliminary advances on account of or in connection with business to which this Agreement relates shall be borne by each of the parties hereto in equal shares and each of the parties hereto shall be entitled to participate equally in the existing Agreements and will offer to the other parties hereto an equal participation with itself in any future loan business falling within the scope of this Agreement. Should one or more of the parties hereto decline a participation in the existing Agreements or any of them or in any such future loan business as aforesaid the party or parties accepting a participation therein shall be free to undertake the same but shall issue on its or their markets only.

5. All Contracts shall so far as possible be made so as not to impose joint liability on the parties hereto but each of the parties hereto shall severally liquidate its own engagements or liabilities. The parties hereto will so far as possible come to an understanding with regard to the realization of the operations but so that such realization in whatever manner this may take place shall be for the separate benefit of each of the parties hereto as regards their respective participations therein and so that each of the parties hereto shall be entitled to realize its participation in the operations only in its own market it being understood that the issues in the respective markets are to be made at substantial parity.

6. Any one or more of the parties hereto who shall have accepted its or their participation in any business hereunder shall be entitled by notice in writing to call upon the other or others of the parties hereto who propose to issue their own respective participations to issue for the account of the party or parties giving such notice or notices either all or one-half of the amount which may constitute the participation of the party or parties giving such notice or notices and the party or parties so called upon shall issue the said amount or amounts (hereinafter called "the Residuary Participation") specified in such notice or notices upon and subject to the terms and conditions following, viz:

(1) Such notice or notices must be received by the other or others of the parties hereto before the execution of the final

Agreement for the issue of the loan or (in the case of an issue of a part only of the loan) of so much thereof as the parties hereto may from time to time agree to issue.

(2) The party or parties to whom such notice or notices shall have been given shall be entitled to decide among themselves and without reference to the party or parties giving such notice or notices as to which one or more of them shall issue the Residuary Participation but in default of any such decision they shall issue the same equally between them.

(3) In issuing the Residuary Participation no distinction shall be made between the Residuary Participation and the amount or amounts issued on its or their own account by the party or parties issuing the Residuary Participation which shall in all respects be subject to the conditions of the respective Syndicates which may be formed for the purpose of effecting the issue.

(4) Each of the parties issuing the Residuary Participation shall be entitled to decide for itself and without reference to the party or parties giving such notice or notices as to what expenses shall be incurred in relation to the issue of the total amount issued by such party.

(5) The party or parties issuing the Residuary Participation shall be entitled between them to charge the party or parties giving such notice or notices with a commission of not exceeding 1½ per cent on the nominal amount of the Residuary Participation and also with a pro rata share of the total expenses which the issuing party or parties may in their sole discretion incur in relation to the whole issue and being in the proportion which the Residuary Participation bears to the total nominal amount of the issue.

(6) The party or parties issuing the Residuary Participation shall not by virtue of this Agreement incur any responsibility to subscribe for the Residuary Participation or to cause the same to be subscribed.

(7) Each party issuing the Residuary Participation shall apply all subscriptions received by it pro rata between the Residuary Participation issued by it and the amount issued by such party on its own account.

(8) Each of the parties issuing the Residuary Participation will apply for and use its best endeavors to obtain a quotation on its market for the total amount issued by it.

(9) No issue of the Residuary Participation or any part thereof shall be made by the party or parties giving such notice or notices unless mutually agreed by the parties hereto.

7. No participation shall be given by any one of the parties hereto outside its own market. Any participation given in its own market by any one of the parties hereto shall be for its own account only or in the event of the issue including any of the Residuary Participation for the accounts pro rata of the issuing Bank and the party or parties giving such notice or notices as aforesaid and in giving any such participation the party giving the same shall use its best endeavors to secure that no part of such participation shall be transferred to parties outside the market of the party giving the same. Any other participation shall be given only with the consent of all parties hereto and shall be borne in equal shares by the parties hereto.

8. This Agreement shall remain in force for the period of five years from the date hereof provided nevertheless that a majority of the parties hereto may by twelve months' previous notice in writing addressed to the other parties hereto terminate this Agreement at any time.

In Witness whereof the duly authorized representatives of the respective parties hereto have set their hands the day and year first above written.[1]

[1] Carnegie Endowment for International Peace, "The Consortium," p. 67.

APPENDIX VI

A Treaty between all Nine Powers relating to Principles and Policies to be followed in Matters concerning China.

The United States of America, Belgium, the British Empire, China, France, Italy, Japan, the Netherlands and Portugal:

Desiring to adopt a policy designed to stabilize conditions in the Far East, to safeguard the rights and interests of China, and to promote intercourse between China and the other Powers upon the basis of equality of opportunity;

Have resolved to conclude a treaty for that purpose and to that end have appointed as their respective Plenipotentiaries: . . . . .
. . . .

Who, having communicated to each other their full powers, found to be in good and due form, have agreed as follows:

ARTICLE I

The Contracting Powers, other than China, agree:

(1) To respect the sovereignty, the independence, and the territorial and administrative integrity of China;

(2) To provide the fullest and most unembarrassed opportunity to China to develop and maintain for herself an effective and stable government;

(3) To use their influence for the purpose of effectually establishing and maintaining the principle of equal opportunity for the commerce and industry of all nations throughout the territory of China;

(4) To refrain from taking advantage of conditions in China in order to seek special rights or privileges which would abridge the rights of subjects or citizens of friendly States, and from countenancing action inimical to the security of such States.

ARTICLE II

The Contracting Powers agree not to enter into any treaty, agreement, arrangement, or understanding, either with one another, or, individually or collectively, with any Power or Powers, which would infringe or impair the principles stated in Article I.

Article III

With a view to applying more effectually the principles of the Open Door or equality of opportunity in China for the trade and industry of all nations, the Contracting Powers, other than China, agree that they will not seek, nor support their respective nationals in seeking

(a) any arrangement which might purport to establish in favor of their interests any general superiority of rights with respect to commercial or economic development in any designated region of China;

(b) any such monopoly or preference as would deprive the nationals of any other Power of the right of undertaking any legitimate trade or industry in China, or of participating with the Chinese Government, or with any local authority, in any category of public enterprise, or which by reason of its scope, duration or geographical extent is calculated to frustrate the practical application of the principle of equal opportunity.

It is understood that the foregoing stipulations of this Article are not to be so construed as to prohibit the acquisition of such properties or rights as may be necessary to the conduct of a particular commercial, industrial, or financial undertaking or to the encouragement of invention and research.

China undertakes to be guided by the principles stated in the foregoing stipulations of this Article in dealing with applications for economic rights and privileges from Governments and nationals of all foreign countries, whether parties to the present Treaty or not.

Article IV

The Contracting Powers agree not to support any agreements by their respective nationals with each other designed to create Spheres of Influence or to provide for the enjoyment of mutually exclusive opportunities in designated parts of Chinese territory.

Article V

China agrees that, throughout the whole of the railways in China, she will not exercise or permit unfair discrimination of any kind. In particular there shall be no discrimination whatever, direct or indirect, in respect of charges or of facilities on the ground of the nationality of passengers of the countries from which or to which they are proceeding, or the origin or ownership of goods or the country from which or to which they are consigned, or the nationality or ownership of the ship or other means of conveying such passengers or goods before or after their transport on the Chinese railways.

The Contracting Powers, other than China, assume a corresponding obligation in respect of any of the aforesaid railways over which they or their nationals are in a position to exercise any control in virtue of any concession, special agreement or otherwise.

ARTICLE VI

The Contracting Powers, other than China, agree fully to respect China's rights as a neutral in time of war to which China is not a party; and China declares that when she is a neutral she will observe the obligations of neutrality.

ARTICLE VII

The Contracting Powers agree that, whenever a situation arises which in the opinion of any one of them involves the application of the stipulations of the present Treaty, and renders desirable discussion of such application, there shall be full and frank communication between the Contracting Powers concerned.

ARTICLE VIII

Powers not signatory to the present Treaty, which have Governments recognized by the Signatory Powers and which have treaty relations with China, shall be invited to adhere to the present Treaty. To this end the Government of the United States will make the necessary communications to nonsignatory Powers and will inform the Contracting Powers of the replies received. Adherence by any Power shall become effective on receipt of notice thereof by the Government of the United States.

ARTICLE IX

The present Treaty shall be ratified by the Contracting Powers in accordance with their respective constitutional methods and shall take effect on the date of the deposit of all the ratifications, which shall take place at Washington as soon as possible. The Government of the United States will transmit to the other Contracting Powers a certified copy of the procès-verbal of the deposit of ratifications.

The present Treaty, of which the French and English texts are both authentic, shall remain deposited in the archives of the Government of the United States, and duly certified copies thereof shall be transmitted by that Government to the other Contracting Powers.

In faith whereof the above-named Plenipotentiaries have signed the present Treaty.

Done at the City of Washington the Sixth day of February One Thousand Nine Hundred and Twenty-Two.[1]

[1] U. S. Congress, 67:2; "Sen. Doc." 126, pp. 893-7.

APPENDIX VII

A Diaz Concession-Contract with the Huasteca Petroleum Co.—Doheny Group.

Secretary of Fomento, Colonization and Industry of the Republic of Mexico. Second Section.—The President of the Republic has been pleased to direct to me the decree which follows: "Porfirio Díaz, Constitutional President of the United States of Mexico, to its people, know ye: That the Congress of the Union has held it well to decree the following:

The Congress of the United States of Mexico decrees: Sole Article.—The contract is approved which was executed on the 22d day of May, 1908, between the Attorney, Olegario Molina, Secretary of State of the Department of Fomento, Colonization and Industry, representing the Executive of the Union, and Mr. Harold Walker, representing the Company called the Huasteca Petroleum Company, for the exploration and exploitation of the deposits of petroleum or gaseous carburets of hydrogen existing in the lands held in the name of the same Company, located in the five northern cantons of the State of Vera Cruz, and in the districts or counties immediately adjacent to the States of Tamaulipas and of San Luis Potosi.—(Signed, Fernando Vega, Deputy President; Luis G. Curiel, Senator; Vice-President, Daniel García, Deputy Secretary; Carlos Flores, Senator Secretary.

Therefore I command that it be printed, published, circulated and that the law be fulfilled.

Given in the Palace of the Executive Power of the Union, in Mexico, on the fourth of June, 1908.—Porfirio Díaz.

To the Attorney Olegario Molina, Secretary of State of the Department of Fomento, Colonization and Industry. And I communicate it to you for your consideration and suitable action. —Mexico, June 4th, 1908.—O. Molina.

The contract to which the preceding decree refers is as follows: Bearing stamps to the value of 2520 pesos, duly cancelled.

CONTRACT

Executed between the attorney Olegario Molina, Secretary of State of the Department of Fomento, Colonization and Industry, representing the Executive of the Union, and Mr. Harold Walker, representing the Company called "Huasteca Petroleum Company," for the exploration and exploitation of the deposits of petroleum and gaseous carburets of hydrogen and their derivatives existing in the lands which the same Company owns in the five northern cantons in the State of Vera Cruz, and in the districts or counties immediately adjacent to the States of Tamaulipas and San Luis Potosi.

Article I.—The Company called Huasteca Petroleum Company is authorized to undertake exploitations of the surface and of the subsoil which belong to it and in those in which it is able to carry on such works by proper legal title, with the object of discovering springs or deposits of petroleum or mineral asphalt, of carburets or hydro-carburets of hydrogen, of natural combustible gas and their derivatives. The authorization to which this article refers deals exclusively with the lands located in the five cantons most northerly of the State of Vera Cruz and of the districts or counties immediately adjacent to the States of Tamaulipas and San Luis Potosi.

Art. 2.—The concessionaire company shall exploit freely the springs and deposits to which the previous article refers, and shall dispose of the products of the same either in their natural state or manufactured or changed in nature; but it shall be obliged to invest in the works of exploration or exploitation a minimum sum of 500,000 pesos within the period of five years reckoned from the promulgation of the present contract. The Company shall be obliged to give evidence before the Secretary of Fomento, and to his satisfaction, that the investment mentioned has been made.

Art. 3.—The concessionaire Company is authorized to establish pipe lines, above or below ground, to conduct where it pleases petroleum or mineral asphalt and the combustible gases, natural or manufactured, and to connect the producing wells with the installations.

Art. 4.—Within the term of two years, reckoned from the date of the promulgation of this contract, the concessionaire Company shall begin the necessary surveys to lay a pipeline for carrying petroleum, asphalt or combustible gases from the points of production of the concessionaire company to a convenient place in the Central Pleateau. The concessionaire company shall give notice to the Secretary of Fomento fifteen days in advance of the day and the place in which they begin the surveys of the land.

Art. 5.—Within the term of one year, reckoned from the date in which they have begun the surveys to which the previous article refers, the concessionaire Company shall present to the Secretary of Fomento, the plans and profiles of the work, in duplicate, and drawn to a decimal metrical scale, accompanied by a descriptive memorandum. If the Secretary of Fomento approves of said plans, he shall return one copy of the same to the concessionaire Company with a corresponding notification, but if in the judgment of the Secretary the plans ought to be modified, he shall come to an agreement by a conference with the engineer of the concessionaire Company.

Art. 6.—Within the term of six months, reckoned from the date of the approval of the plans, the concessionaire Company shall be obliged to begin works of construction of the pipeline to the Central Plateau, being under obligation to construct 20 kilometers at least during the first year, and 50 kilometers in each of the subsequent years.

Art. 7.—For the installation of the pipeline to which the preceding articles refer, there is granted to the Company a right-of-way of a width of 20 meters as a maximum, this being determined in each instance by the Secretary of Fomento. In view of the circumstances, the Secretary shall be empowered to authorize the occupation of a greater extent of ground, when necessity occurs, for establishing depots, gasometers, stations, pump plants and other accessories for the service of the pipeline.

Art. 8.—The Company shall be empowered to construct in such time and place as is convenient to it, other lines parallel to that mentioned in the previous article, always provided that those lines are laid within the right-of-way of 20 meters set down in the same article. Moreover the same Company shall be empowered to establish other pipelines parallel to those which are indicated above, outside the right-of-way of 20 meters, but in this case, they shall be installed at a minimum distance of 100 kilometers from each other. In every instance, the plans relating to these, shall be submitted for the approval of the Secretary of Fomento.

Art. 9.—The concessionaire Company is obliged to construct such ways and bridges as the traffic, whether general or elsewhere, requires, whenever this traffic is in any manner disturbed by the course of the pipeline. For this reason, the concessionaire Company shall be obliged to present plans of the said ways and bridges for the approval of the Secretary of Communications and Public Works, or of the local competent authority.

Art. 10.—For the establishment and conservation of the pipeline to the Central Plateau, the concessionaire Company shall have the right of establishing ways or roads which are necessary, and of constructing and operating a light railroad line confined exclusively to the proper necessities of the enterprise.

Art. 11.—During the period of the execution of the works referred to in Article 6, the Secretary of Fomento shall have the right to order inspections of them whenever he considers it advantageous, for which purpose, from the beginning of the work until the completion of the line, the concessionaire Company shall deposit each month in the Treasury General of the Republic, the sum of 300 pesos on account of the expenses of inspection.

Art. 12.—Every time that the concessionaire Company, in conformity with this contract, desires to modify its systems of pipelines, or to extend them, it shall have the right to do it by previous authorization of the Secretary of Fomento and his subsequent approval of the respective plans.

Art. 13.—For the execution of the works and the establishment of the services to which Articles 3, 4, 6, 7, 8, 10 and 12 of the present contract refer, the concessionaire Company shall have the right to occupy national lands, paying for them the price which the respective tariff has fixed for alienation of unoccupied lands according to the terms in force at the time for the transfer. The same Company is authorized to expropriate for the purposes indicated lands owned by individuals, observing for this purpose the following regulations:

A.—The concessionaire Company shall present to the Secretary of Fomento a plan of works with which the lands are to be occupied whose expropriation is desired, accompanied by all the necessary data to show the necessity of said works.

B.—The Secretary being informed by the Inspector what is intended, and taking account of the data which he has the right to demand from the authorities, from the concessionaire Company and from the proprietors of the lands which it is desired to expropriate, shall base his decision upon his approval of the plans presented.

C.—If the decision of the Secretary should be in the sense that he does not approve of the plans, he shall make to the concessionaire Company suggestions to the end that the plans may be duly modified, if that should be possible, and in view of the reply of the concessionaire Company, the Secretary shall determine definitely upon the propriety or impropriety of the expropriation.

D.—If the plans are approved, with or without modification, it shall be considered that for this case alone the expropriation of the lands described in the plan or plans approved is declared and established.

E.—With these plans and the final verdict of approval, the concessionaire Company shall apply to the District Judge within whose jurisdiction the lands are which are being expropriated. The concessionaire Company in the legal capacity which, according to the Code of Federal Procedure, is granted to the expropriation authority, and to the Public Minister on his part, shall proceed to arrange the procedure proper for expropriation in accordance with what is laid down in said code.

F.—If the owner of the property to be expropriated is absent, or ignorant of the proceedings, he shall receive notification in the manner provided in Article 194 of the Code of Procedure already cited. If he does not present himself, the judgment shall proceed nevertheless and the amount of the indemnification determined upon shall be deposited in accordance with the decision of the court.

G.—If the owner of the land is unknown or doubtful for whatever cause, the judgment shall proceed with the person or persons who present themselves in opposition, and the amount of indemnification shall be deposited in the same manner as is set down in the other case, the deposit shall be paid over for him who shall later show right to it.

H.—For the initiation of this kind of suit it shall not be necessary that the concessionaire Company previously attempt to reach an agreement with the owner or owners of the land to be expropriated.

Art. 14.—The concessionaire Company shall enjoy, for a term of ten years reckoned from the promulgation of the present contract, the following exemptions:

1.—The capital invested in the enterprise to which this contract refers, as well as the products which the Company obtains or manufactures, so long as they do not pass into the ownership of a third person, shall be exempt from every Federal tax with the exception of those which are paid in the form of stamps.

2.—The concessionaire Company shall have the right to export, free of all dues and charges, the natural products, crude, refined, or manufactured, which are obtained from the exploitations to which the present contract refers.

3.—The same Company shall be permitted to import, free of taxes, the machinery and accessories for boring wells, for producing, refining, or manufacturing every kind of products which have petroleum as a base, natural combustible gas, carburets or hydro-carburets of hydrogen or their derivatives, the necessary pipes for these industries and for the lines of communication with the Central Plateau, as well as the accessories for one and all; pumps and their accessories; tanks and barrels of iron, steel or wood; gasometers; materials for buildings intended for the exploitation, and the fixed material and rolling stock for the light railroad of the enterprise.

Art. 15.—For the enjoyment of the exemptions which are mentioned in the third paragraph of the previous article, the concessionaire Company shall present in every case to the Secretary of Fomento, complete detailed lists of the materials which it is proposed to import, specifying the number, quantity and quality of said materials, and accompanying them with drawings and explanatory notes. The Secretary of Fomento shall reach his decision in the premises in the understanding that the concessionaire Company shall subject itself in making its importations to the dispositions and regulations which the Secretary of Hacienda shall lay down.

Art. 16.—The materials imported for the aid of the concession which is the object of this contract, may not be sold by the Company without a previous authorization by the Secretary of Hacienda, and the failure by the Company to observe this requirement shall incur condemnation for the crime of smuggling and shall subject it to the penalties which the laws prescribe.

Art. 17.—The concessionaire shall guarantee the fulfilment of its obligations by a deposit of 20,000 pesos in bonds of the Public National Debt. This deposit shall be made in the National Bank of Mexico within eight days following the date of the promulgation of this contract, and while the deposit remains the Company shall have the right of disposing of the matured coupons attached to the bonds.

Art. 18.—The deposit to which the previous article refers shall be forfeited by the concessionaire Company in case the present concession is declared forfeit. For the return of the same deposit, the following rules shall be observed:

1.—On the proof by the Company that it has invested the sum of 500,000 pesos in the period stated in the second article, there shall be returned 50% of the said deposit.

2.—The remaining 50% shall be returned when the Secretary of Fomento declares that the Company has fulfilled all the stipulations of this contract.

Art. 19.—If the Company shall not complete the construction of the pipeline to the Central Plateau in the period stipulated, it shall lose 50% of the deposit and the authorization which is granted under this contract to construct the said pipeline shall expire.

Art. 20.—The obligations which the concessionaire Company undertakes in respect to the terms fixed in this contract, shall be suspended in case of accident or of force majeur which prevents the fulfilment of such obligations. The suspension shall endure for the time that the interruption lasts and two months longer, the concessionaire Company being obliged, however, to give notice to the Secretary of Fomento when the occasion for suspension occurs.

Art. 21.—The concessionaire Company shall maintain always in this capital a representative duly authorized, to treat with the Government upon all the matters dealt with in the present concession.

Art. 22.—The concessionaire Company shall have the right to transfer, in whole or in part, the concessions granted in the present contract, to one or more companies organized in conformity with the laws of the Mexican Republic, but in every instance the previous approval of the Secretary of Fomento will be required in order to effectuate any such transfer. In no case shall transfer be made to a foreign government or State, nor shall they or their agents be admitted as associates, and any such transfer, stipulation or agreement to this effect shall be null and void.

Art. 23.—The concessionaire Company shall be considered as Mexican, being subject, both as to the Company itself and as to the foreigners who have part in its business in the character of stockholders, employes, or in whatever other character, to the laws and courts of the Republic. Never can it allege in respect of the property and business of the enterprise any right of extra-territoriality, under whatever pretext, and it shall have solely the right and means of making them valid which the laws of the Republic concede to Mexicans. It shall consequently not be able to make any appeal under the said business to foreign diplomatic agents.

Art. 24.—This contract shall be forfeit by failure to deposit the guarantee within the time fixed in the 17th Article and shall be made void by any of the following reasons:

1.—By failure to invest the sum of 500,000 pesos in accordance with the second article.

2.—By selling or hypothecating any or all of the concessions granted by the present contract in violation of the stipulation of Article 22.

3.—By employing the railroad which is constructed in accordance with Article 10 for uses different from those which the said article authorizes.

4.—By transferring this contract or hypothecating any of its concessions to any foreign government or State or agent for the same.

Art. 25.—If the forfeit is declared, for any of the reasons given in paragraphs 1, 2 and 3, the Company shall lose the deposit as well as the concessions and franchises which this contract grants. If the forfeit is declared for the reasons which are given in the 4th paragraph, the Company shall incur a total loss of its rights, goods, and properties of whatever kind referred to in this contract. The forfeit shall be declared administratively by the Secretary of Fomento, but before making such declaration of forfeit there shall be granted to the concessionaire Company a reasonable period for setting forth its defense.

Art. 26.—This contract shall last ten years, reckoned from its promulgation. When the said term is completed the Company shall have the right to continue the exploitation of its installations and other properties in conformity with the general law of the Republic.

Art. 27.—This contract shall be submitted for the approval of the Congress of the Nation.

Art. 28.—The stamps of this contract shall be paid for by the concessionaire Company.

Done in the city of Mexico, on the 22d day of the month of May, 1908.

O. MOLINA.

HAROLD WALKER.

(Rúbricas.)

A true copy.—Mexico, June 4, 1908.—The Sub-Secretary, A. Aldasoro.[1]

[1] "Mexican Review," v. III, p. 32 ff.

APPENDIX VIII

MEXICAN DEPARTMENT OF INDUSTRY, COMMERCE, AND LABOR

Petroleum Section

CONCESSION granted by the Executive of the Union, represented by C. Leon Salinas, Secretary of Industry, Commerce and Labor, to the Petroleum Company of Sonora, Incorporated, for the exploration for petroleum in the zones specified in the first clause of this concession, and for the exploitation of deposits of petroleum or hydro-carbons that are discovered in the zones referred to in the second clause of the same.

FIRST—The Petroleum Company of Sonora, Incorporated, hereinafter called the concessionaire, is authorized, without prejudice to a third who may have a better right, to carry out, for a period of four years from the date of this permission, labors of surface exploration for petroleum on the subsoil of lakes, lagoons, gulfs, national territories which may be unoccupied or those whose title of property leaves the subsoil rights to the Federal Government; as well as on the beaches, maritime zone, and federal zones, margins and beds of rivers, streams, marshes and bays of federal jurisdiction: within the Districts of Hermosillo, Guaymas, Alamos, and Altar, of the State of Sonora, with the exception of a square, sixty kilometres on each side, which is in the centre of one of them, the place called Point Tepoca on the shore of the District of Altar, situated with two sides parallel to the general coast line.

SECOND—At the end of the first two years of the period mentioned in the preceding clause, the Concessionaire shall be obliged to withdraw from the Districts of Hermosillo and Guaymas, reserving the parcels of land that it may have decided to exploit; at the end of the third year, it shall have to withdraw from the District of Alamos; and at the end of the fourth year it shall have to withdraw from the District of Altar.

At the close of each period of time of the three mentioned, the

Concessionaire must have presented to the Department of Industry, Commerce, and Labor, a statement in which shall appear all the allotments which the same Concessionaire wishes to reserve for exploitation, with their respective locations.

THIRD—The Concessionaire is authorized to elect, within each of the periods of time marked in the preceding clause, the precise places in which it proposes to drill wells, and in that case shall have the right, which is conceded it, for each place designated, to an area in the form of a square of two thousand hectares and whose centre is precisely the place designated for the well.

If any or part of the allotments of two thousand hectares should be on private property, the Concessionaire shall have the right to denounce the part of the private property which may be necessary, respecting the preferences established by the Petroleum Law.

FOURTH—Once the allotments of two thousand hectares which it intends to reserve are chosen by the Concessionaire, and their location approved by the Secretary of Industry, Commerce, and Labor, the Concessionaire may drill within each allotment the number of wells which it believes proper after the corresponding authorization has been requested for each well, of the Secretary of Industry, Commerce, and Labor.

FIFTH—For a period of twenty years from the date of this concession the Concessionaire shall have the right to carry out all kinds of petroleum exploitation in the places selected in conformance with the preceding clause.

SIXTH—The Concessionaire is obliged to begin the labor of drilling at the latest within the fifth year of the life of this concession.

SEVENTH—At the expiration of the term referred to in the preceding clause and the labor once begun, the Concessionaire shall be obliged to drill one productive well each year at the least, or to drill one thousand metres.

EIGHTH—The Concessionaire is obliged to pay the Federal Government, as its share, ten per cent of the gross production of petroleum of each one of its wells, and as long as petroleum is found in any of the wells drilled in each allotment, the Company shall pay the Federal Government five dollars annually per hectare.

The payment of this share shall be made in specie or metal, as may suit the Government, the Concessionaire holding itself subject to what the corresponding laws and regulations dispose in this matter.

NINTH—At the end of the period of twenty years referred to in the Fifth Clause, a new concession may be granted on conditions dictated by the Executive, and in this case the present Concessionaire or its successor shall enjoy the right of preference provided it has fulfilled in a satisfactory manner the obligations imposed on it by this Concession.

TENTH—If the new concession should not be granted to the present Concessionaire or its successor, it may, the one or the other, as may be the case, take away its installations, leaving to the Federal Government the wells in the process of being drilled as well as the productive ones in a condition of perfect and immediate utilization.

ELEVENTH—The Concessionaire shall guarantee the fulfillment of the stipulations of this concession with a deposit of $5000, national gold, which it shall deposit in the General National Treasury within fifteen days of the date of this concession; with the understanding that if such deposit is not made, this concession shall not go into effect.

TWELFTH—The periods indicated in this concession shall be suspended in case of accident or unforeseen circumstances which directly and positively impede the fulfillment of the stipulated obligations, the Secretary of Industry, Commerce, and Labor having the power in such cases, to prolong the periods by the time that may be considered necessary.

In order that the Concessionaire may use this privilege it shall justify before said Secretary the accident or case of unforeseen circumstances that has impeded or which impedes the fulfillment of its obligations, presenting the respective proofs. The notification and the justification before the Secretary of the case of accident or unforeseen circumstances must be made by the Concessionaire within one month of the date of such case.

THIRTEENTH—The Concessionaire is obliged to carry out its labors of exploration and exploitation subject to all the conditions dictated by the Executive through the Department of Communication and Public Works, Department of the Treasury and Public Credit, and the Departments of War and Marine, in respect to matters falling within their jurisdiction.

FOURTEENTH—The Concessionaire agrees to invest in labors of exploration within a period of seven years from the date of this concession, the sum of one million dollars, national gold, this obligation taking effect as long as no petroleum is found, and the Secretary of Industry, Commerce, and Labor having the power to recognize, through whatever medium he deems opportune, said expenditure.

FIFTEENTH—At the close of the two year period conceded for the Districts of Hermosillo and Guaymas, the Concessionaire may explore these same Districts without any preference whatsoever for three years more; at the end of the three year period conceded for the District of Alamos, the Concessionaire may explore the same District without any preference whatsoever for two years more, and at the end of the four years conceded for the District of Altar, the Concessionaire may explore this last District without preference whatsoever for one year more. If, within any of these additional periods, the Concessionaire should find some free land suitable for its exploitation, that land shall be included in this same concession and shall be subject to all the stipulations indicated herein.

SIXTEENTH—In case the labors of exploration, or subsequently, those of exploitation, should result in the discovery of a petroleum well with a total daily production of four thousand cubic metres at the minimum, for the period of one year, the Concessionaire shall be obliged to install a petroleum refinery wherever it may itself choose within the Mexican Territory.

In matters appertaining to the installation of said refinery the Concessionaire shall send to the Department of Industry, Commerce, and Labor, for its approval, plans for its situation, and all details, accompanied by the rest of the documents which the applicable provisions require, said work being subject thereafter to all the provisions that rule such matters.

SEVENTEENTH—The Concessionaire shall have the right:

A—To have rented to it under the same conditions as the general public, the part of the beaches and federal maritime zones which it needs to carry out the labors of exploration and exploitation to which this concession refers.

B—To lay out pipe-lines which conduct petroleum from the wells to the nearest storing places.

EIGHTEENTH—The concessionaire shall also have the right of expropriation, in conformance with the dispositions of the corresponding laws.

NINETEENTH—In no case may the Concessionaire mortgage or in any way pledge this concession or any of the rights or privileges contained in it, to foreign corporations or governments, nor may it admit them as associates, any operation made in this sense being declared null and void.

The Concessionaire may transfer this concession to an individual or corporation organized in conformance with the laws of Mexico, with previous notification to this Department, this obligation being permanent for all companies that in the future or in any manner acquire this concession.

TWENTIETH—The Concessionaire is obliged to render annually to the Department of Industry, Commerce, and Labor, a report on the production of the well or wells drilled, on the contracts that it enters into in relation to their production, as well as a general statement of the works executed during the past fiscal year, expenses of exploration and exploitation, general balance, statistics of production, and all the other data designated by said Department. This report should be rendered within two months of the close of the year to which it refers. Failure of fulfillment of this obligation shall be punished by a fine of one hundred to five hundred dollars, according to the gravity or frequency of the omissions, at the discretion of the same Department.

TWENTY-FIRST—The Executive may declare administratively the forfeit of this concession for any of the following reasons:

(a) Failure of the Concessionaire to submit to the dispositions of new laws or regulations on petroleum;

(b) Failure to begin the labors of drilling within the period indicated in the sixth clause;

(c) Failure to make the payment referred to in the eighth clause for a period of one year;

(d) Failure to submit to the conditions imposed by the Departments of Communication and Public Works, Treasury and Public Credit, and War and Marine for the execution of the work within the indicated period;

(e) Failure to make the expenditure stipulated in the fourteenth clause;

(f) Failure to comply with the nineteenth clause;

(g) Establishment of proof that the Concessionaire, or its successors, is guilty of financial irregularity, in matters appertaining to the works of exploration and exploitation referred to in this concession.

TWENTY-SECOND—In all cases of forfeiture, the Concessionaire shall lose the deposit of guarantee and the privileges that this concession grants, the productive wells and those in process of drilling passing to the ownership of the Federal Government.

If the present concession should be transferred to any foreign corporation, state or government, or if one of these is admitted as associate, the Concessionaire shall lose, besides the guarantee and its privileges, all the property which it has and all installations it may have executed in relation with the executed labors.

Before making the definitive declaration of the forfeiture of this concession, the Department of Industry, Commerce, and Labor shall indicate a period of sixty days in which the Concessionaire may present its defense.

TWENTY-THIRD—This concession is granted with the understanding that the Concessionaire shall hold itself subject to all that new laws and regulations on petroleum may provide in regard to it.

TWENTY-FOURTH—The taxes (stamp) borne by this concession shall be for the account of the Concessionaire.

Issued in duplicate, in the city of Mexico, on March twelfth, nineteen hundred and twenty.

LEON SALINAS,
Secretary of Industry, Commerce, and Labor.
CHESTER H. WESGOLL,
for the Petroleum Company of Sonora, Inc.

BY THE PRESIDENT OF THE UNITED STATES OF AMERICA,

A PROCLAMATION.

Whereas a convention between the United States of America and the Dominican Republic providing for the assistance of the United States in the collection and application of the customs revenues of the Dominican Republic, was concluded and signed by their respective Plenipotentiaries at the City of Santo Domingo, on the eighth day of February, one thousand nine hundred and seven, the original of which convention, being in the English and Spanish languages, is word for word as follows:

Whereas during disturbed political conditions in the Dominican Republic debts and claims have been created, some by regular and some by revolutionary governments, many of doubtful validity in whole or in part, and amounting in all to over $30,000,000 nominal or face value;

And Whereas the same conditions have prevented the peaceable and continuous collection and application of National revenues for payment of interest or principal of such debts or for liquidation and settlement of such claims; and the said debts and claims continually increase by accretion of interest and are a grievous burden upon the people of the Dominican Republic and a barrier to their improvement and prosperity;

And Whereas the Dominican Government has now effected a conditional adjustment and settlement of said debts and claims under which all its foreign creditors have agreed to accept about $12,407,000 for debts and claims amounting to about $21,184,000 of nominal or face value, and the holders of internal debts or claims of about $2,028,258 nominal or face value have agreed to accept about $645,827 therefor, and the remaining holders of internal debts or claims on the same basis as the assents already given will receive about $2,400,000 therefor, which sum the Dominican Government has fixed and determined as the amount which it will pay to such remaining internal debt holders; making the total payments under such adjustment and settlement, including interest as adjusted and claims not yet liquidated, amount to not more than about $17,000,000.

And Whereas a part of such plan of settlement is the issue and sale of bonds of the Dominican Republic to the amount of $20,000,000 bearing five per cent interest payable in fifty years and redeemable after ten years at 102½ and requiring payment of at least one per cent per annum for amortization, the proceeds of said bonds, together with such funds as are now deposited for the benefit of creditors from customs revenues of the Dominican Republic heretofore received, after payment of the expenses of such adjustment, to be applied first to the payment of said debts and claims as adjusted and second out of the balance remaining to the retirement and extinction of certain concessions and harbor monopolies which are a burden and hindrance to the commerce of the country and third the entire balance still remaining to the construction of certain railroads and bridges and other public improvements necessary to the industrial development of the country;

And Whereas the whole of said plan is conditioned and dependent upon the assistance of the United States in the collection of customs revenues of the Dominican Republic and the application thereof so far as necessary to the interest upon and the amortization and redemption of said bonds, and the Dominican Republic has requested the United States to give and the United States is willing to give such assistance:

The Dominican Government represented by its Minister of State for Foreign Relations, Emiliano Tejera, and its Minister of State for Finance and Commerce, Federico Velásquez H., and the United States Government, represented by Thomas C. Dawson, Minister Resident and Consul General of the United States to the Dominican Republic, have agreed:

I. That the President of the United States shall appoint, a General Receiver of Dominican Customs, who, with such Assistant Receivers and other employees of the Receivership as shall be appointed by the President of the United States in his discretion, shall collect all the customs duties accruing at the several customs houses of the Dominican Republic until the payment or retirement of any and all bonds issued by the Dominican Government in accordance with the plan and under the limitations as to terms and amounts hereinbefore recited; and said General Receiver shall apply the sums so collected, as follows:

First, to paying the expenses of the receivership; second, to the payment of interest upon said bonds; third, to the payment of the annual sums provided for amortization of said bonds including interest upon all bonds held in sinking fund; fourth, to the purchase and cancellation or the retirement and cancellation pursuant to the terms thereof of any of said bonds as may be directed by the Dominican Government; fifth, the remainder to be paid to the Dominican Government.

The method of distributing the current collections of revenue in order to accomplish the application thereof as hereinbefore provided shall be as follows:

The expenses of the receivership shall be paid by the Receiver as they arise. The allowances to the General Receiver and his assistants for the expenses of collecting the revenues shall not exceed five per cent unless by agreement between the two Governments.

On the first day of each calendar month the sum of $100,000 shall be paid over by the Receiver to the Fiscal Agent of the loan, and the remaining collection of the last preceding month shall be paid over to the Dominican Government, or applied to the sinking fund for the purchase or redemption of bonds, as the Dominican Government shall direct.

Provided, that in case the customs revenues collected by the General Receiver shall in any year exceed the sum of $3,000,000, one half of the surplus above such sum of $3,000,000 shall be applied to the sinking fund for the redemption of bonds.

II. The Dominican Government will provide by law for the payment of all customs duties to the General Receiver and his assistants, and will give to them all needful aid and assistance and full protection to the extent of its powers. The Government of the United States will give to the General Receiver and his assistants such protection as it may find to be requisite for the performance of their duties.

III. Until the Dominican Republic has paid the whole amount of the bonds of the debt its public debt shall not be increased except by previous agreement between the Dominican Government and the United States. A like agreement shall be necessary to modify the import duties, it being an indispensable condition for the modification of such duties that the Dominican Executive demonstrate and that the President of the United States recognize that, on the basis of exportations and importations to the like amount and the like character during the two years preceding that in which it is desired to make such modification, the total net customs receipts would at such altered rates of duties have been for each of such two years in excess of the sum of $2,000,000 United States gold.

IV. The accounts of the General Receiver shall be rendered monthly to the Contaduria General of the Dominican Republic and to the State Department of the United States and shall be subject to examination and verification by the appropriate officers of the Dominican and the United States Governments.

V. This agreement shall take effect after its approval by the Senate of the United States and the Congress of the Dominican Republic.

Done in four originals, two being in the English language, and two in the Spanish, and the representatives of the high contracting parties signing them in the City of Santo Domingo this 8th day of February, in the Year of our Lord 1907.

THOMAS C. DAWSON
EMILIANO TEJERA
FEDERICO VELÁZQUEZ H.

[Signed by Theodore Roosevelt, July 25, 1907.]

APPENDIX X

THE HAITIAN TREATY OF 1915

By the President of the United States of America.

A PROCLAMATION.

Whereas a Treaty between the United States of America and the Republic of Haiti having for its objects the strengthening of the amity existing between the two countries, the remedying of the present condition of the revenues and finances of Haiti, the maintenance of the tranquillity of that Republic, and the carrying out of plans for its economic development and prosperity, was concluded and signed by their respective Plenipotentiaries at Port-au-Prince. on the sixteenth day of September, one thousand nine hundred and fifteen, the original of which Treaty, being in the English and French languages, is word for word as follows:

TREATY BETWEEN THE UNITED STATES AND THE REPUBLIC
OF HAITI

Preamble

The United States and the Republic of Haiti desiring to confirm and strengthen the amity existing between them by the most cordial coöperation in measures for their common advantage;

And the Republic of Haiti desiring to remedy the present condition of its revenues and finances, to maintain the tranquillity of the Republic, to carry out plans for the economic development and prosperity of the Republic and its people;

And the United States being in full sympathy with all of these aims and objects and desiring to contribute in all proper ways to their accomplishment;

The United States and the Republic of Haiti have resolved to conclude a Convention with these objects in view, and have appointed for that purpose, Plenipotentiaries,

The President of the United States, Robert Beale Davis, Junior, Chargé d'Affaires of the United States;

And the President of the Republic of Haiti, Louis Borno, Secretary of State for Foreign Affairs and Public Instruction, who, having exhibited to each other their respective powers, which are seen to be full in good and true form, have agreed as follows:—

ARTICLE I

The Government of the United States will, by its good offices, aid the Haitian Government in the proper and efficient development of its agricultural, mineral and commercial resources and in the establishment of the finances of Haiti on a firm and solid basis.

ARTICLE II

The President of Haiti shall appoint, upon nomination by the President of the United States, a General Receiver and such aids and employees as may be necessary, who shall collect, receive and apply all customs duties on imports and exports accruing at the several custom houses and ports of entry of the Republic of Haiti.

The President of Haiti shall appoint, upon nomination by the President of the United States, a Financial Adviser, who shall be an officer attached to the Ministry of Finance, to give effect to whose proposals and labors the Minister will lend efficient aid. The Financial Adviser shall devise an adequate system of public accounting, aid in increasing the revenues and adjusting them to the expenses, inquire into the validity of the debts of the Republic, enlighten both Governments with reference to all eventual debts, recommend improved methods of collecting and applying the revenues, and make such other recommendations to the Minister of Finance as may be deemed necessary for the welfare and prosperity of Haiti.

ARTICLE III

The Government of the Republic of Haiti will provide by law or appropriate decrees for the payment of all customs duties to the General Receiver, and will extend to the Receivership, and to the Financial Adviser, all needful aid and full protection in the execution of the powers conferred and duties imposed herein; and the United States on its part will extend like aid and protection.

ARTICLE IV

Upon the appointment of the Financial Adviser, the Government of the Republic of Haiti, in coöperation with the Financial Adviser, shall collate, classify, arrange and make full statement of all the debts of the Republic, the amounts, character, maturity and condition thereof, and the interest accruing and the sinking fund requisite to their final discharge.

ARTICLE V

All sums collected and received by the General Receiver shall be applied, first, to the payment of the salaries and allowances of the General Receiver, his assistants and employees and expenses of the Receivership, including the salary and expenses of the Financial Adviser, which salaries will be determined by previous agreement; second, to the interest and sinking fund of the public debt of the Republic of Haiti; and, third, to the maintenance of the constabulary referred to in Article X, and then the remainder to the Haitian Government for purposes of current expenses.

In making these applications the General Receiver will proceed to pay salaries and allowances monthly and expenses as they arise, and on the first of each calendar month, will set aside in a separate fund the quantum of the collection and receipts of the previous month.

ARTICLE VI

The expenses of the Receivership, including salaries and allowances of the General Receiver, his assistants and employees, and the salary and expenses of the Financial Adviser, shall not exceed five per centum of the collections and receipts from customs duties, unless by agreement by the two Governments.

ARTICLE VII

The General Receiver shall make monthly reports of all collections, receipts and disbursements to the appropriate officer of the Republic of Haiti and to the Department of State of the United States, which reports shall be open to inspection and verification at all times by the appropriate authorities of each of the said Governments.

ARTICLE VIII

The Republic of Haiti shall not increase its public debt except by previous agreement with the President of the United States, and shall not contract any debt or assume any financial obligation unless the ordinary revenues of the Republic available for that purpose, after defraying the expenses of the Government, shall be adequate to pay the interest and provide a sinking fund for the final discharge of such debt.

ARTICLE IX

The Republic of Haiti will not without a previous agreement with the President of the United States, modify the customs duties in a manner to reduce the revenues therefrom; and in order that the revenues of the Republic may be adequate to meet the public debt and the expenses of the Government, to preserve tranquillity and to promote material prosperity, the Republic of Haiti will cooperate with the Financial Adviser in his recommendations for improvement in the methods of collecting and disbursing the revenues and for new sources of needed income.

ARTICLE X

The Haitian Government obligates itself, for the preservation of domestic peace, the security of individual rights and full observance of the provisions of this treaty, to create without delay an efficient constabulary, urban and rural, composed of native Haitians. This constabulary shall be organized and officered by Americans, appointed by the President of Haiti, upon nomination by the President of the United States. The Haitian Government shall clothe these officers with the proper and necessary authority and uphold them in the performance of their functions. These officers will be replaced by Haitians as they, by examination, conducted under direction of a board selected by the senior American officer of this constabulary and in the presence of a representative of the Haitian Government, are found to be qualified to assume such duties. The constabulary herein provided for, shall, under the direction of the Haitian Government, have supervision and control of arms and ammunition, military supplies, and traffic therein, throughout the country. The high contracting parties agree that the stipulations in this Article are necessary to prevent factional strife and disturbances.

ARTICLE XI

The Government of Haiti agrees not to surrender any of the territory of the Republic of Haiti by sale, lease, or otherwise, or jurisdiction over such territory, to any foreign government or power, nor to enter into any treaty or contract with any foreign power or powers that will impair or tend to impair the independence of Haiti.

ARTICLE XII

The Haitian Government agrees to execute with the United States a protocol for the settlement, by arbitration or otherwise, of all pending pecuniary claims of foreign corporations, companies, citizens or subjects against Haiti.

ARTICLE XIII

The Republic of Haiti, being desirous to further the development of its natural resources, agrees to undertake and execute such measures as in the opinion of the high contracting parties may be necessary for the sanitation and public improvement of the Republic, under the supervision and direction of an engineer or engineers, to be appointed by the President of Haiti upon nomination by the President of the United States, and authorized for that purpose by the Government of Haiti.

ARTICLE XIV

The high contracting parties shall have authority to take such steps as may be necessary to insure the complete attainment of any of the objects comprehended in this treaty; and, should the necessity occur, the United States will lend an efficient aid for the preservation of Haitian Independence and the maintenance of a government adequate for the protection of life, property and individual liberty.

ARTICLE XV

The present treaty shall be approved and ratified by the high contracting parties in conformity with their respective laws, and the ratifications thereof shall be exchanged in the City of Washington as soon as may be possible.

ARTICLE XVI

The present treaty shall remain in full force and virtue for the term of ten years, to be counted from the day of exchange of ratifications, and further for another term of ten years if, for specific reasons presented by either of the high contracting parties, the purpose of this treaty has not been fully accomplished.

In faith whereof, the respective Plenipotentiaries have signed the present Convention in duplicate, in the English and French languages, and have thereunto affixed their seals.

Done at Port-au-Prince, Haiti, the 16th day of September in the year of our Lord one thousand nine hundred and fifteen.

> Robert Beale Davis, Jr. [SEAL]
> *Chargé d'Affaires of the United States*
> Louis Borno [SEAL]
> *Secrétaire d'Etat des Relations Exterieures et de l'Instruction Publique.*

[Signed by Woodrow Wilson, May 3, 1916.]

By the President of the United States of America,

A PROCLAMATION.

Whereas a Convention between the United States of America and the Republic of Nicaragua granting to the United States the exclusive proprietary rights for the construction and operation of an interoceanic canal by a Nicaraguan route, the lease of certain islands, and the right to establish a naval base on the Gulf of Fonseca, was concluded and signed by their respective Plenipotentiaries at Washington, on the fifth day of August, one thousand nine hundred and fourteen, the original of which Convention, being in the English and Spanish languages is, as amended by the Senate of the United States, word for word as follows:

The Government of the United States of America and the Government of Nicaragua being animated by the desire to strengthen their ancient and cordial friendship by the most sincere cooperation for all purposes of their mutual advantage and interest and to provide for the possible future construction of an interoceanic ship canal by way of the San Juan River and the great Lake of Nicaragua, or by any route over Nicaraguan territory, whenever the construction of such canal shall be deemed by the Government of the United States conducive to the interests of both countries, and the Government of Nicaragua wishing to facilitate in every way possible the successful maintenance and operation of the Panama Canal, the two Governments have resolved to conclude a Convention to these ends, and have accordingly appointed as their plenipotentiaries:

The President of the United States, the Honorable William Jennings Bryan, Secretary of State; and

The President of Nicaragua, Señor General Don Emiliano Chamorro, Envoy Extraordinary and Minister Plenipotentiary of Nicaragua to the United States;

Who, having exhibited to each other their respective full powers, found to be in good and due form, have agreed upon and concluded the following articles:

ARTICLE I

The Government of Nicaragua grants in perpetuity to the Government of the United States, forever free from all taxation or other public charge, the exclusive proprietary rights necessary and convenient for the construction, operation and maintenance of an interoceanic canal by way of the San Juan River and the great Lake of Nicaragua or by way of any route over Nicaraguan territory, the details of the terms upon which such canal shall be constructed, operated and maintained to be agreed to by the two governments whenever the Government of the United States shall notify the Government of Nicaragua of its desire or intention to construct such canal.

ARTICLE II

To enable the Government of the United States to protect the Panama Canal and the proprietary rights granted to the Government of the United States by the foregoing article, and also to enable the Government of the United States to take any measure necessary to the ends contemplated herein, the Government of Nicaragua hereby leases for a term of ninety-nine years to the Government of the United States the islands in the Caribbean Sea known as Great Corn Island and Little Corn Island; and the Government of Nicaragua further grants to the Government of the United States for a like period of ninety-nine years the right to establish, operate and maintain a naval base at such place on the territory of Nicaragua bordering upon the Gulf of Fonseca as the Government of the United States may select. The Government of the United States shall have the option of renewing for a further term of ninety-nine years the above leases and grants upon the expiration of their respective terms, it being expressly agreed that the territory hereby leased and the naval base which may be maintained under the grant aforesaid shall be subject exclusively to the laws and sovereign authority of the United States during the terms of such lease and grant and of any renewal or renewals thereof.

ARTICLE III

In consideration of the foregoing stipulations and for the purposes contemplated by this Convention and for the purpose of reducing the present indebtedness of Nicaragua, the Government of the United States shall, upon the date of the exchange of ratification of this Convention, pay for the benefit of the Republic of

Nicaragua the sum of three million dollars United States gold coin, of the present weight and fineness, to be deposited to the order of the Government of Nicaragua in such bank or banks or with such banking corporation as the Government of the United States may determine, to be applied by Nicaragua upon its indebtedness or other public purposes for the advancement of the welfare of Nicaragua in a manner to be determined by the two High Contracting Parties, all such disbursements to be made by orders drawn by the Minister of Finance of the Republic of Nicaragua and approved by the Secretary of State of the United States or by such person as he may designate.

ARTICLE IV

This Convention shall be ratified by the High Contracting Parties in accordance with their respective laws, and the ratifications thereof shall be exchanged at Washington as soon as possible.

In witness whereof the respective plenipotentiaries have signed the present treaty and have affixed thereunto their seals.

Done at Washington, in duplicate, in the English and Spanish languages, on the 5th day of August, in the year nineteen hundred and fourteen.

WILLIAM JENNINGS BRYAN [SEAL.]
EMILIANO CHAMORRO [SEAL.]

And whereas, the advice and consent of the Senate of the United States to the ratification of the said Convention was given with the following proviso: *"Provided,* That, whereas, Costa Rica, Salvador and Honduras have protested against the ratification of the said Convention in the fear or belief that said Convention might in some respect impair existing rights of said States; therefore, it is declared by the Senate that in advising and consenting to the ratification of the said Convention as amended such advice and consent are given with the understanding, to be expressed as a part of the instrument of ratification, that nothing in said Convention is intended to affect any existing right of any of the said named States;"

And whereas, the said understanding has been accepted by the Government of Nicaragua;

And whereas, the said Convention, as amended by the Senate of the United States, has been duly ratified on both parts, and the ratifications of the two governments were exchanged in the City of Washington, on the twenty-second day of June, one thousand nine hundred and sixteen;— —

[Signed by Woodrow Wilson, June 24, 1916.]

APPENDIX XII

(Excerpts made from the full contract. Omitted sections contain detailed agreement regarding form of bonds, method of replacing, drawing and retiring bonds, etc.)

REPUBLIC OF NICARAGUA
and
CENTRAL UNION TRUST COMPANY
OF NEW YORK
and
BROWN BROTHERS AND COMPANY AND J. AND W. SELIGMAN
AND COMPANY

BOND TRUST AND FISCAL AGENCY CONTRACT

Dated: October 5, 1920

As modified by the ratifying Act passed by the Nicaraguan Congress on December 6, 1920, and promulgated by Executive Decree on December 7, 1920.

BOND TRUST AND FISCAL AGENCY CONTRACT

Contract made at the City of New York, this fifth day of October, nineteen hundred and twenty, between the REPUBLIC OF NICARAGUA (hereinafter called the "Republic"), party of the first part; CENTRAL UNION TRUST COMPANY OF NEW YORK, a corporation organized under the laws of the State of New York (hereinafter called the "Trustee"), party of the second part; and BROWN BROTHERS AND CO. and J. & W. SELIGMAN & CO., copartnerships doing business in the City of New York (who, acting together, are hereinafter called the "Fiscal Agent"), parties of the third part;

WHEREAS, the Republic desires to obtain a Loan for the purpose

324

(a) Of aiding in the construction and equipment of a railroad to connect the Lake of Nicaragua with the Atlantic Coast at Monkey Point (hereinafter referred to as the "Atlantic Railroad"); and

(b) Of refunding a part of the Republic's outstanding indebtedness and for other purposes; and

WHEREAS, in order to carry out the above purposes, the Republic proposes to create and issue its Bonds to the aggregate principal amount of nine million dollars ($9,000,000), United States gold, to be secured under this Contract and as hereinafter stated; and

WHEREAS, the Republic desires the Central Union Trust Company, of New York, to act as Trustee under this Contract, and as Transfer Agent of such Bonds; and desires Brown Brothers & Co. and J. & W. Seligman & Co. to act jointly as Fiscal Agent of the Republic in respect of the proposed Loan, with the powers and duties hereinafter prescribed:

Now, THEREFORE, in consideration of the premises and of the mutual covenants and undertakings hereinafter contained, the parties hereto covenant and agree to and with each other as follows:

ARTICLE FIRST

THE BONDS

Section 1. The Republic shall issue its Bonds to the aggregate principal amount of nine million dollars ($9,000,000), United States gold, which shall be designated and known as the "Seven per cent. 15-Year Sinking Fund Gold Bonds of the Republic of Nicaragua," herein, for brevity, called the "Bonds of 1920" or the "Bonds." The total amount of Bonds to be issued shall not exceed the principal sum of nine million dollars ($9,000,000)...........

Section 4. The Bonds, both as to the principal and interest, shall be payable at the office of the Fiscal Agent in the City of New York; except that the Bonds payable in Pounds Sterling, if so issued, may be payable in London.........................

The text of each Bond and Coupon may be either in English or in both the English and Spanish languages, as the Fiscal Agent may determine, but in each and every case the English text shall govern..........The printing and engraving of both the temporary and definitive Bonds shall be under the direction of the Fiscal Agent..

Section 12. The Loan represented by the proposed Bonds shall constitute and is hereby declared to be a direct liability and obligation to the Republic irrespective of any security provided hereunder; and the Republic hereby pledges its faith and credit for the due and punctual payment of the principal and interest of the Loan and of all amounts required for or incident to the service of the Loan, and for the performance of all the undertakings herein contained on its part to be performed.

Section 13. The expenses of printing and engraving the provisional and definitive Bonds, the cost involved in the listing of those Bonds on the Exchanges, the cost of such foreign stamp taxes as may be incurred on the issue, including any taxes which may be payable in the United States, the compensation and expenses of the Trustee for authenticating the Bonds, and the shipping and insurance expenses, if any, shall be paid by the Bankers for account of the Republic out of the moneys to be provided in accordance with subdivision (2) of Section 1 of Article Second of the Financial Plan of 1920.

Section 14. The Bonds shall always be exempt both as to principal and interest, from any and all imposts, contributions or other taxes now or hereafter levied or collected by or in the Republic, whether they be on said Bonds, the income derived therefrom or on the holder thereof; and whether the latter be a Nicaraguan citizen or a citizen of a State friendly or hostile to the Republic of Nicaragua. The Republic shall furthermore pay and discharge any and all imposts or other taxes now leviable or collectible, or which may hereafter be levied or collected, on said Bonds by the Republic or by any political authority within the Republic; whether such impost or tax be on said Bonds, the income derived therefrom, or on the holder thereof; and whether the latter by a Nicaraguan citizen or a citizen of a State friendly or hostile to the Republic of Nicaragua.

All stamp or other duties and taxes to which this Contract and all other documents, whether public or private, and whether executed in the Republic of Nicaragua or in the United States of America under the terms of this Contract, or in execution thereof, may be subject, as well as all notarial, registry and other expenses connected with the execution and recording of said instruments, shall be paid by the Republic out of the portion of its Surplus Revenues available for public works and other expenses . . .

ARTICLE SECOND

SECURITY

Section 1. The principal and interest of the Bonds, the instalments of the Sinking Fund hereinafter provided for, and all other amounts required for or incident to the service of the Loan, as also the performance by the Republic of all of its obligations under this Contract, shall be secured as follows:

(a) By a lien and charge, hereby constituted, upon all customs duties receivable by or for the Republic on and after the date of the Bonds to be issued hereunder, whether such customs duties be imposed upon exports or imports, subject only to the prior liens referred to in subdivisions (1) to (4) inclusive of Section 1 of Article Second of the Financial Plan of 1920, and excepting from said lien and charge that portion of the customs revenues known as the "12½% Surtax."

(b) By a first pledge of such of the Republic's bonds of 1909 as may be acquired by the Republic, or for its account, under the terms of an Agreement bearing even date herewith between the Republic and Brown Brothers & Co. and J. & W. Seligman & Co. (hereinafter referred to as "Bankers Agreement of 1920"), which Bonds the Republic will deposit or cause to be deposited with the Trustee as and when so acquired; ....

(c) By a mortgage and lien upon all the property and earnings of the Ferrocarril del Pacifico de Nicaragua, including its franchises, concessions, equipment and other appurtenances, subject only to a prior mortgage and lien thereon in favor of the Treasury Bills, Series A, as set forth in the Treasury Bills, Series A, Trust and Fiscal Agency contract bearing even date herewith. In order that said mortgage and lien may be duly constituted, the Republic, as soon as it shall have acquired all of the stock of the Ferrocarril del Pacifico de Nicaragua, as provided in the Bankers Agreement of 1920, and in any event on or before December 15, 1920, shall cause that company to execute and duly record in favor of the Trustee, a mortgage in form satisfactory to the Trustee and deliver to the Trustee a duly certified copy thereof.

It shall be provided in said mortgage that, so long as any of the Treasury Bills of 1920, Series A or Series B, referred to in the Bankers Agreement of 1920, shall be outstanding, and until the completion of the proposed Atlantic Railroad, the earnings of the Ferrocarril del Pacifico de Nicaragua (after setting aside for betterments and improvements such sum as the Railroad Commission referred to in the Bankers Agreement of 1920 may determine, and after setting aside from any dividends declared the sum of 12,500 cardobas semi-annually, or such portion thereof as may be necessary to pay for transportation services rendered to the Republic by the Ferrocarril del Pacifico de Nicaragua), shall, either directly or as dividends, be devoted first, to the payment of the principal and interest of Treasury Bills, Series A, and thereafter to the payment of principal and interest of Treasury Bills, Series B, and / or to the construction of said proposed Atlantic Railroad; but it shall also be provided in said mortgage that the right to utilize said earnings for the retirement of Treasury Bills, Series B, and / or said railroad construction shall be subject to the prior lien in favor of the Republic's Bonds of 1920 if the customs revenues shall be insufficient to meet the charges on the loan represented by those Bonds, it being the intention that said customs revenues shall be primarily liable to meet those charges.

(d) By a first mortgage and lien upon all the property and earnings of the Atlantic Railroad, as and when constructed including its franchises, concessions, equipment and other appurtenances.
. . . .

(e) By mortgages upon all improvements, extensions, additions and equipments which may hereafter be made on or added to the existing Pacific Railroad, subject only as to the former to prior mortgages and liens in favor of Treasury Bills, Series A.

For the purpose of making the securities provided in this paragraph and paragraphs (c) and (d) above more effective, and so long as such securities shall exist, the Republic shall be obliged to maintain in full force, the provisions of Article I of Law of November 29, 1920, which provides: "Property devoted to a service which cannot be paralyzed without prejudice to the public, such as railroads, tramways or municipal light, drinking water or draining enterprises, etc., may be attached but the attachment shall not interfere with the continuance of the functioning of said service." [1]

(f) By a pledge of the entire capital stock of the Ferrocarril del Pacifico de Nicaragua, or its successor, subject to the prior rights of the Treasury Bills, Series A, and by a pledge of the entire capital stock of the Ferrocarril del Atlantico de Nicaragua. . . . . .

Section 2. In order to fully protect the value of the various mortgages, liens and pledges mentioned in Section 1 above, the Republic hereby reaffirms the provisions of Section 3 of Article Seventh of the Concession granted by the Republic to the Ferrocarril del Pacifico de Nicaragua, dated June 19, 1912, whereby the Republic agreed that it would under no pretext grant concessions to construct any other railroad, to other persons or companies, within a zone of twenty miles on each side of the company's lines, without the company's consent. In compliance with said provision, the Republic hereby agrees that a concession recently solicited

[1] As modified by the ratifying Act passed by the Nicaraguan Congress on Dec. 6, 1920, and promulgated by Executive Decree of Dec. 7, 1920.

by one Keilhauer to construct a railway from Chinandega to the Gulf of Fonseca via El Viejo will be refused.

Section 3. The Annual Budget of the Republic shall be paid as provided in the Financial Plan of 1920, a copy of which marked "Schedule D" is annexed to and forms a part of the Bankers Agreement of 1920; and the liens at present existing or created hereunder and simultaneously herewith on the Customs Revenues, Internal Revenues and other internal taxes of the Republic, and upon the 12½ per cent Customs Surtax in favor of the Guaranteed Customs Bonds of the Republic shall continue in effect; but, except for the charge of said Annual Budget, and except for said liens, the Customs revenues, Customs surtax, the Internal Revenues, and all other taxes of the Republic shall, so long as any of the Republic's Bonds of 1920 shall be outstanding, be and continue free and clear of all liens, charges or encumbrances; and no such liens, charges or encumbrances shall be placed thereon except with the consent of the High Commission and of the Secretary of State of the United States; and even then only in case that a preferential lien upon such revenues and taxes shall first be created in favor first of the Treasury Bills, Series A, and second, of the Bonds of 1920. The Republic accordingly covenants not to permit any liens or charges to be placed on such revenues so long as any of its Bonds of 1920 are outstanding, except as aforesaid. If, at any time, the Customs revenues and the dividends of the Ferrocarril del Pacifico de Nicaragua, or of its successor, and of the proposed Ferrocarril del Atlantico de Nicaragua, should be insufficient to meet the service of the 1920 Bonds, any sum which may be required to make up the deficit shall be provided by the Republic out of such of its Surplus Revenues as are not subject to prior charges.

ARTICLE THIRD

COLLECTION OF CUSTOMS

Except as may otherwise be expressly provided under the Financial Plan of 1920, the Customs duties of the Republic shall continue to be collected and administered by the Collector General of Customs in manner and form as provided in Agreement dated September 1, 1911, between the Republic of Nicaragua and Brown Brothers & Co. and J. & W. Seligman & Co.; and such collection and administration shall continue until the payment in full of the Loan represented by the Republic's Bonds of 1920 and until the full discharge of all the obligations of the Republic under this Contract. ....

ARTICLE FIFTH

EXPENSES AND COMPENSATION OF FISCAL AGENT AND TRUSTEE

At the end of each six months during the life of this Contract, on the written request of the Trustee and of the Fiscal Agent respectively made to Brown Brothers & Co. and J. & W. Seligman & Co. as Bankers under the Financial Plan of 1920, and as Fiscal Agent of the Republic, there shall be paid to them respectively out of the moneys to be provided under subdivision (2) of Section 1 of Article Second of said Financial Plan, all expenses incurred by them or either of them in good faith in the service of the Loan, or in the performance of any duty imposed upon them, or either of them, under this Contract, and also such further amounts as either of them shall estimate may be required by them respectively to meet all expenses reasonably incident to the immediate further service of the Loan, or to the discharge of said duties, which expenses shall be paid by the Bankers out of said moneys against proper vouchers. The reasonable and customary compensation of the Trustee and of the Fiscal Agent for all services rendered by them or either of them hereunder shall likewise be paid by the Bankers out of said expense fund at the end of each six months during the life of this Contract. ....

ARTICLE SEVENTH

ENFORCEMENT OF PLEDGE OF RAILROAD STOCK UPON DEFAULT

In case default shall be made in the payment of any bond or default shall be made in the due performance of any of the other covenants of the Republic hereunder, and such last mentioned default shall continue for a period of thirty (30) days after written notice thereof and demand of performance, the Trustee may and, if thereunto requested by the holders of a majority in amount of the Bonds issued and outstanding hereunder, and if indemnified to its satisfaction for its costs and expenses in so doing, shall proceed to sell the shares then held by it hereunder.
....

ARTICLE EIGHTH

CONCERNING THE TRUSTEE AND THE FISCAL AGENT

Section 1. The Republic hereby appoints Central Union Trust Co. of New York, Trustee for the Bondholders and Transfer

Agents of the Bonds, and hereby appoint Brown Brothers and Co. and J. & W. Seligman & Co., jointly, Fiscal Agent of the Republic hereunder, in the United States of America and in Europe, with full power to appoint agents, in the United States and in Europe or elsewhere, to act for it in respect hereof; and the Central Union Trust Co. of New York and Brown Brothers & Co. and J. & W. Seligman & Co., respectively, accept such appointments. The Republic covenants that, during the life of the Bonds, the Republic will at all times maintain in the City of New York, United States of America, a Fiscal Agency, and also a Transfer Agency of the Bonds, and any successor to the Central Union Trust Company of New York, as Trustees, shall always be a trust company organized under the laws of the State of New York and carrying on business in the Borough of Manhattan, in said city, and having a capital and surplus aggregating at least two million dollars.

Section 2. The Trustee and the Fiscal Agent, respectively, in the execution of the trusts and duties incumbent upon them hereunder shall be under full legal liability except as in this Contract provided. They respectively may at any time, instead of acting personally, employ and appoint such agent or agents, and attorney or attorneys, as they may deem desirable.

Section 3. Neither the Trustee nor the Fiscal Agent shall be answerable for the default or misconduct of any agent, attorney, bank or banker appointed or selected by them or either of them in pursuance hereof, if such agent, attorney, bank or banker shall have been selected with reasonable care; or for anything whatever in connection with this trust, except for their own wilful misconduct.

Section 4. The Trustee and the Fiscal Agent, or either of them, may at any time, and from time to time, take such steps as they may deem proper for the enforcement of the provisions hereof and for the protection of the rights of the Bondholders hereunder.

. . . .

ARTICLE TENTH

GENERAL PROVISIONS

Section 4. In case any controversy, question, dispute or difficulty whatsoever shall arise regarding the interpretation, performance or otherwise in connection with this agreement, such controversy, question, dispute or difficulty so arising shall, unless otherwise provided in this Contract or in the Financial Plan of 1920, immediately be referred by any of the parties hereto to the

Secretary of State of the United States for determination, decision and award and any such determination, decision and award when made after such reference shall be accepted by the parties hereto as final and conclusive.

Section 5. This Contract has been submitted to the Secretary of State of the United States who perceives no objection thereto from the standpoint of the Department of State of the United States. Within 10 days after the ratification of this Contract by the Executive and the Congress of the Republic, the Republic shall file with the Department of State of the United States of America an original executed counterpart of this contract.

Section 6.[1] This Contract shall take effect and become operative when ratified and approved by the Executive and Congress of the Republic.

IN WITNESS WHEREOF, the REPUBLIC OF NICARAGUA has caused this Contract to be subscribed on its behalf by Señor Don Octaviano Cesar, Minister of Finance and Financial Agent of the Republic of Nicaragua; the CENTRAL UNION TRUST COMPANY OF NEW YORK has caused this Contract to be subscribed in its name by one of its Vice-Presidents, and its corporate seal to be hereunto affixed and attested by one of its Assistant Secretaries; and said BROWN BROTHERS & CO. and said J. & W. SELIGMAN & CO. have hereunto set their hands and seals the day and year first above written.

This contract is executed in quadruplicate.

OCTAVIANO CESAR
Minister of Finance and Financial Agent of
the Republic of Nicaragua
CENTRAL UNION TRUST COMPANY OF NEW YORK
BY F. J. FULLER
Vice-President

(Corporate Seal)

Attest:

C. P. STALLKNECHT
Assistant Secretary

BROWN BROTHERS & Co.   (L.S.)
J. & W. SELIGMAN & Co.   (L.S.)

---

[1] As modified by the ratifying Act passed by the Nicaraguan Congress on Dec. 6, 1920 and promulgated by Executive Decree of Dec. 7, 1920.

BIBLIOGRAPHY

BOOKS AND PAMPHLETS

Adams, J. Q. Memoirs; Comprising Portions of His Diary from 1795–1848. Philadelphia: Lippincott, 1874–77. 12 v.

American Economic Association. Papers and Proceedings of the Thirty-third Annual Meeting. . . . December, 1920. Princeton: Am. Econ. Ass., 1921. (American Economic Review, v. 11, no. 1; Supplement.)

American History Leaflets. Edited by A. B. Hart and E. Channing. New York: P. P. Simmons, 1906–14. 36 v.

Annuaire Général de la France et de l'Etranger. Paris: Comité du Livre. [Annual.]

Baker, R. S. Woodrow Wilson and World Settlement. New York: Doubleday, Page, 1923. 3 v.

Bankers Trust Company. Our United States. New York: Bankers Trust Co., 1917. 32 p.

Barron, C. W. The Mexican Problem. Boston: Houghton, Mifflin, 1917.

Bau, M. J. The Foreign Relations of China: A History and Survey. New York: Revell, 1921.

Beals, Carlton. Mexico; an Interpretation. New York: Huebsch, 1923.

Beard, C. A. Contemporary American History. New York: Macmillan, 1914.

Bierstadt, E. H. The Great Betrayal: A Survey of the Near East Problem. New York: McBride, 1924.

Blaine, J. G. Letter Accepting the Nomination for President. Albany: Republican State Committee, 1884. 23 p.

Blakeslee, G. H., ed. Latin America. New York: Stechert and Co., 1914.

—— Mexico and the Caribbean. New York: Stechert and Co., 1920.

—— Recent Developments in China. New York: Stechert and Co., 1913.

Bland, J. O. P. Recent Events and Present Policies in China. Philadelphia: Lippincott, 1912.

333

Bolivia. Ministerio de Hacienda. Memoria. 1922. La Paz: Escuela Tipografica Salesiana, 1922.

Bowman, Isaiah. The New World. Yonkers-on-Hudson, N. Y.: World Book Company, 1921.

Canada. Commercial Intelligence Service. Canada as a Field for British Branch Industries. Ottawa: Department of Trade and Commerce, 1922.

Canada. Statistics Bureau. The Canada Year Book. Ottawa: F. A. Acland. [Annual.]

Carnegie Endowment for International Peace. Division of International Law. The Consortium: the Official Text of the Four-Power Agreement for a Loan to China and Relevant Documents. Washington: The Endowment, 1921. 76 p. (Its Pamphlet Series no. 40.)

Coolidge, A. C. The United States as a World Power. New York: Macmillan, 1908.

Crichfield, G. W. American Supremacy. New York: Brentano, 1908. 2 v.

Croly, H. D. Willard Straight. New York: Macmillan, 1924.

Culbertson, W. S. International Economic Policies; a Survey of the Economics of Diplomacy. New York: Appleton, 1925.

Curtis, G. T. Life of Daniel Webster. New York: Appleton, 1870. 2 v.

Davenport, E. H., and Cooke, S. R. The Oil Trusts and Anglo-American Relations. London: Macmillan, 1923.

De Bekker, L. J. The Plot Against Mexico. New York: Knopf, 1919.

Delaisi, Francis. Oil: Its Influence on Politics . . . London: Labour Publishing Co., 1922. 94 p.

The Democratic Text-Book. 1912. Issued by the Democratic National Committee. 1912.

Dewey, John. China, Japan and the U. S. New York: Republic Publishing Co., 1921. 64 p. (New Republic Pamphlet no 1).

Dunn, R. W. American Foreign Investments. New York: Huebsch, 1925.

Eckel, E. C. Iron Ores. New York: McGraw-Hill, 1914.

Egan, M. F. Ten Years Near the German Frontier. New York: Doran, 1919.

Elliot, Jonathan. The American Diplomatic Code. Washington: Printed by J. Elliot, Jr., 1834. 2 v.

Elliott, C. B. The Philippines to the End of the Commission Government. Indianapolis; Bobbs-Merrill, 1917.

Federal Reporter. v. 272. St. Paul, Minn., West Publishing Co., 1921.

The Federalist. A Collection of Essays by Alexander Hamilton, John Jay and James Madison. New York: The Colonial Press, 1901.

The Financial Post Survey. 1925. Winnipeg: MacLean Publishing Co.

Fish, C. R. American Diplomacy. New York: Holt, 1915.

Fisk, H. E. Inter-Ally Debts. New York: Bankers Trust Co., 1924.

Foreign Policy Association. The Seizure of Haiti by the United States. New York: Foreign Policy Association, 1922. 15 p.

Great Britain. Foreign Office. Correspondence Between His Majesty's Government and the United States Ambassador Respecting Economic Rights in Mandated Territories. London: H. M. Stationery Office, 1921. 13 p. [Its Miscellaneous no. 10 (1921). Cmd. 1226.]

—— Correspondence Respecting the New Financial Consortium in China. London: H. M. Stationery Office, 1921. 56 p. [Its Miscellaneous no. 9 (1921). Cmd. 1214.]

—— Memorandum of Agreement Between M. Philippe Berthelot . . . and Professor Sir John Cadman . . . London: H. M. Stationery Office, 1920. [Its Miscellaneous no. 11 (1920). Cmd. 675.]

Harrison, F. B. The Corner-Stone of Philippine Independence. New York: Century, 1922.

Hart, A. B. The Monroe Doctrine. Boston: Little, Brown, 1916.

—— New American History. New York: American Book Co., 1917.

Havana Electric Railway, Light and Power Company. Annual Report to the Stockholders. 1921. Havana, Cuba.

Hawaiian Branches of the Sons of the American Revolution. . . . Address to Their Compatriots in America Concerning the Annexation of Hawaii. Washington, 1897. 7 p.

Haworth, P. L. The United States in Our Own Times, 1865–1920. New York: Scribner's, 1920.

Heitman, B. F. Historical Register and Dictionary of the United States Army. Washington: Govt. Ptg. Off., 1903. 2 v. (United States. War Dept.)

Hendrick, B. J. The Life and Letters of Walter H. Page. New York: Doubleday, Page, 1922. 2 v.

Hilferding, Rudolph. Finanzkapital. Wien: Verlag der Wiener

Volksbuchhandlung. 1910. (Separatabdruck aus den Marx-Studien, III Band.)

Hill, D. J. Greater America. Address Delivered December 8, 1898. Washington: Judd and Detweiler, printers, 1898. 10 p.

Hobson, C. K. Export of Capital. London: Constable, 1914.

Hobson, J. A. Evolution of Modern Capitalism. New York: Scribner's, 1917.

—— Imperialism. New York: James Pott & Co., 1902.

Hughes, C. E. Foreign Relations. Republican National Committee, 1924. 80 p.

Hutcheson, Robert. Expansion the Traditional Policy of the United States. Speech before the Ohio Republican Association, September 25, 1899. Washington: G. E. Williams, 1899. 27 p.

"I Took the Isthmus." Ex-President Roosevelt's Confession, Colombia's Protest and Editorial Comment by American Newspapers on "How the United States Acquired the Right to Build the Panama Canal." Compiled by Francisco Escobar, Consul-General of Colombia. New York. 1911.

Ingalls, W. R. Wealth and Income of the American People. 2nd ed. York, Pa.: G. H. Merlin Co., 1923.

Inman, S. G. Problems in Pan Americanism. New York: Doran, 1921.

Jefferson, Thomas. Writings. Collected and Edited by P. L. Ford. New York, Putnam's, 1892–99. 10 v.

Johnson, J. W. Self-Determining Haiti. New York: The Nation, 1920. 48 p.

Johnson, W. F. Four Centuries of the Panama Canal. New York: Holt, 1907.

Jones, C. L. Caribbean Interests of the United States. New York: Appleton, 1919.

Keynes, J. M. The Economic Consequences of the Peace. New York: Harcourt, Brace, 1920.

Knowles, L. C. A. The Economic Development of the British Overseas Empire. New York: Boni, 1925.

Knox, P. G. The Spirit and Purpose of American Diplomacy; Address at the Commencement Exercises of the University of Pennsylvania, June 15, 1910. 57 p.

Lamont, T. W. Preliminary Report on the New Consortium for China. Privately Printed, 1920. 18 p. [Furnished through the courtesy of J. P. Morgan & Co.]

Latané, J. H. America as a World Power. New York: Harper, 1907.

—— From Isolation to Leadership; Revised. New York: Doubleday, Page, 1922.

—— The United States and Latin America. New York: Doubleday, Page, 1920.

Lawrence, David. The True Story of Woodrow Wilson. New York: Doran, 1924.

Lee, Higginson & Co. Circular regarding Dominican Republic 5½ % Sinking Fund Gold Bonds, dated March 1, 1922.

Lenin, Nikolai. Imperialism, the Final Stage of Capitalism. Boston: Progress Ptg. Co., 1917. 66 p.

L'Espagnol de la Tramerye, Pierre. The World-Struggle for Oil. New York: Knopf, 1924.

Lingley, C. R. Since the Civil War. New York: Century, 1920.

MacDonald, William. Documentary Source Book of American History, 1606–1913. New York: Macmillan, 1916.

MacMurray, J. V. A., ed. Treaties and Agreements With and Concerning China, 1894–1919. New York: Oxford University Press, 1921. 2 v.

McMaster, J. B. A History of the People of the United States. New York: Appleton, 1883–1913. 8 v.

Mahan, A. T. Naval Strategy. Boston: Little, Brown, 1911.

Mahony, T. H. The Monroe Doctrine. Boston: Knights of Columbus Historical Commission, 1921. 91 p.

The Mineral Industry: Its Statistics, Technology and Trade. Edited by G. A. Roush. New York: McGraw-Hill. [Annual.]

Moody's Analyses of Investments. 4 parts: Railroad Investments; Industrial Investments; Public Utility Investments; Government and Municipal Securities. New York: Moody's Investors' Service. [Annual.]

Moore, J. B. A Digest of International Law. Washington: Govt. Ptg. Off., 1906. 8 v.

Moulton, H. G. and McGuire, C. E. Germany's Capacity to Pay. New York: McGraw-Hill, 1923.

Munro, D. G. The Five Republics of Central America. New York: Oxford University Press, 1918. (Carnegie Endowment for International Peace. Division of Economics and History.)

Ogg, F. A. National Progress, 1907–1917. New York: Harper, 1918. (The American Nation: a History. v. 27.)

O'Shaughnessy, Edith. A Diplomat's Wife in Mexico. New York: Harper, 1916.

Overlach, T. W. Foreign Financial Control in China. New York: Macmillan, 1919.

Paisch, George. Trade Balance of the United States. (In United States. National Monetary Commission. Publications. v. 20. Washington: Govt. Ptg. Off., 1910. pp. 153–213.)

Pan American Financial Conference. Proceedings. May 24–29, 1915. Washington: Govt. Ptg. Off., 1915.

Pan, Shü-Lun. The Trade of the United States with China. New York: China Trade Bureau, 1924.

Pereyra, Carlos. El Mito de Monroe. Madrid: Editorial-América, 1916.

Pettigrew, R. F. Triumphant Plutocracy. New York: The Academy Press, 1922.

Philippine Islands. Commerce and Industry Bureau. Statistical Bulletin No. 3. 1920. Manila: Bureau of Printing, 1921.

Plebs League. An Outline of Modern Imperialism. London: Plebs League, 1922. (Plebs Textbooks no. 2.)

Polk, J. K. Diary. Chicago: McClurg, 1910. 4 v. (Chicago Historical Society. Collection. v. 6–9.)

Price, M. P. Germany in Transition. London: Labour Publishing Co., 1923.

Prinsen Geerligs, H. C. The World's Cane Sugar Industry. Altringham (Manchester) Eng.: Norman Rodger, 1912.

Reid, Whitelaw. Problems of Expansion. New York: Century, 1900.

Reinsch, P. S. World Politics at the End of the Nineteenth Century as Influenced by the Oriental Situation. New York: Macmillan, 1916.

Reyes, J. S. Legislative History of America's Economic Policy Toward the Philippines. New York: Columbia University, 1923. (Studies in History, Economics and Public Law. Ed. by the Faculty of Political Science of Columbia University. v. CVI, no. 2.)

Rhodes, J. F. History of the United States. New York: Macmillan, 1906. 7 v.

—— The McKinley and Roosevelt Administrations. New York: Macmillan, 1922.

Robinson, E. E. and West, V. J. The Foreign Policy of Woodrow Wilson, 1913–1917. New York: Macmillan, 1917.

Roig de Leuchsenring, Emilio. La Enmienda Platt. (In Sociedad Cubana de Derecho Internacional. Anuario. 1922. pp. 323–462.)

Roosevelt, Theodore. The Works of Theodore Roosevelt. Presidential Addresses and State Papers. Executive Edition. New York: Collier and Son, 1910. 8 v.

Root, Elihu. The Military and Colonial Policy of the United States. Cambridge: Harvard University Press, 1916.

Ross. E. A. The Social Revolution in Mexico. New York: Century, 1923.

Russia. Foreign Affairs Commissariat. Secret Diplomatic Documents and Treaties. v. 1. Petrograd, 1918. 47 p.

Scott, J. B. ed. President Wilson's Foreign Policy. New York: Oxford University Press, 1918.

Sociedad Cubana de Derecho Internacional. Anuario. 1922. Habana: El Siglo XX, 1922.

Speyer & Co. and Equitable Trust Company of New York. Circular regarding Dominican Republic 8% Sinking Fund Gold Bonds dated June 1, 1921. New York, June 20, 1921.

Straight, Willard. The Politics of Chinese Finance. New York: Privately Printed, 1913. 29 p.

Stuart, G. H. Latin America and the United States. New York: Century, 1922.

Taft, W. H. and Bacon, Robert. Cuban Pacification. Report of W. H. Taft, Secretary of War, and Robert Bacon, Assistant Secretary of State, of What was Done Under Instructions of the President in Restoring Peace in Cuba. (In United States. War Dept. Annual Report. 1905 / 06. pp. 444–543.)

Taussig, F. W. Some Aspects of the Tariff Question. Cambridge: Harvard University Press, 1915.

Tumulty, J. P. Woodrow Wilson as I Know Him. New York: Doubleday, Page, 1921.

United States. Attorney General. Opinions. v. 31. 1916–19. Washington: Govt. Ptg. Off., 1920.

—— Census Bureau. Estimated National Wealth. 1922. Washington: Govt. Ptg. Off., 1924. 34 p.

—— Congress. 32: 1. Message from the President and Accompanying Documents. December 2, 1851. Washington, 1851. (Sen. Ex. Doc. 1. Serial 611.)

—— —— 39: 1. French Occupation of Mexico. Washington, 1866. (Sen. Ex. Doc. 6. Serial 1237.)

—— —— 50: 1. American Rights in Samoa. Washington: Govt. Ptg. Off., 1888. (House Ex. Doc. 238. Serial 2560.)

—— —— 52: 2. Annexation Treaty with the Hawaiian Islands. Washington: Govt. Ptg. Off., 1893. 69 p. (Sen. Ex. Doc. 76. Serial 3062.)

—— —— 55: 3. A Treaty of Peace Between the United States and Spain. Washington: Govt. Ptg. Off., 1899. (Sen. Doc. 62. Serial 3732.)

—— —— 56: 1. Communications Between the Executive Departments of the Government and Aguinaldo, etc. Washington: Govt. Ptg. Off., 1900. (Sen. Doc. 208. Serial 3854.)

——— —— 57:1. Affairs in the Philippine Islands. Hearings before the Committee on the Philippines of the United States Senate. Washington: Govt. Ptg. Off., 1902. 2 vols. (Sen. Doc. 331. Serials 4242–4243.)

——— —— 57:1. Cession of Danish Islands in the West Indies. Washington: Govt. Ptg. Off., 1902. 25 p. (Sen. Doc. 284. Serial 4239.)

——— —— 57:1. Documents Relating to the Interoceanic Canal. Washington: Govt. Ptg. Off., 1902. 68 p. (Sen. Doc. 357, Serial 4245.)

——— —— 57:1. Payments to F. B. Thurber out of Cuban Funds. Washington: Govt. Ptg. Off., 1902. 24 p. (House Doc. 679. Serial 4377.)

——— —— 57:1. Reciprocity with Cuba. Washington: Govt. Ptg. Off., 1902. 3 p. (Sen. Doc. 405. Serial 4245.)

——— —— 63:2. The Panama Canal and Our Relations with Colombia. Washington: Govt. Ptg. Off., 1914. 75 p. (Sen. Doc. 471. Serial 6594.)

——— —— 66:1. Treaty of Peace with Germany. Hearings before the Committee on Foreign Relations, United States Senate. Washington: Govt. Ptg. Off., 1919. (Sen. Doc. 106. Serial 7605.)

——— —— 66:2. Virgin Islands. Report of Joint Commission Appointed under Authority of the Concurrent Resolution Passed by Congress January, 1920. Washington: Govt. Ptg. Off., 1920. 38 p. (House Doc. 734. Serial 7768.)

——— —— 66:2. Investigation of Mexican Affairs. Washington: Govt. Ptg. Off., 1920. 2 v. (Sen. Doc. v. 9–10. Serials 7665–7666.)

——— —— 67:2. Conference on Limitation of Armament. Washington: Govt. Ptg. Off., 1922. (Sen. Doc. 126. Serial 7976.)

——— —— 67:2. Treaty Between China and Japan for the Settlement of Outstanding Questions Relating to Shantung. (Sen. Doc. 166. Serial 7987.)

——— —— 67:4. Filipino Appeal for Freedom. Washington: Govt. Ptg. Off., 1922. 90 p. (House Doc. 511. Serial 8215.)

——— —— 68:1. Claims for the Death of Several Nicaraguans. Washington: Govt. Ptg. Off., 1924. 5 p. (Sen. Doc. 24. Serial 8253.)

——— —— 68:1. Oil Concessions in Foreign Countries. Washington: Govt. Ptg. Off., 1924. (Sen. Doc. 97. Serial 8241.)

——— —— 68:1. To Provide for a Civil Government for the

Virgin Islands and for Other Purposes. Washington: Govt. Ptg. Off., 1924. (Senate Bill 2786.)

—— Foreign and Domestic Commerce Bureau. Foreign Commerce and Navigation of the United States. Washington: Govt. Ptg. Off. [Annual.]

—— —— Trade Information Bulletin—no. 194. The Bolivian Public Debt. Washington: Govt. Ptg. Off., 1924. 27 p.

—— —— Trade Information Bulletin—no. 340. The Balance of International Payments of the United States in 1924. Washington: Govt. Ptg. Off., 1925. 28 p.

—— Foreign Relations of the United States. Washington: Govt. Ptg. Off. [Annual.] (State Department.)

—— Haiti and Santo Domingo, Select Committee on. Inquiry into Occupation and Administration of Haiti and Santo Domingo. Hearings . . . 67 Cong. 1 and 2 Sess. Washington: Govt. Ptg. Off., 1922. 2 v.

—— House. Foreign Affairs Committee. Cession of Danish West Indian Islands. Hearings . . . 64 Cong., 2 Sess. Washington: Govt. Ptg. Off., 1917. 27 p.

—— Marine Corps. Report on Affairs in the Republic of Haiti, June 1915 to June 30, 1920. Washington, 1920. (Mimeographed.)

—— National Monetary Commission. Publications. v. 20. Washington: Govt. Ptg. Off., 1910.

—— Navy Department. Annual Reports. Washington: Govt. Ptg. Off.

—— Philippine Commission. Report. Washington: Govt. Ptg. Off., 1900–01. 4 v.

—— Philippine Islands, Special Mission to the. Report of the Special Mission on Investigation to the Philippine Islands to the Secretary of War. Washington: Govt. Ptg. Off., 1921. 58 p.

—— Senate. Foreign Relations Committee. The Convention Between the United States and Nicaragua. Hearings . . . 63 Cong. 2 Sess. Washington: Govt. Ptg. Off., 1914. (Confidential.)

—— —— —— Nicaraguan Affairs. Hearing . . . 62 Cong. 2 Sess. Washington: Govt. Ptg. Off., 1913. 92 p.

—— —— —— Revolutions in Mexico. Hearing . . . 62 Cong. 2 Sess. Washington: Govt. Ptg. Off., 1913.

—— State Department. Treaty Series No. 629. Convention Between the United States and Denmark. Cession of the Danish West Indies. Washington: Govt. Ptg. Off., 1919.

—— Statistical Abstract of the United States. Washington:

Govt. Ptg. Off. [Annual.] (Foreign and Domestic Commerce Bureau.)
—— Statutes. Statutes at Large. Washington: Govt. Ptg. Off.
—— Treasury Dept. Annual Report . . . on the State of the Finances. Washington: Govt. Ptg. Off.
—— Treaties, Conventions, International Acts, Protocols and Agreements Between the United States of America and Other Powers. Compiled by W. M. Mallory and others. 1776–1923. Washington: Govt. Ptg. Off., 1910–23. 3 v. (61 Cong. 2 Sess. Sen. Doc. 357; 67 Cong. 4 Sess. Sen. Doc. 348. Serials 5646–5647, 8167.
—— Virgin Islands, Commission to the. Report of the Federal Commission Appointed by the Secretary of Labor to Investigate Industrial and Economic Conditions in the Virgin Islands, U. S. A. February 29, 1924. Washington: Govt. Ptg. Off., 1924. 35 p.
—— War Department. Annual Reports. Washington: Govt. Ptg. Off.
—— World War Foreign Debt Commission. Great Britain. Proposal, dated 18th day of June, 1923 by His Britannic Majesty's Government to Government of United States regarding funding of debt of Great Britain to United States [and acceptance] 1923. 13 p.
Veblen, Thorstein. The Engineers and the Price System. New York: Huebsch, 1921.
Viallate, Achille. Economic Imperialism and International Relations During the Last Fifty Years. New York: Macmillan, 1923.
Washington, George. The Writings of G. Washington, edited by J. Sparks. Boston: Little, Brown, 1855. 12 v.
Willoughby, W. W. and Fenwick, C. G. Types of Restricted Sovereignty and of Colonial Autonomy. Washington: Govt. Ptg. Off., 1919. (United States. State Department.)
Wilson, Woodrow. A History of the American People. New York: Harper, 1902–03. 5 v.
Wissler, Clark. Man and Culture. New York: Crowell, 1923.
Woolf. L. S. Economic Imperialism. London: Swarthmore Press, 1920. (The Swarthmore International Handbooks. v. 5.)
Yearbook of the Exchange Rates of the World; ed. by Emil Diesen. Christiania: A / S Økonomisk Literatur.
Zelaya, J. S. La Revolución de Nicaragua y los Estados Unidos. Madrid: B. Rodríguez, 1910.

PERIODICALS

Academy of Political Science. Proceedings. 1917–18.

Borchard, E. M., "Commercial and Financial Interests of the United States in the Caribbean." (v. 7, pp. 383–91.)

Hart, A. B., and Wicker, C. F., "The Caribbean Question" (v. 7, pp. 423–32.)

Howe, F. C., "Dollar Diplomacy and Imperialism." (v. 7, pp. 597–603.)

Shaw, Albert, "The Monroe Doctrine and the Evolution of Democracy." (v. 7, pp. 471–8.)

Shepherd, W. R., "The Attitude of the United States toward the Retention by European Nations of Colonies in and around the Caribbean." (v. 7, pp. 392–405.)

American Academy of Political and Social Science. Annals. 1899, 1916, 1924.

Ford, W. C., "The Commercial Relations of the United States with the Far East." (v. 13, Supplement, pp. 107–130.)

Hobson, C. K., "British Oversea Investments, Their Growth and Importance." (v. 68, pp. 23–35.)

Skelton, O. D., "Canadian Capital Requirements." (v. 68, pp. 216–25.)

Hughes, C. H., "The Centenary of the Monroe Doctrine." (v. 111, Supplement, pp. 7–19.)

Culbertson, W. S., "Raw Materials and Food Stuffs in the Commercial Policies of Nations." (v. 112, pp. 1–145.)

American Economist. 1923.

Austen, G. W., "Americanization of Canadian Industry." (v. 71, pp. 77–8.)

American Journal of International Law. 1913.

"The Passing of Dollar Diplomacy." (v. 7, pp. 335–41.)

Annalist. 1920, 1923, 1924.

"Jacob H. Schiff the Pioneer of American Foreign Financing." (v. 16, p. 452.)

Chalmers, F. S., "American Capital in Canada." (v. 22, p. 208.)

Hodges, Charles, "The Business Background of the Philippine Question." (v. 23, p. 159.)

Argentina. Boletin Oficial, June 27, 1918.

Cuba. Camara de Comercio, Industria y Navegacion. Boletin Oficial, 1909.

Cuba. Estado, Secretaria de. Boletin Oficial, 1917.

Cuba. Gaceta Oficial, July 17, 1906.

Cuba. Hacienda, Secretario de. Boletin Oficial, 1917.

Current History Magazine of the New York Times. 1917, 1922–23.
"Japanese-American Agreement." (v. 7, pp. 547–50.)
Gruening, E. H., "Conquest of Haiti and Santo Domingo." (v. 15, pp. 885–96.)
Joachim, Maurice, "America's Attitude Toward India's Revolt." (v. 16, pp. 1028–34.)
Mayer, H. B., "America Again Defenseless." (v. 17, pp. 393–402.)
Woodhouse, Henry, "The Chester Concession as an Aid to New Turkey." (v. 18, pp. 393–400.)
Buell, R. L., "International Capitalism and Its Control." (v. 19, pp. 483–8.)
Robb, Walter, "The Filipino's Demand for Independence." (v. 19, pp. 281–7.)
Economic World. 1922.
Crissinger, D. R., "The Financial Contribution of the United States to the Rehabilitation of the World Since the War." (n.s.v. 24, p. 413.)
Far Eastern Review. 1915.
Rea, G. B., "Roads Towards Peace." (v. 11, pp. 273–84.)
Foreign Affairs. 1923.
Hughes, C. E., "Recent Questions and Negotiations." An Address Before the Council on Foreign Relations, New York, January 23, 1924." (v. 2, no. 2. Special Supplement. pp. i–xxii.)
Literary Digest. 1904.
"Panama and the President." (v. 29, pp. 551–2.)
Manchester Guardian Commercial. 1923–24.
Delaisi, Francis, "The Comité des Forges de France." (3 pts. Pts. 1–2 in Supplement: European Reconstruction, sections 15–16, pp. 846–9, 879–82. Pt. 3 in v. 7, pp. 197–8.)
King, W. L. M., "Canada." (v. 7, p. 370.)
Sclater, A. G., "The Progress of Manufacturing." (v. 9, Supplement, Sept. 18, 1924, p. 38.)
Mexican Review. 1919.
"A Sample Oil Concession." (v. 3. pp. 32–6).
Monetary Times. 1925.
"Summary Bond Sales in All Markets, 1911–1924." (v. 74, no. 2, p. 80.)
Nation. 1919–20, 1923.
De Bekker, L. J., "The Plot against Mexico." (v. 109, pp. 36–7, 107–9.)
"Why Haiti Has No Budget." (v. 111, pp. 307–8.)
Warner, Arthur, "Bayonet Rule for Our Colonial Press." (v. 116, p. 267.)

—— "Political Peonage in the Virgin Islands." (v. 116, pp. 650–2.)

Outlook. 1911.

Roosevelt, Theodore, "How the United States Acquired the Right to the Panama Canal." (v. 99, pp. 314–18.)

Pacific Era. 1909.

Kaneko, Baron, "Expansion Program of Nippon after the War." (v. 1, pp. 13–18.)

Pan American Union. Bulletin. 1924.

Political Science Quarterly. 1924.

Earle, E. M., "The Turkish Petroleum Company—A Study in Oleaginous Diplomacy." (v. 39, pp. 265–79.)

Review of Economic Statistics. 1919.

Bullock, C. J., and others, " The Balance of Trade of the United States." (v. 1, pp. 215–54.)

Review of Reviews. 1916.

Ham, C. D., "Americanizing Nicaragua." (v. 53, pp. 185–91.)

United States. Congressional Record.

United States. Federal Reserve Board. Federal Reserve Bulletin. 1921, 1924.

"Foreign Loans Placed in the United States." (v. 7, pp. 942–51.)

"Foreign Loans Placed in the United States, 1919–1923." (v. 10, pp. 92–3.)

United States. Foreign and Domestic Commerce Bureau. Commerce Reports.

"Record Foreign Borrowing in 1924." (Jan. 26, 1925, pp. 184–6.)

University of California Chronicle. 1920.

Priestley, H. I., "The Relations of the United States and Mexico since 1910." (v. 22, pp. 47–60.)

World Peace Foundation. 1923.

"Reparation: Part 5. The Dawes Report." (v. 6, no. 5, pp. 325–500.)

World's Work. 1914.

Middleton, James, "Mexico, the Land of Concessions." (v. 27, pp. 289–98.)

Hale, W. B., "Our Moral Empire in America." (v. 28, pp. 52–8.)

"Our Arms and Aims in Mexico." (v. 28, pp. 129–35.)

Yale Review. 1900.

Bacon, N. T., "American International Indebtedness." (v. 9, pp. 265–85.)

INDEX

347